CRIME
FRAUD

JOHN CADER

Johnny Words
PO Box 8181
Pelham, NY 10803
johnnywords.com

ISBN 978-0-578-91761-0

Cover Design by 100Covers.com
Interior Design by FormattedBooks.com

For Mary Alice and John

CHAPTER ONE

The Hotdog

"Do you like boxing? Hey, do you like boxing? Who do you like?" I was sweating through the back of my shirt and staring into my hand at an uneaten hotdog. The August sun was getting ready to disappear on the other side of the Hudson River. I could see him out of the corner of my eye without turning my head. Polished black combat boots. Olive green army fatigue pants and jacket. Who the hell wears a jacket on a day like this? I was about to melt. And a black beret with wraparound sunglasses. His uniform was military, but there was nothing militant about him. He was loose and somehow on this blazing hot day he was cool. Not breaking a sweat about anything.

Total whacko. I didn't respond. Cars whizzed by on the West Side Highway near where I was sitting. It was the same place I sat every time I needed to get away from the office, and no one had ever noticed me before. I had been working at Smith Stevens for sixteen months and it could be maddening. Long stretches of boredom spiked with periods of intense stress.

It was the same as a lot of other law firms, and I had worked at a couple, except this place was richer and more cold-blooded. I was in litigation—a department with big corporate clients with big problems. The defense of big tobacco, big industry and big banking were on the menu daily. And those clients wouldn't be on Smith Stevens' roster if they couldn't pay the firm's billing rates. They could and they did.

I didn't belong. I was surrounded by Ivy-Leaguers with pedigrees I couldn't imagine until I worked with them. I should've been emptying the firm's trash cans after hours. I went to a less prestigious law school in Boston. Few of us had realistic hopes of working for a big law firm. And none of us dreamed of working at Smith Stevens. It was often a small personal injury firm or busting your hump as an assistant district attorney if you were lucky.

After graduation I fell into Feinberg & Bowser, a boutique litigation shop in Boston handling small lawsuits for Wampanoag Bank, which had branches in and around the city. The cases were frequently the same. Someone stopped making payments on a loan and the bank sued to collect. It wasn't what I planned on doing when I went to law school, but the cases got me into court almost every week. Typically, we settled for pennies on the dollar because receiving something was better than getting nothing. I didn't enjoy dragging some poor schlepp into court, but if there was a silver lining, it was that the schlepp usually only had to pay a fraction of the original debt and got to move on with his life.

After a couple of years at Feinberg & Bowser, Wampanoag was swallowed by a bigger bank, National Union Bank & Trust from New York. And the firm was swallowed by Johnson Lewis, a preeminent Boston firm that wanted to take over all of National Union's legal work in Massachusetts. With that takeover I entered the world of white-shoe law firms. White shoes because they normally didn't get grimy dealing with street-level legal work like suing on loan defaults.

But there I was suing on loan defaults and continuing to strike low-value settlements with debtors. Now I was doing it around attorneys with impressive pedigrees and Brahmin names. My address and salary changed, but so did my hours at work. My 8:00 to 6:00 job suddenly became an 8:00 to 8:00 job, unless there was an emergency. Then I had to be ready to camp out. There was a shower in the office and a cot inside my coat closet. More than once I found myself pulled into a disaster and ended up using both.

Litigation wasn't the firm's main focus, but the attorneys that litigated were usually in federal court where the cases were more complex, the stakes were higher, and the money involved was much more significant than in state court. Where my cases were frequently worth tens of thousands of dollars each, the cases Johnson Lewis handled were worth millions. Trade secrets, securities, and class actions. It was where most trial attorneys wanted to be, but I never got the invitation to that party.

After eight months at Johnson Lewis, the firm's managing partner called a firm meeting on a Thursday morning and announced the firm was merging with Smith Stevens the following Monday. Attorneys and staff with conflicts of interest with Smith Stevens' clients wouldn't be coming. And although it was called a merger, there was little doubt that it was a takeover. Johnson Lewis was going to be picked apart like a Thanksgiving bird. Anyone without a firm grip on a juicy leg or a wing was going to be on the street. And within a week, every decent law firm in Boston was going to be flooded with the resumes of dozens of attorneys with the same story: pushed out of Johnson Lewis with barely a scrap of business, if that.

As of the following Monday, Johnson Lewis ceased to exist. And those of us that cleared conflicts were officially employees of Smith Stevens LLP. I wasn't a partner of the firm, just an associate. So, I wasn't an owner, only an employee, and knew nothing about the details of the merger in advance, but discussions had been going on for months. Smith Stevens had a reputation as one of the best firms in the United States with a ruthless approach to handling deals and disputes. It also had a reputation for its ruthless approach to dealing with employees like me.

Most associates lasted less than two years at the firm. A combination of long hours, stress and being treated with utter contempt by partners and clients alike doomed most attorneys' careers at the firm. Those that succeeded had seven-figure incomes, luxury cars and beautiful homes they rarely spent time in. It was the carrot that kept drawing new attorneys into the firm, despite its high attrition rate and reputation for mistreating associates. The news of the merger pulled the rug out from underneath me, but I had no choice except to go. I didn't have a turkey leg or even a scrap to hang onto.

I showed up to work that Monday, as usual. But now as an employee of Smith Stevens. On Wednesday, all of the associates working for National Union in Boston were called into a meeting with the managing partner of the New York office. He informed us that all of National Union's legal work, including my loan lawsuits, would be run out of New York effective immediately. And all personnel handling cases for National Union would be based in New York. Not only had my firm changed out from underneath me, but if I wanted to keep my job, I had to relocate. While Smith Stevens' culture was known as cold, uncaring, and ruthless throughout its offices, the New York office had a national reputation for cruelty to associates.

The best of the best of Smith Stevens' partners were seated in the "Temple" in the middle of Manhattan in Times Square. It was a glittering glass and steel monument designed to rub the noses of competitors in its success while intimidating opponents with its vast and seemingly infinite resources. If you were a young attorney and found yourself at the Temple, you had a rabbi—a partner with influence at the firm who liked you—and likely a future at the firm. And if your rabbi was a whale—a partner with a big book of business—you had a golden ticket and probably a very bright future ahead of you. Your office had a window either overlooking Times Square to the east or the Hudson River to the west.

For all of the other attorneys and staff of Smith Stevens in New York, there was another office known as the "Backwater." The Backwater was located in an old manufacturing building on Eighth Avenue between 54th and 55th Streets with barely any windows. It was not glittery and there was no steel or glass. Instead, there was aging brick, a decrepit façade and no outside sign or symbol revealing Smith Stevens had an office inside. There was no receptionist and few offices. With little sunlight and grey paint covering the walls, the office had the charm of the department of motor vehicles.

The Backwater had a large open area called the "Pit" with long folding tables and metal chairs set up for reviewing documents. Surrounding the Pit was a maze of cubicles. And in each cubicle was a lawyer or lawyers deemed unworthy to be seated in the Temple. This is where all the unsexy work took place. The grunts in the Backwater reviewed documents for any reason to keep them private from a court. It was also where low-profile cases were managed and prepared for trial. It was a place where no Smith Stevens client would ever enter. And it is where the firm put me after I moved to New York.

After months of running cases from the Backwater as I had at Feinberg & Bowser and Johnson Lewis, National Union took a new approach to its loan cases, one that was more in line with Smith Stevens' usual litigation practices. I would no longer be offering low-dollar settlements in my cases and any new cases would be handled by local attorneys, rather than me. I would be directing those attorneys to take their cases to trial to win judgments that would be used to seize assets, such as cars, bank accounts, and homes from the bank's customers. Wearing the black hat didn't sit well with me.

David Bell was Smith Stevens' relationship partner with National Union. That meant he was the main point of contact with the bank and all significant communications went through him. David was notoriously hard to reach, especially if you were calling from the Backwater. I tried several times, but his assistant was never able to connect us. Unable to reach him, I made the trek from Eighth Avenue over to the Temple. It was a longshot, but I wasn't getting anywhere sitting at the Backwater.

After fighting my way through crowds and cartoon characters in Times Square, I found myself outside of the building that housed the Temple. Building security wouldn't let me enter with my Backwater security pass. Instead, they photographed me and issued a temporary paper pass after I showed my driver's license. And once I arrived inside the Temple, the receptionist stared at me blankly and wouldn't let me in until I showed the temporary pass. I was reduced to a tourist.

I arrived at David's office just as he was putting on a black overcoat while striding towards the door. He was in his 50's, physically fit with a full head of silvering hair always slicked back. A double Ivy-Leaguer—Harvard University undergrad and law school—David started at the firm in Los Angeles, eventually returning east to open up the New York office twenty years ago. He was seldom in court, barely at his desk and never seemed to be doing anything that appeared to be actual legal work. His pedigree gave him the right connections, though, and that's all it took to succeed at Smith Stevens.

"David, do you have a couple of minutes for me?" He shrugged, looking bored.

"Walk with me." I trailed him down the hallway just off of his shoulder as he walked quickly towards a bank of elevators.

"I want to talk to you about National Union."

"About what?," he growled.

"About the loan default litigation. I think the new approach is going to be trouble. We're going to force people into bankruptcy and who knows what we'll get. We're going to lose more money taking these cases to trial than just settling them. It just doesn't make sense to me."

"Listen, you have to look at the big picture." His feet shuffled impatiently in front of the elevators. I glanced down and saw the reflection of the overhead lights in the shine of his Valentino loafers. His Patek Philippe watch gleamed as it punctuated his sentences.

"And what's that?"

"You're working on cases involving branches that aren't profitable and aren't desirable. Think of where your cases come from. Dorchester. Hyde Park. Roslindale. Roxbury. South Boston. Do you think National Union's paying Smith Stevens' rates because it wants to be in those neighborhoods?"

He didn't come out and say it, but he didn't have to. Each of those neighborhoods was largely populated by working class people. And few of them were wealthy. The wealthy folks historically left those areas as soon as they could. South and North of Boston were loaded with people generations removed from Southie, Dorchester, and other urban neighborhoods.

"Your job is to push the cases. Be a hard-ass and collect. And above all, bill your fucking time. All of it. You think about them on the subway, you bill it. You have to justify your existence here. Every day. You make your bones with National Union, maybe you can work your way out of the Annex. The only reason those branches exist is because regulators forced National Union to keep them after the merger with Wampanoag. They're fucking losers and their customers are a bunch of bums. National Union doesn't want them. If they shutter, even better."

I tried to respond, but stammered incoherently. An elevator door opened, and David disappeared from view without another word. After he slipped away, I felt as though someone was watching me. I turned around, but was alone in the elevator bank. A large silver Smith Stevens sign loomed over me. And so did a security camera. Somewhere someone was making sure I wasn't stealing pencils. I didn't belong in the Temple and it seemed as though Smith Stevens was determined to make sure I knew it.

"You like boxing?" I continued staring at the paver stones under my polished work shoes, trying my best to act like I was ignoring him. But it was pointless. "Who's your favorite boxer?" My voice felt stuck. No words wanted to come out.

"Yeah, I like boxing," I finally croaked while clearing my throat.

"Well, who do you like?"

"Canelo. I like Canelo Alvarez."

"Really, you like Canelo?"

"I do."

"Well, who else?"

"I can't remember his name, but that big Mexican guy from Los Angeles. You know, that guy that beat the English champion and took his belt. He didn't look like he was in shape, but he had those fast hands. The champ wasn't ready for those hands."

"I'm taking courses to be a trainer."

"A trainer?"

"Yeah, a personal trainer. Y'know, at the gym." He suddenly looked distracted and pulled a phone out of a backpack sitting next to him and began to type.

My thoughts trailed back to where I was and what I was doing on a park bench instead of being in my cubicle at 6:35 on a Tuesday evening. My brief conversation with David rattled through my head. When I moved to New York I didn't bank on becoming a cog in a scheme targeting my former neighbors. I wanted to walk away from the firm, but it wasn't so simple.

There were no saddlebags of sweat under my armpits, but there might as well have been. The August humidity weighed heavily on me and moisture covered my entire body. My pants, which were crisp with defined creases at the start of the day, were now hot and sweaty. My body pressed them into the park bench. New lines and creases crisscrossed my legs. Where I looked sharp and ready for battle in the morning, now I was a rumpled mess. Like I belonged in the Backwater.

I hadn't even eaten my hotdog, which was now the same temperature as the air outside. And sweating as much as me. It wasn't an attractive look for either of us. I peeled myself off of the bench and trudged from the edge of the Hudson River back to my cubicle in the Backwater. I didn't want to return, but there were hours to bill and I had to get back to billing.

CHAPTER TWO

Shine

"Hey, where you going you fucking nickelbagger?" Aaron Goldberg sat in a cubicle close to mine. He also worked on cases the firm didn't advertise to the outside world. But unlike me, he acted like he owned the place. While I took my sanity breaks alone by the river, Aaron took his at his favorite shoeshine and preferred company, especially if that company could fill him in on firm gossip. No one was more tapped into the comings and goings of Smith Stevens. He was at least two steps ahead of every other attorney on Eighth Avenue.

"I'm taking a squirt. What's it to you?"

"We're getting a shine. C'mon. Push it out!"

"Man, I can't. I'm slammed." I was behind on paperwork and phone calls after being in Boston on one of my loan cases. If Smith Stevens had all of the resources in the world, you wouldn't know it in the Backwater. Aside from occasionally being needled by Chuck MacPherson, a junior partner tasked with managing National Union's lawsuits around the country, I had little oversight and little assistance from anyone else at the firm.

Chuck's main skills were figuring out how to circumvent the firm's firewall to get a golf game installed on his computer and thinking of punitive work assignments for his underlings. Seeking his input or advice was a last resort only to be used when all other options had failed. Visiting his office frequently meant interrupting his backswing and then reflexively being assigned some time-consuming project to be completed on an impossibly tight deadline.

He flipped questions back onto their askers with vomit-inducing corporate double-speak. "I'm going to kick it back to you." "Research it some more, then tee it up." "I'll be out of pocket for that." "Let's double-back on this after some more deep thought." Each answer a non-answer. Always vaguely off to the side, he never took a stand or a strong position on a client issue or strategy. And he rode this approach out of the associate ranks to a position as a junior partner. While he wasn't yet an owner of the firm, he was on the right track, albeit in the Backwater. I couldn't fathom that his strategy worked. He must've know where the bodies were buried.

I shared my assistant, Randall, with four other attorneys. He sat on the other side of the Backwater from my cubicle and peered at me over his reading glasses with only a vague sense of recognition when I asked him to do something. Randall was my only other living connection in the Backwater beyond Chuck who could confirm I worked for National Union. And that was only because he saw the firm's bills before they went out to the bank.

Even without any consistent human oversight, one system made sure I was working. It was our big brother: BAMS. The Billing Automated Management System. It was a calendar open at all times on my firm laptop constantly reminding me to bill. Every day I had to bill a minimum of ten hours to paying clients. And I had to enter that time into the calendar by noon the following day. I'd receive an unpleasant email from accounting if I didn't. A couple of those and it could be out the door. But my building pass kept working, so I took it as a sign of my continued employment.

"Why do you have to be like that? I bust my balls all day to keep your ass out of trouble. And this is how you repay me? Where's the fucking loyalty? Or at least a little love? I'd take either!"

"I'll squeeze really hard. How about you come and milk my prostate to speed it up?" I couldn't afford to spend time away from the Backwater, but there was no saying "no."

"Fuck you! You don't have enough money for that. But call me when you do."

Aaron was right. I didn't have enough for that, but I did have enough for a shine. His favorite was in the basement of Grand Central Terminal, normally a twenty-five minute walk from the Backwater. Factoring in our conversational pace and occasional beer along the way, it could easily take an hour just to get there, let alone to get your shoes shined and back.

"Alright, alright. Seriously, give me a minute. I gotta piss."

"Don't take too long. Tripper's going to meet us midway in Times Square."

Great. Bowdin Williams Crowninshield, III, Esq. Everyone called him Tripper. If I was the kind of guy the firm wanted to hide in the Backwater, he was the kind of guy they wanted to put on the front page of the firm's website. And, in fact, they did. One of the first things you'd see on Smith Stevens' homepage was a picture of Tripper helping villagers install a water collection and filtration system in a remote village in Tonga. His family had been in New York since it was a colony and just about all of them attended Yale since the 1700's.

Where Aaron pried intel from his sources, the firm voluntarily shared it with Tripper. Earmarked as a future star during law school, he sat in the firm's prestigious corporate department in the Temple. He never appeared in court and would never have to. Instead, he sat in on negotiations with senior partners and clients, controlled the papers in massive deals, and managed other attorneys and paralegals reviewing mind-boggling amounts of documents as part of the firm's due diligence process. He had a reputation for being cruel and arrogant to his underlings. I wasn't excited about wasting a trip outside the Backwater on him.

As Aaron and I walked through Times Square, Tripper stood on the corner of 46th Street and Broadway basking in the bright January sun. Six feet tall and wiry, his blonde hair and high cheek bones looked bronzed and radiant in the midday glow. He was a veteran of multiple marathons and regattas and it showed on his taut physique.

"Oh, so in love! It warms my heart and makes me so jealous at the same time. Is there room in there for a throuple?" Tripper laughed as the words left his mouth.

"Fuck you," Aaron retorted. "I'm not letting you in on any of this until you show us that little cocktail weenie you're hiding behind that Zegna suit, you fucking fraud. No one can have it all." Maybe true, but Tripper seemed like he did.

We began to stroll across Seventh Avenue and continued on until we were finally seated in black leather chairs elevated off of Grand Central Terminal's basement floor. The comforting aroma of shoe polish enveloped us. Shiners dutifully polished and buffed until artfully snapping at their quarry's shoes with an oily rag. A shine was a relaxing break from the office.

"So, how's bottom-feeding for National Union treating you?" It was a playful slap, but stung coming from Tripper.

"I'm just living the dream. So hard. Every single day."

"You better get some new running shoes." Tripper smiled.

"How's that?"

"You're going to be chasing ambulances soon. That's the next step, right?" Tripper chuckled, but I wasn't laughing. I could feel my face getting hot.

"And why exactly am I going to be chasing ambulances soon?" Clearly Aaron knew something I didn't know, but wanted me to hear it from Tripper. It was no accident that he brought the two of us together for a shine.

"You don't know?"

"No Tripper, I have no fucking idea what you're talking about."

"Oh, shit." He sighed and then took a deep breath. "Check cashing? Payday loans?" I stared at him blankly. "I thought you all knew. Fuck."

"Maybe we should discuss this in a less public forum," Aaron suggested looking around the basement's glowing marble. With shoes sparkling like polished glass, the three of us headed over to St. Pat's on 46th Street. We took a booth across from the bar and ordered a pitcher of lager.

"I thought you knew. I thought everyone knew."

"I still don't know what the fuck you're talking about." My face felt like it was burning.

"National Union's taking over Live Payday Check Loan. They're going to acquire it, then expand its operations into the northeast."

Live Payday Check Loan was located in the Midwest and gave payday loans to people in need of cash. The company also provided check-cashing services. Its customers were typically people in desperate need of money, people who didn't trust banks and people who didn't have access to a bank in their neighborhood. All of its storefronts were located in residential neighborhoods in Cleveland, Chicago, Detroit, and Indianapolis.

If you watched daytime television or late-night re-runs in any of those cities, you would inevitably see an advertisement for livepaydaycheckloan.com. And if you read the newspaper, you'd find the company's print ads. It was a lucrative business founded on taking advantage of some of the most vulnerable members of the communities where it operated. And National Union wanted to move that business into New York, New Jersey, Connecticut, Rhode Island, and Massachusetts.

"This is going to happen. But not directly through National Union, of course," Tripper continued.

As was typical of a lot of banks, National Union believed in making itself difficult to pin a lawsuit or a judgment on through a maze of subsidiaries and related companies. And it would take more than an amateur sleuth to connect the dots between it and all of its affiliated sibling and child companies. The acquisition would happen through a subsidiary of a subsidiary. And the subsidiary acquiring Live Payday Check Loan would be operating out of the Cayman Islands.

"And within nine to eighteen months, National Union plans on replacing more than seventy-percent of its urban branches with Live Payday Check Loan offices. I thought you were in on it." Aaron sat gazing into space.

"Nah, it's ok. I'm . . . I'm just surprised," I replied.

"Don't worry about it. I'm sure you'll be doing work for Live Payday Check Loan as soon as the National Union lawsuits dry up." Tripper seemed satisfied at my stunned expression.

My marching orders from David Bell were coming into sharper focus. I was hammering away on the loan lawsuits to drive "undesirable" clients away from National Union while setting the stage for branch closures. And once customers closed their accounts and branches shuttered, Live Payday Check Loan would be there to fill the void. Shutting down branches and replacing them with Live Payday Check Loan storefronts was a devious scheme. It wasn't surprising Smith Stevens was paving the way.

As the news sank in, my face was closer to grey than red. "I gotta go." I didn't have to go. I lived alone and there wasn't anyone waiting for me back at my apartment on Charles Street. Not even a dog. I staggered out of St. Pat's onto 46th Street and headed towards Sixth Avenue. The air was filled with the sound of car horns and the buzz of engines. People washed past me in both directions as I walked down the sidewalk where the smell of vending cart nuts and hot dogs drifted through the evening. I turned left onto Sixth Avenue and headed south towards the West Village.

Suing people on defaulted loans for Wampanoag almost seemed quaint. Being moved to New York and directed to aggressively go after people and their possessions was a "sea change" as they like to say in law firms. I don't think Tripper ever had a second thought about wiping out bank branches and replacing them with predatory check cashers. Generations of his family never touched money without gloves on if they ever did at all.

Like other lawyers at Smith Stevens, Tripper's life was so different from the tens of thousands of people that would be impacted by National Union's plans they might as well have been aliens from another planet. In reality, inside the walls of the firm and the bank, those customers were only numbers and not people. And once their humanity was removed it was easy to do things that were inhumane.

When I arrived in the West Village I was exhausted. I peeled off my clothes after scaling the three flights of stairs leading to my apartment in an old brownstone building. The neighborhood was quiet except for the occasional distant sound of a siren or the rumble of a junky old taxi heading towards Bleecker Street to find a fare. In the stillness of the night my troubled mind was an arena where my fear of losing my job tangled with regret over working for National Union.

CHAPTER THREE

A Bit of a Surprise

A shy knock drew my attention away from a pile of papers sitting in front of me. "Are you the lawyer for a day?" A lanky man cautiously stepped inside the doorway.

"I'm one of them. How can I help you? I'm Will Duggan."

As I stood up he turned his back to me and shut the door. There was the faint sound of a button being pushed through a denim eyelet followed by the unmistakable sound of a zipper being pulled downwards. The man slipped his blue jeans to his thighs revealing saggy black underwear covering his thin frame. He bent down and unfastened a bundle of papers wrapped around his wiry leg with several large rubber bands. Then holding the papers under his armpit, he pulled his pants back up to his waist and rebuttoned and zipped them. He turned around and looked in my eyes.

"I'm Desmond Baines, but everyone calls me 'Desi.'"

I was only mildly surprised by the partial disrobing. I volunteered every quarter to serve as an attorney for the day at the Vanderbilt Houses, a homeless shelter in the Bronx. Every large firm in the city boasted about its commitment to *pro bono* service. It was just a fancy legal way of saying free service. Clients for the day at the Vanderbilt Houses had problems ranging from back child support to criminal matters.

One thing they all had in common was they were homeless and in recovery for substance or alcohol addiction and were trying to put their lives back together. It was our job to help them on their way. Usually it was a one-time deal, and I would answer some questions or help fill out paperwork. Another thing they all had in common was creativity in protecting their most important documents. Because when you're homeless, you frequently don't have any safe place to keep them.

"Can I call you 'Desi?'"

"That's what I said. Everyone calls me 'Desi.'"

"OK, Desi. Please have a seat. Let me get organized. What brings you in today?" I sat back on an old squeaky wooden desk chair and took an intake sheet off of a pile sitting on a well-worn metal desk.

"Well, it's kind of a long story."

"That's ok. I'm here to listen." In fact, it was more than ok. If I spent my entire day at the Vanderbilt Houses I wouldn't have to go to the Backwater.

"You see. I'm trying to get a job, but I can't."

"All right. How can I help with that?"

"I have a bit of a problem."

He ruffled through his papers, which were now sitting on his lap. He held up several sheets stapled together and began to pull them against the edge of the desk. He did his best to remove the curl caused by them being wrapped around his leg.

"Would you look at this?"

His slid the papers towards me and I picked them up. They were frayed and the paper felt soft from being scuffed between denim and skin. It was a New York State Criminal History Record, commonly referred to as a "rap sheet." I reviewed the pages, which included incidents going back some decades. Mainly minor infractions. Drunkenness, disturbing the peace and shoplifting. Every incident was closed except for two: grand larceny of a vehicle and criminal possession of a controlled substance. Both on the same date more than a dozen years ago.

"Tell me what's going on?"

"I'm in recovery, you see. I've been clean for over a year now. I was diagnosed with bipolar and was self-medicating. If I want to move on with my life I have to come to grips with my past. I applied for a job in a kitchen. I love to cook. Always have. And a couple of weeks later I get a call from the manager and he says they can't hire me on account of there being an open warrant for my arrest. I said I didn't know what he was talking about. He told me I better check my record.

"So I spoke to my counselor here and he helped me get it. And to my surprise I have an open case. I swear to you I didn't know. I was pretty messed up back then. I was drinking. I was smoking. I was self-medicating. I guess I forgot. I haven't been in trouble since. My counselor said I should come talk to you and I could trust you. So here I am."

"I'm not exactly a criminal lawyer, but let's see if we can come up with a game plan for what to do. If you're going to see a judge, you gotta have a good story. But keep in mind that these judges in state court see tons of people every day and they hear lots of stories every week. And they can sniff out bullshit pretty quickly."

"Mr. Duggan, I got that right?"

"Please, just Will."

"Nah, Mr. Duggan. I ain't gonna bullshit you. I've been out of trouble. I came here a few years ago to stay for a night. And they made me attend group."

"Like therapy?"

"Yeah. Exactly. Group therapy. I like this place and I kept coming back. Every time I came back to stay there was more time with the group. Eventually they gave me a counselor. He had me see a shrink."

"And did you keep seeing the . . . Was it a psychiatrist or a psychologist?"

"He's a psychiatrist. And yeah. I did. I've been seeing him for a couple of years now. And I was diagnosed with bipolar. I take medicine and I stopped drinking and drugging. Like I said, I've been clean for more than a year. No more self-medication. I want to get a job and get out of here. I want my own place. But I can't get a job or a place with a warrant hanging over me. That's why I need you."

"Ok, ok. Back up with me a little. Everything you're telling me is good so far, but we have to talk about what happened with the warrant and the charges. You need to explain to the judge why you didn't show up. The car theft could be sticky."

"Well, you see. That wasn't my fault." I could feel the needle on my bullshit meter starting to move.

"You have to take responsibility for what happened. If the judge thinks you believe it's no big deal, he might show you it's a big deal to him."

"I'm serious, Mr. Duggan."

"Just, Wi—"

"I'm really serious. A friend of mine told me he bought a car and it died. He couldn't get it started. He asked me to help him move it. So we're pushing it down Third Avenue."

"In Manhattan?"

"Nah. Third Avenue in Mount Vernon. In Westchester County."

"All right."

"Next thing a cruiser pulls up and two cops step out asking what's happening. My friend gives some lip and says he just bought this car and it broke down and we're pushing it to his apartment. One of the cops says he'll call a tow and my friend says he doesn't have money to pay for it. That gets the cops curious and next thing they're running the VIN because there were no plates on it."

"Uh oh."

"Yeah. Uh oh. And guess what? The fucking thing's stolen. We both end up in cuffs and the cops find two joints in my pocket."

"Jesus. And what happened next?"

"I was scared shitless and my mind was whacked out on a bunch of stuff. I got a defender and a court date. I never made it."

"Well, I'm relieved it was weed and not something hard. That we can deal with. Grand theft, though. Nothing anywhere else? Not in another state or something?"

"Nah, Mr. Duggan. Nowhere. I've been good. And I'm doing real good right now. My counselor and my shrink say they'll vouch for me. They'll do anything you need."

"I can help you work on the story for the judge, but you need a criminal lawyer."

"Nah, Mr. Duggan. I need you. I went once to talk to a defender and told him I wanted to surrender and he wouldn't listen to my story. He told me to go home and get a toothbrush. I can't go back to jail. I need your help." I could feel my face getting flush. I was scared to fuck up a case when only money was at stake.

"Ok. I'll see what I can do. But I can't promise you anything. My firm doesn't handle criminal cases, so I don't even know if I can do it, but I'll ask. How can I get in touch with you?"

"I don't have a phone, but you can leave a message here and I'll call you back."

"That works. Here's my card. I'll call you as soon as I know. Probably in a couple of days."

"Thanks, Mr. Duggan."

"Please, just Wi—"

"Nah, Mr. Duggan. My lawyer."

"Well, we'll see." With that Desi turned his back to me and put the documents back in their hiding place and headed out the door. He looked back and gave an enthusiastic thumbs-up as he disappeared from view.

At the end of the afternoon at the Vanderbilt Houses I retreated to my apartment in the West Village. I sat down at my tiny two-seat kitchen table and looked at a thick legal folder with the name "Mickey" written across the top on a white label. I opened the folder and looked at the latest letter from Kevin Sullivan, whom everyone around Boston called "Knuckles." Refusing to give into email and disliking putting anything in writing, the letter simply said, "Call me."

I leafed through the file, including defense motions, appellate briefs, and letters to the parole board. Each document containing arguments and case precedents explaining that Michael "Mickey" Glynn was wrongfully incarcerated and should be released from prison. Mickey was my older brother by six years. We had different fathers—he never knew his and mine disappeared into a haze of alcohol, drugs, and dog tracks before I was in Kindergarten. We shared a roof with our mother, Alice, until she died of liver disease when I was twelve.

Mickey kept our triple-decker apartment afloat working on any construction site that would hire him. With no other family, he was desperate to keep me out of Boston's beleaguered foster care system. While he had multiple run-ins with the police as a youth, he managed to mostly keep himself out of trouble after Alice died. He had been a father figure to me since I was little and became even more of one after her death.

I thought of Mickey when Desi told me the story of his arrest. One afternoon I came home from school and Mickey wasn't there. It sometimes happened when he had the chance to make some extra cash working overtime. As afternoon turned to evening he didn't return and didn't call. That night Mickey never came home. Tears streamed down my thirteen-year-old face as I lay in bed with the lights on imagining the worst had happened to him.

Eventually the bell rang followed by thumping on the old front door of our dingy first floor apartment. I cautiously pulled the sheets down from my face and peered towards the door. Through the glass I saw two police officers and feared Mickey was dead. I opened up and they told me he was arrested, but everything was going to be all right. They took me to a police station. In the middle of the night a woman from social services arrived and took me to a house where I stayed for a few nights.

I didn't see Mickey again for three years. I bounced from foster home to foster home in the Boston neighborhoods of Dorchester and Roslindale until an elderly couple in suburban Quincy took me in. They were kind and were the first foster family to take me to see my brother at MCI-Cedar Junction. Every time I visited, Mickey told me the same story. His friend Chris "Higgs" Higgins called him and asked for a ride from the Lucky 88 Donut Shop outside of Fields Corner in Dorchester. Mickey dutifully picked him up in his decrepit maroon 1986 Chrysler LeBaron.

Mickey waited in the parking lot for Higgs, who ran out of the donut shop, yanked the door open and yelled, "let's get the fuck out of here," as he slammed the door shut. Less than ten minutes later they were pulled over by multiple police cars on Dorchester Avenue. Mickey and Higgs were cuffed against a cruiser. Police searched the LeBaron and found a Colt Python revolver on the floor in the back of the car.

The police separated Mickey from Higgs and interrogated him. Secure in his innocence, nineteen-year-old Mickey waived his right to an attorney and admitted to picking Higgs up, but denied knowing Higgs had just emptied the cash register and unloaded the contents of the Python into the chest of the donut shop's teenage cashier. Higgs never said a word to the police.

Unfortunately for Mickey, as Higgs' crime was a murder committed in furtherance of a felony—the holdup of the donut shop—it was a felony murder. Anyone charged as an accomplice faced the same penalty as Higgs: life in prison with no possibility of parole. Mickey and Higgs were tried together. At the close of the prosecution's case, Mickey's shaky public defender told him there was no way he was going to beat the felony murder charge.

Instead of putting up a defense and allowing Mickey to testify, the attorney convinced the teenager to take a deal. Staring at life in prison, Mickey pled guilty to second degree murder and received a life sentence with eligibility for parole after fifteen years. But after eighteen years, Mickey was still in prison and could be there much longer, if not for the rest of his life.

He was the reason I went to law school. I thought I could find a way to get him out. During my first year I worked hard in all of my classes, but none more so than Criminal Law. Of all the long hours I spent in the library, most were spent studying that subject—the assigned material and more. And I began a daily ritual of searching for a case or a parole board decision that could help win Mickey's freedom.

At the end of the year I received the highest grade in the class and the professor recommended me for an unpaid internship with the Suffolk County District Attorney's Office in Boston. I jumped at the chance and enthusiastically appeared at the office in the middle of June for an eight-week internship. After a brief orientation I was assigned to the "Murder Squad" and thrown into the mix to handle grunt work, including organizing evidence files in murder and rape cases. I sat at a long table with two investigators and quickly learned there was a huge difference between the almost philosophical study of criminal law in a law library and the actual practice of criminal law, especially in violent crimes.

One of my first assignments was to review a file in a rape case, which was going to be used in a new case against the same defendant. I began by sorting through photographs of a woman's bruised and battered body. The two investigators ate lunch and discussed their cases as I sifted through the box.

"Look at this," one of them said. He held up a photograph and I squinted to understand what I was looking at. As he chewed, he began to smile at my confusion. "Look closer." He held the picture closer to my face.

"Ah. That's a man's head and is that a carjack? And what are those on the ground?"

He smiled wider. "That's a dent puller. You don't recognize those things."

"I don't know. What are they?"

His chin flicked upwards. "They're his eyes."

"What?" Both of the investigators were now smiling. I refocused on the picture and realized they were eyes with blood vessels and tendons dangling on the ground behind them. "Holy shit. Someone took out his eyes?"

"Nah. He got hit in the back of his head with the dent puller and his eyes popped out." My chin recoiled into my Adam's apple when he said it. "Happens all the time."

"This is a two-fer," the other investigator added with satisfaction.

"A two-fer?"

"Yeah. Two for the price of one. You know? One bad guy killed another."

"Holy shit."

"Don't sweat it. You'll get used to it."

They turned back to their sandwiches and continued reviewing photographs of victims and gruesome crime scenes. As they talked, I pulled a large yellow envelope out of a box and felt something soft inside. I twisted a fastener open and aimed the mouth of the box at the table. Faded pink panties slid out in front of me.

"What's that?"

"Someone's underwear, I think."

"That should be in an evidence bag." The underwear was stained with dried blood and other fluids. "I'll take care of it, hold on." Moments later the investigator returned with a plastic bag. "Well, we can't say this has been preserved, but it shouldn't sneak up on anyone again." He used a pair of tongs and placed the garment in a clear bag, which he sealed and labeled. The two investigators resumed eating and talking as if nothing happened.

Unlike my co-workers, the day-to-day horrors witnessed working on the Murder Squad followed me home and tormented me nightly. After a summer of reviewing scenes of murdered children, gang members beaten and raped to death and more disembodied eyeballs than I could count, I buried my plans for entering the world of criminal law. Instead of trying to free Mickey on my own, I decided to hire the best criminal lawyer I could afford as soon as I had a job.

I got lucky when Knuckles agreed to take on Mickey's case. Ending up at Smith Stevens was another lucky break, as my salary allowed me to fund the cost of turning over every possible stone to free Mickey. As out of place as I was at the firm, I was determined to do everything I could to get him out. It was the fuel that motivated me, even if years of pursuing Mickey's freedom had yet to yield any results.

Perhaps I couldn't get Mickey out of prison by myself, but after everything I had researched and read about Mickey's case, maybe I could help keep Desi out of jail, even if I was scared of the consequences of messing up. As my last legal act of the day, I opened my laptop and tapped out an email to Smith Stevens' conflicts committee requesting permission to represent him. I copied the firm's *pro bono* committee hoping they could push the decision my way and began waiting for a response.

CHAPTER FOUR

The Senator

I slipped into the Backwater early with an egg and cheese sandwich in one hand and the handle to a black carry-on suitcase in the other. Every quarter I provided National Union with a status report of my Massachusetts cases along with any upcoming events that would have legal significance to the bank. I normally completed it the day before it was due, but was behind after sneaking away with Aaron and Tripper followed by a day at the Vanderbilt Houses. My report would be incorporated into a board report given to all of the members of the board of directors and used for planning and budgeting over the upcoming quarters.

As I unwrapped my sandwich, I noticed the red light on my desk phone was blinking. I tapped the message button. "You have two new messages. First message received today at 7:43 a.m. Beep. Bangkok Tailors will be in New York in the month of February and has a special offer for you. We will come to your office and measure you for custom suits—"

I freed my right hand from the egg and cheese and deleted the message with my greasy index finger. "You have one new message. Message received yesterday at 11:14 a.m. Beep. Hello, this is Andrew Bertrand calling for William Duggan. Mr. Duggan, I'm calling from Senator John Galvin's office concerning National Union Bank & Trust. I understand you're the bank's lawyer in some lawsuits pending in Boston. Please call me back."

Fuck. John Galvin was a short, bald-headed cannonball of a man who grew up in housing projects in South Boston. He survived by being the toughest son of a bitch in his neighborhood. Smart as a whip, he attended the Boston campus of the University of Massachusetts while supporting himself working the graveyard shift as a mechanic's apprentice at the Fore River Shipyard. After U-Mass, he received a law degree from New England School of Law and began a lifelong career in politics, first as an aide, then eventually running for office himself and becoming a state senator representing the First Suffolk District, which included Southie.

He won his two-year senate term a dozen times, rarely facing a challenger. With no term limits restricting his membership in the senate, he was as much of an institution in Massachusetts as Fenway Park. Beloved throughout his constituency, he took a punch-first approach to fighting for their rights and benefits. I knew as soon as I heard his name his office wasn't calling to get my address to send me a birthday card. Almost twenty-four hours had passed since the message.

I stuffed the last bit of my sandwich into my mouth and headed for Chuck's office, chewing as I walked. He wasn't there and didn't arrive until just before noon. When I finally caught him at his desk he had his back to the door. His tasseled loafers were crossed and resting on his credenza. As usual, the golf game was open on his computer screen. I knocked tentatively. Pushing off the credenza with his loafers, Chuck wheeled his chair around. He held up one finger and then pointed at a chair in front of his desk.

"Right. Right. Alright. Let me know. Relax. Nothing will happen. I promise. Ok, see you later." Chuck hung up the phone. "What's up?"

"Well, I got a phone call from John Galvin's office about my National Union cases." Chuck stared blankly, raising his eyebrows and puckering his lips. "Oh. John Galvin is a state senator in Massachusetts. From South Boston. His aide called and said they want to talk to me about the cases."

"About what, specifically?" Chuck looked irritated.

"I don't know. They didn't say. But I wanted to talk to you before I called back. This seems a little above my pay grade."

"Call them back and see what they want. But don't commit to anything."

"Do you want to be on the call with me?"

"I wish I could, but I'm going to be out of pocket this afternoon. I'm about to head out to see a client for lunch." Bullshit, but also typical. He was more likely heading over to GolfLand to swing some clubs or the Roosevelt Hotel to drift off into oblivion.

After returning to my cubicle I looked down at my desk phone and hoped for a blackout. Then it rang. Six. One. Seven. Oh, shit! I quickly steeled myself and grabbed the receiver. "Hello, this is Will Duggan."

A voice boomed from the other end of the line. "William Duggan! Is that you?"

"Yes, it's me."

"Hey, Andy! You sure you called the right numbah? I called one time and guess who I got? You're not lyin' to me, ahh you Andy?"

My stomach sank through the floor. Holy Fuck. I cleared my throat. "Senator Galvin, it's Will Duggan. Andy called me, but I was out of the office. I was literally just about to call him back."

"Sure, you were," the senator spat back at me. "I'm glad you're not a liar, Andy. You had me worried. So Duggan, you must be a busy guy. I'd think if a senator called me I'd get back to him pretty quickly."

"As I said, I was out of—"

"Yeah, yeah. And I'm sure a place like Smith Stevens doesn't have the technology to permit you to check your messages from outside the office or to make a call back. You weren't foxholing on me, Duggan. Were you?"

"Um, what?" If I hadn't noticed I was sweating up a storm, surely anyone walking past my cubicle could see it.

"Ya'know, foxholing. Hiding out in a foxhole, hoping I'd forget about you. Is that your thing?"

"No, I promise—"

"How'd you end up at Smith Stevens? Andy just showed me your bio. It definitely wasn't based on looks." He chuckled.

"It's a long story—"

"No time for that. Andy called because my office received complaints about National Union closing branches in Roxbury, Dorchester, and Southie. He also did some research showing most of National Union's lawsuits are in Boston. And it looks to me like almost all of the people sued by National Union live in only a handful of neighborhoods. As I see it, the cases are coming out of Southie, Dorchester, Mattapan, and Roxbury. This makes me curious. Do you know why I'm curious, Duggan?"

I knew exactly why he was curious. "No. No, I don't, sir."

"Because it doesn't look like National Union has filed a single suit in Norfolk County. And there are only a few in Middlesex—in Cambridge. And I don't see any in Essex. And only some in Plymouth—looks like there are some in Brockton. And it doesn't look like National Union has closed branches in those counties, either. I get that there are more people in Boston—but it looks like National Union is picking on us city people. Can you tell me why that is?"

"Um, well, I only handle the cases that are sent to me and I can't speak to the bank's litigation strategy. And I think we're getting into some areas of attorney-client privilege."

"Bullshit! You know why, Duggan! You know who lives in these neighborhoods! Immigrants and minorities! And they're hardworking people that are part of the fabric of Boston. You know what this is? The R word! Redlining! This is just the kind of thing the attorney general would love to sink her teeth into."

Beads of sweat were rolling from my hairline down my forehead. "I don't know anything about that. Listen, they don't bring me in on high level decision-making and I can't speak to branch closures."

"Well, who the hell can? Someone can explain this."

"I'll run it up the chain," I stammered.

The senator shrugged audibly. "When can I expect to hear from you?"

"Give me a few days and I'll follow up with you."

"I'll be waiting." And with that the line went dead. In the stillness of my cubicle the only sound I could hear was the beating of my heart throbbing through my eardrums.

I hurried back down to Chuck's office, but he was already gone. The golf game wasn't even open on his computer screen. As usual, the voicemail on his cellphone was full. He had perfected the art of avoidance. I could try to take it to David Bell, but that would surely end in disaster. David would call Chuck, and if Chuck hadn't told David about our discussion, Chuck would get blasted. And if Chuck got blasted, I was going to get it even worse in return. And the longer it all took to reach David, the worse it was going to be for everyone.

I grabbed my jacket and bolted out of the Backwater into cold January daylight. My first stop was GolfLand. I scanned the store and didn't see him driving balls into video fairways. He wasn't chipping onto the artificial greens. A salesperson asked if he could help me find a club, but I'd rather go naked beekeeping than golfing. Chuck was nowhere to be seen on the floor. My lower back seized.

My only hope was the Madison Club Lounge at the Roosevelt Hotel. If he wasn't there, I was going to have to call David. Fifth Avenue was crowded following the December holidays. In my growing panic I was out of sync with the masses of people walking together in clusters and found myself bouncing off of their shoulders. Clouds of cigarette smoke wafted around the hotel's taxi entrance. I wove my way through European tourists wearing leather jeans and scarves who didn't seem to notice my existence.

Up the stairs and through the gilded lobby I worked my way towards the lounge, dodging wheelie bags and legs dangling from plush leather chairs. I stepped inside and immediately lost hope. It was buzzing with chatter. Chuck wasn't on a barstool, where he could often be found nursing a beer and picking at French fries. I stepped deeper into the dark and atmospheric space, which was partially illuminated by stained-glass windows.

I'm fucked. I turned around, hoping I might catch him returning from the men's room. Instead, I caught a glimpse of the back of his head on the other side of the lounge seated at a small, low table across from a woman. As I approached, his fingertips were resting on her hand. I could only see the outline of her long blonde hair, as Chuck's head blocked her face. It wasn't his wife. She didn't have blonde hair. At least that's what I remembered from meeting her once at a firm holiday party.

As the woman's face became clear she said, "Hi, Will." At that, Chuck quickly swiveled in his chair, his fingers jumping off of hers. It was Julia Mancuso, a junior attorney from the Backwater.

"Will, how's it going?" Chuck acted as if he expected my arrival. "Why don't you grab a chair and sit with us?" His face betrayed his graciousness. Even in the shadows I could see its color had washed away. If I thought I was fucked before, I was absolutely fucked now.

"Actually, I can't stick around, but I need to talk to you. Can I steal you for a moment?"

"Of course." We stepped away from the table and at the end of the bar I filled him in on the senator's call.

"Should I call David or anyone from National Union?"

"How much time do we have?" I told Chuck a few days. "Then, no. Let me tell David and we'll handle it from there. Circle back with me next week, and I'll fill you in." This wasn't reassuring given that Chuck was already out of the office drinking and canoodling with a young associate, but I wasn't going to attempt to go around him.

"I have to submit my quarterly report to National Union today. Should I footnote the call in the report?"

"No, don't put it in yet. Wait until next week and you can submit a supplement. Let's have a plan in place first. No need to unnecessarily raise any alarm bells. And you don't want to get ahead of your skis on this with David. He's in Tahoe for a long weekend and if he hears about it from National Union first it will be a career-defining moment for you. And if he hears about it from you while he's away, it might also be a career-defining moment. This will blow over, so don't worry about it for now. Understood?" Chuck headed back to his table and I returned to the Backwater relieved and uneasy at the same time.

The suitcase stared at me from the floor when I sat down in my cubicle. At least I had the weekend before whatever shit-show the senator's call would cause next week. I picked the last nits from the report and sent it to National Union. As soon as I received a blind copy of the email, I snapped my laptop shut, threw it in my briefcase and headed to the Port Authority.

CHAPTER FIVE

Street Level

The aura of a life of smoking hung in the air six feet around Catherine Corcoran. Footsteps echoed on the marble floors of Suffolk Superior Court in Boston as we stood a cautious distance from one another. Somewhere within the sagging white cotton cardigan draped over her bony frame was a crumpled pack of menthol cigarettes. She was from Savin Hill, otherwise known as "Stab n' Kill." My guess was they were Parliaments. Her friends called her "Cath," but to me she would always be "Ms. Corcoran." She rarely looked up from her shoes and only made glancing eye contact when she did.

Minutes before, the Honorable Donald J. Butler ordered us out of his wood-paneled courtroom into the chilly hallway to discuss settlement. I arrived before 9:00 for a status conference. When I asked his clerk Debbie how heavy the docket was she grunted. "Stacked." There was no telling when we'd be in front of the judge. I resigned myself to an uncomfortable wooden bench in the gallery. Judge Butler grew increasingly impatient as he churned through the docket and chewed on attorneys. My confidence faded as morning turned into afternoon. By the time Debbie ordered everyone to return after lunch, it had drained completely from my body.

Just after 2:00 a court officer entered the courtroom. "All rise!" Judge Butler marched imperiously to his bench trailed by Debbie and his interns. The pristine white collar of his dress shirt peeked out from underneath his robes and framed a thick Windsor knot. Athletic and solidly built at fifty-something, the shine of his wingtips was only matched by the shine of his balding head, which was crowned with silvering hair and reflected the overhead lights. Debbie whispered something into his ear and the judge became visibly agitated. She then pointed towards the gallery full of attorneys.

Debbie followed with, "Hickey & Schultz versus Red Lotus Flower LLC!" As the attorneys arranged themselves, Judge Butler looked intently at a large stack of papers sitting on the edge of his bench.

Before they could get comfortable, he bellowed, "Counselors!" Everyone looked up as a court reporter typed rapidly. The air in the courtroom was heavy and reeked of nervous sweat. "Do you see this thick stack of papers sitting in front of me?" The attorneys watched silently. "These papers are just the cases I have to deal with today. And tomorrow there'll be another stack of papers just like it. And I have so many cases lined up for trial it would make an air traffic controller's head explode. I don't have time for trivial nonsense. I hear we have a settlement, but there's a minor hang-up. Could someone enlighten me?"

Attorneys at both tables stood up and stammered incoherently looking helplessly towards each other and then at the judge. "Well, since it looks like the cat got both your tongues, let me help." He looked at the Plaintiffs' table where attorneys from Hickey & Schultz were stationed. "So we have a settlement for twenty-five K, but you want the money up front and not over time. Could you refresh my memory as to how many months that is?"

A gangly man in a grey suit and tassel loafers stood up and brushed a mane of thick brown hair to the side. "Your Honor, James Hickey on behalf of Hickey & Schultz. The proposed payment plan is over five months."

"So, twenty-five over five months. That doesn't seem unreasonable to me. You understand how busy this Court is? And you won't be going to trial within those five months?"

"I'm sensitive to that, Your Honor. But if we don't get paid up front, there's risk of nonpayment and default. And if that happens we're going to be back in this courtroom tangling over an unpaid settlement amount. We want security that we're going to get paid."

"Ok, Ok. Well I'm interested in hearing the other side of this. Red Lotus? Do you have anything to say?"

Slowly, a younger attorney stood up from behind the Defendants' table and took a sip of water from a plastic bottle and carefully tightened the white cap. "Good morning, Your Honor. Gerry Schroder of Gerry Schroder, P.C. on behalf of Red Lotus Flower LLC d/b/a Bang Bang House. Your Honor, it's a matter of cash flow. My client is a restaurant and it doesn't have $25,000 laying around. Money comes in and it's used to pay bills.

"It's very much a hand-to-mouth business. Paying twenty-five at once wouldn't just be a hardship, it would put my client out of business. And, Your Honor, with all due respect, this is a contested case and my client has a counterclaim for malpractice. If the case can't be settled with payments over time, my client's going to fight. This is a matter of life or death. And a lump-sum means death."

"That point is well-taken, counselor. But what about Mr. Hickey's desire for security?" For a moment Judge Butler seemed to be enjoying the dialogue.

"Your Honor, if this case goes to trial, there's no security. I firmly believe Red Lotus will defeat Hickey & Schultz if this goes to a jury. And I further believe Red Lotus will win its malpractice case. My client isn't settling because it believes it's going to lose. My client's settling because litigation is too expensive and time-consuming. And for purposes of argument only, suppose Hickey & Schultz wins and the firm gets a judgment against Red Lotus in the full amount of its claim, $45,000. Well, that judgment is just a piece of paper, Your Honor. And they would need to enforce it. I'm telling you in all candor that paying twenty-five at once right now could shut down Bang Bang House because it represents a major cash-flow problem. And it doesn't get easier with forty-five."

Judge Butler interrupted. "I don't want to steal your thunder counselor, but as I understand it there's more security in a payment plan because the restaurant can actually pay it."

"In essence, yes, Your Honor."

The judge looked towards the Plaintiff's table. "Any response?"

James Hickey stood up and cleared his brown hair from his eyes again. "Your Honor, we're also confident we're going to win. And I understand the point about a judgment being a piece of paper, but when the bank freezes your accounts people often find a way to pay."

"Or file for bankruptcy," blurted Gerry Schroder.

"Your Honor . . ." James Hickey sighed and his shoulders sagged.

The judge's eyes darted at the young lawyer. "Mr. Schroder, you've had a chance to speak. Now it's his turn. I can't hear either of you if you talk over each other. Proceed, Mr. Hickey."

"Your Honor, I was just trying to explain that judgments have a way of encouraging resolution. And we'd prefer to have an enforceable judgment in hand than settle for less. And then possibly be back in court fighting over the unpaid settlement."

"Ok. Mr. Schroder, anything to add?"

"Judge, my client respectfully asks for an opportunity to be heard."

"Well, that's a bit unusual at a status conference." The judge peered at Plaintiff's table, his bald head reflecting sunlight that was now pouring through a large window next to his bench. "Any objection?"

"No objection, Your Honor, provided we have an opportunity to respond."

"Ok, then. Mr. Schroder . . ."

"Your Honor, may I please introduce Hong Nguyen, the owner of Red Lotus Flower LLC d/b/a Bang Bang House."

A middle-aged man stood up at the defense table. "Judge, I'm Hong Nguyen. I own Bang Bang House and have been in the restaurant business since I moved here as a teenager more than thirty years ago. I started as a dishwasher, then worked as a busboy and a waiter. Finally, I opened my own restaurant. I pay my debts, but these guys screwed up. They fuc—"

"Your Honor!" James Hickey leapt to his feet.

Before another word came out, Judge Butler held his finger in the air. "Mr. Nguyen, this isn't a time for evidence. I'm giving you an opportunity to discuss the proposed settlement. There will be a time for evidence later if this isn't resolved. Ok?"

Gerry Schroder whispered something into his client's ear. "I'm sorry, Judge," Mr. Nguyen replied. "I pay my debts. If we settle, I will pay it. But I have a cash-flow problem. I can't pay all of it now. I don't want to pay, but paying attorneys is so expensive, so I agree to settle."

"Anything else, Mr. Schroder?"

"No, Judge."

"Mr. Hickey?"

"Your Honor, we've been trying to get payment for over a year from Mr. Nguyen. And malpractice never came up until we filed suit. I need a lump-sum payment. If he isn't going to pay all at once, then we don't have a settlement. And in that case, we want a trial date."

Judge Butler took a deep breath and looked sternly at James Hickey. "You're entitled to a trial date, but as I told you before, this Court is very busy and very booked up with trials. I can't force you to settle, but I'm frustrated five months is too much time for Mr. Nguyen to pay you." He paused and looked towards his clerk. "Debbie, could you tell me how my trial calendar looks in eighteen months?"

"Eighteen months, Your Honor?" James Hickey was in disbelief as the words escaped his mouth.

The judge's eyes darted in his direction. "Do we have a problem, Mr. Hickey?"

"Uh, uh, no no, Your Honor. My apologies."

"Debbie, how does my calendar look in twenty-four months?" James Hickey was silent this time.

"Judge, the first two weeks are clear."

"And that is?"

"The first week of January. Right after the holidays."

"Perfect. I love a trial just after the holidays. The lawyers can really use that time to get ready." He sneered as the words left his mouth. James Hickey looked furious, but didn't sass the judge this time. "Anything else?" The judge scanned the silent courtroom with satisfaction. "Well, good then. Just to let you know…" He leaned towards Debbie and said something in a muffled tone and shook his head. "The attorneys' conference room down the hall is open if you want to try to resolve this before you leave today. I'll be here until 4:30 if you have good news to report."

Full-blown anxiety replaced my depleted confidence and I began to brace myself. My marching orders from National Union were to go to trial and the only compromise I could reach was on payment timing, but not amount. At 4:15 Debbie called National Union's case and her words echoed in the now-empty courtroom. I was sore from the wood bench, but relieved any torture wouldn't be witnessed by a gallery full of attorneys.

Judge Butler glared at me as I passed through the bar. "How much are you billing National Union per hour to be here?"

"Your Honor, that's a client matter I can't divulge."

He shot me a hard look as I put down my briefcase. "Coming from Smith Stevens in Manhattan it's probably somewhere around five or six hundred an hour. Being conservative at five hundred per . . . You've been here since 9:00. My guess is you've billed at least $3,500 just to sit here all day, plus your tickets to come from New York and travel time. And that's on top of the cost of preparing for a trial. I don't understand it. Maybe you can enlighten me?"

"Enlighten you, Your Honor?" Debbie smirked at me.

"I don't understand what we're doing in this courtroom, counselor? You got a $26,000 case and you're going to run up more than $50,000 in legal fees. It simply makes no sense. Why hasn't this case settled long before?"

"With all due respect, Your Honor, I think we're getting into areas of confidential strategy I can't divulge. And we're talking about strategy decisions I wasn't a part of. I just litigate the cases."

The judge's eyebrows looked like they would crawl over his balding head and down the back of his neck. "You just litigate the cases? Don't you have a duty to think about your client's best interests? Don't you think you have a conflict billing your client more than the case is worth?"

"Again, there are decisions I'm not a part of. I take my direction from the client and my understanding is the client understands the dynamics of this case." It was hard to sound convincing, especially when the judge was making the same point I tried to make to David Bell months before.

Catherine Corcoran continued to look at her feet. "I can't pay you what I don't have. I can't promise to pay you $26,000 I don't have. I paid every month until I lost my job. I was late by sixty days and you sued me. I still

40

can't believe it. I've always been a loyal customer. I was with Wampanoag before you guys became National Union. I just don't have the money. I'll start paying again as soon as I get another job.

"I used to be able to go to the branch and explain if I was going to be late and we always worked it out. I knew everyone in there. But you closed the branch. Every time I call the bank's number they put me on hold for an hour. And when I finally get through, I know it's not anybody even in this country. And they don't know me. They don't care. I'm just some number. If I want to talk to anyone in person I have to take a bus to the Red Line to downtown Boston and I don't know anyone there."

At 4:45 we re-entered the courtroom, which was completely empty except for a court officer. "We're ready to report back to Judge Butler." I expected to get blasted.

"Hold on." He disappeared into a doorway behind the bench.

A few minutes later Debbie appeared and walked to the edge of the bar. "What's the latest?"

"We didn't settle."

"Great," she replied sarcastically. "The judge is gone for the day. Can you come back on Monday?" Relief washed over me.

"I can't. I have to be back in Manhattan."

I looked at Ms. Corcoran then at Debbie. I had no interest in appearing before the judge again anytime soon. "Is there any chance we could set up an informal mediation in front of you?"

Debbie shrugged and looked to Ms. Corcoran. "Can you be back here in ninety days?"

"I might be working, but ok."

"See you in ninety days."

While it had been a long and pointless day in court, I nearly skipped past building security having avoided Judge Butler's wrath for now, at least.

CHAPTER SIX

Tough Nut

A thick fog coated the windows and obscured the view from outside. Loud chatter leaked onto the sidewalk and the fragrance of body heat and beer wafted out as soon as I pulled the bright blue wooden door open. I craned my neck as I navigated the crowd.

"There he is!" Knuckles' thin lips parted into a wide smile revealing gleaming white teeth. He clutched a short glass half full of brown liquid floating a couple of surviving pieces of ice. The rest were being victimized by his unbreakable habit of chewing frozen water. "Step inside my office." His eyes flashed as he took his coat and briefcase off an adjacent barstool. As I sat down and peeled off my grey tweed overcoat, he shook his glass at me. "What do you want for lunch?"

"Harpoon."

"You can take a Dot Rat out of Boston, but you can't take the Boston out of a Dot Rat." He chuckled and smiled. It was an insult, but coming from Knuckles it felt like a compliment or maybe even a badge of honor. And no one in New York ever accused me of being a Dorchester street urchin.

The surging crowd lapped against the bar all around us. "Petey! Another brown and a Harpoon for my friend here!" He turned to me. "How was court?"

"Total shit-show."

"Who you got?"

"Butler."

"Shit. Dismiss the case and get the fuck out of there while you still have a law license."

"Tell me about it. Called us last, sent us out to discuss settlement and left before we finished."

"Sounds about right. Good luck in his court, New York."

"I'm no New Yorker." Knuckles grinned.

After more than thirty years practicing in every criminal court in Massachusetts, Knuckles knew everything about everyone in the legal system. He started as an assistant district attorney and worked his way into trying serious felonies. After half a decade working for the prosecution, he switched teams and briefly worked for a preeminent criminal defense firm before hanging a shingle as a solo.

His big break came when Tony "Rings" DiCiaccio retained him in a complex racketeering case. "Rings" because his fingers were too thick to wear them. He faced a lengthy prison sentence for bookmaking, money laundering and collections. The unpredictability of juries coupled with the consequences of failing Tony Rings scared away other defense attorneys. Despite the risk, Knuckles took the case, which involved dozens of defendants and witnesses and thousands of pieces of evidence.

The prosecution closed its case after months of testimony and a mountain of exhibits. With chests puffed they withdrew a plea deal offered to Tony Rings carrying a ten-year prison sentence. Then Knuckles stood up at the defense table and nonchalantly walked over to a podium in front of the witness stand and cleared his throat. He introduced himself to the jurors and sized up the prosecution's lead witness, a turncoat mobster who traded testimony for leniency, Bobby DeFabio. He then led Bobby through an extensive and detailed history of Bobby's criminal activities. Much of it surprised the prosecution.

Hours into Knuckles' cross-examination in front of Tony Rings' glare, Bobby looked like he would've sworn he was wearing panties to get off the witness stand. With beads of sweat rolling down his forehead and the attentive eyes of the jury trained on him, Bobby's memory began to faulter and Knuckles punched holes through his story. And the case began to crumble. Not just against Tony Rings, but also against every other defendant in the courtroom.

With their case suddenly falling apart, the prosecutors decided the only way to avoid wasting years of preparation and months of trial time was to get Knuckles out of the courtroom. After a hasty sidebar with the judge, in front of the stunned faces of the other defendants and their counsel, Tony Rings walked out of federal court in downtown Boston a free man with Knuckles by his side matching him stride for stride. The image was front page news in every newspaper in New England. And at exactly that moment Knuckles' star shot into the stratosphere and he became the go-to attorney whenever someone was in a hairy situation.

"When did you get in?"

"Last night."

"Fly?"

"Nah, bus."

"You took the fucking bus?" Knuckles was incredulous. "Wait, you have a job, right? You're still an attorney? At Smith Stevens, no? You're fucking with me. I knew it."

"Kevin, I took the bus. I like the bus. I chilled. I read. It had Wi-Fi and I played on my phone."

"Can't you afford a car? Or Jesus, rent a car? Or take the train? Anything would be better than being on a bus with bus people and fucking chickens running all over the place shitting everywhere."

"There were no chickens on the bus, Kevin. I'm serious, it's not that bad. And it's cheap." I didn't own a car. I barely left Manhattan, let alone the west side of the city.

"Hey, Petey! Did you hear that?"

"Nah, Kev, what's up?" Pete sidled over to us and leaned across the bar.

"My friend here works at a white-shoe law firm in Manhattan and takes the goddamn bus. Can you believe that?"

"Why do they call it 'white shoe?'"

"Well, normally it's because they don't have to pick up dog shit in their own backyard, but my friend here seems to love it." Knuckles laughed hardily, but Pete looked puzzled and increasingly disinterested.

Pete asked, "Another round?" Knuckles lifted his glass. The drink Pete had just poured was disappearing quickly.

Knuckles looked at me and I looked at my beer. I had barely touched it. "What? Surgery tomorrow? After today I'd be crying into my drink if I were you. Pete, get him another."

"Nah, nah. I'm good."

"Screw that. Put a little hair on your chest. I'm buying." He was buying, but it was with my money.

"All right. Another Harpoon."

"Good for you. How's the talent in here?" Knuckles scanned the room smiling. He responded to a loud "Kevin" with a wave. He turned his stool sideways. "How's Mickey?"

"I'm seeing him tomorrow."

"He's a tough one," Knuckles commented.

"He is. He's going to be ok."

"Eighteen years. I think he's going to be all right. But what I meant was he's a tough nut to crack."

"True."

"A lot of people would say anything to get out after that much time. All he has to say is 'sorry.' Can you finally talk some sense into him?"

"I've tried. You know I've tried. But he won't apologize for something he didn't do. Nothing I've said has changed his mind."

"You gotta keep trying. He'll never get to live his life if he doesn't ask the parole board for forgiveness"

"He's not going to do it. Can you keep digging? Is there anything we can do?"

"I've had PI's on it and questioned everyone that might have seen anything. People are gone. Witnesses are dead. If I could dig up Chris Higgins' body and make it answer questions, I would." Nine months after his conviction, Higgs died of a brain aneurysm after repeatedly smashing his head into the wall of his cell. Unfortunately for Mickey, Higgs never discussed his crime with anyone before his death. Any chance of exoneration evaporated with his suicide.

"I can have my investigator cover old ground, but there's nothing out there. And if I go before the parole board again without an acknowledgement of guilt and a show of remorse, he's just going to go right back to Cedar Junction. And the same thing is going to happen over and over until long after I retire." It was kinder than saying until Mickey died.

I looked down at my beer as the noise of the bar washed around me. "Nothing else?"

"No. Well, not unless the governor owes you a favor." I shook my head and grimaced.

"Kevin, I have something for you." Knuckles looked down at my hands suspiciously. I reached into my briefcase and pulled out a thick white envelope.

"There's fifteen inside in fifties." It was why I took a bus to Boston. No one in a bus terminal would ever know I was carrying $15,000 in cash. If I tried to move through LaGuardia with that kind of stash, I likely would've gotten to spend some quality time with drug enforcement agents in one of the airport's backrooms.

Knuckles' eyes released from the envelope and he looked back at me. "You know I love taking your money. But nothing's going to change. I can save you fifteen grand right now. The PI will sniff around. He won't find anything new. Then I'll make my pitch to the parole board. Basically the same as last time—he was a teenager, didn't rob the donut shop and unwittingly picked up his friend after the robbery. They'll look at Mickey. He'll say he's innocent and refuse to apologize. They'll deny parole and he'll go back to jail for a few more years until he's eligible for his next hearing."

I listened to Knuckles' precap with pursed lips while nodding my head. "I know, I know. But I gotta do my part. Even if he doesn't play ball. I won't sleep at night if I'm not at least trying to do something. So are you in? Would you prefer a check?"

Knuckles feigned anger, looked at me then the envelope. "Give me that thing. Check. Christ! You already paid taxes on it, why should I?" His eyes sparkled as I handed it over. Without checking the bills, he tucked it into an inside pocket of his suit jacket. Pete materialized close to Knuckles, who was thrilled to have new money in his pocket.

"Another beer for my young friend!"

"Nah, I gotta go. Getting up early."

Knuckles nodded his head and smiled. "All right. Now you stay out of trouble."

I dismounted the barstool, grabbed my briefcase in my left hand and slung my overcoat across my elbow. "Thanks for the drinks."

Before he turned back to the bar, Knuckles held out his hand. "It's up to Mickey. Don't let it beat you up. You're a good kid."

I wiggled my way through the steamy crowd and into the relief of a cold January night in Boston. The next morning I waited in line for the first round of security at Cedar Junction. The conversation with Knuckles rang in my head. The morning air was cold and my breath hovered under a blue sky. A half dozen visitors stood in line ahead of me, including some small children.

A woman was turned away because she didn't submit a Visitor Information Form in advance. The guards had no tolerance for surprise drop-ins. I submitted mine long ago and received a handbook of protocol for visiting the prison. It included a laundry list of information about who could visit, visiting hours, behavior, physical contact, and dress code—dressing like a prisoner wasn't permitted. I had the routine down cold, but not everyone got the memo.

I passed through the humiliation of an exterior security entrance, which offered only a taste of the humiliations rendered daily to the residents on the inside. I walked down an asphalt path leading to the next security checkpoint at the perimeter fence. A guard waved a wand around my body and I was patted down from my ankles to my Adam's apple. I pushed through tinted glass doors, which concealed the stale smell of too many men living together in an enclosed space. Inside, another security guard checked my identification and pointed me towards a waiting room with rows of bare metal chairs held to the floor by heavy bolts.

I waited to be ushered into the visiting room. While Mickey expected my visit, the guards didn't track him down until after I was seated. The air was stagnate. The door to the visiting room finally buzzed open. "Mr. Duggan." I looked up and a muscular guard nodded at me to follow him. The visiting room smelled of bleach. Windows covered in heavy chicken wire lined one side of the room. Tinted windows surrounded a metal door coated in chipped green paint on the other side.

I sat quietly until the chipped green door buzzed open and Mickey walked through. He was a wire coat hanger under an oversized white tee shirt. Green hospital scrubs revealed white tube socks bleeding into white slip-ons. Mickey wasn't a problem prisoner or a gang member. Unlike many other prisoners, he had never been transferred and spent his entire incarceration inside Cedar Junction. Due to his good behavior, he neither wore handcuffs nor shackles. I stood up and gave him a quick hug. A fading shiner circling his left eye attracted my gaze.

Mickey noticed my stare. "I slipped."

"You're full of shit," I replied. He smirked a little, but shook off sharing the details. "How's the wife and kids?"

He smiled at me. "Fucker! How about yours?"

I laughed. "Same as yours. What's new?"

"I just got back from Monte Carlo. Last night me and the boys had a big feast to celebrate. The guards brought in filet mignon, lobster . . . Johnnie Walker Black. Met this great girl. Fucking amazing." Mickey's blue eyes scanned my face. His hair was fading from a dark brown. Silver hairs were increasingly popping up around his temples. The heaviness of his living situation weighed on me. "It's all right. I'm doing fine. I work out. I watch television. I go to therapy. I got a routine. There's some good guys in here. And thanks for the books and for putting money in my account."

"No problem, Mick." Mickey could buy snacks, paper, envelopes, soap, and shampoo from the commissary as long as he had money in his account. "I saw Knuckles last night."

"Social call?"

"C'mon, Mickey."

"They ain't letting me walk out of here."

"But they will if you own it and show remorse."

"I got no remorse. I'm not sorry for something I didn't do."

"Well fuck what you did or didn't do. Knuckles is going to take it to the parole board."

"I'm not going through the story again. I didn't fucking do anything wrong. And what if I did apologize? Then I'm a fucking admitted murderer. And I walk out of here to what? I'm almost forty. I haven't had a job in almost twenty years. What does that life look like? I'll have no job and no place to live. I'll be a fucking bum on the streets."

"You can come live with me and we'll figure it out."

"They ain't letting me out of Massachusetts if I'm paroled."

"Then I'll move back and get a job here."

"Just like that?" Mickey snapped his fingers.

"This is your fucking life! Do you really want to spend the rest of it in here?" My face was bright red. Mickey looked stern.

"No. Will. I don't want to spend the rest of my life in here. But at least I have a life here. I got nothing on the outside."

"Fuck you. You got me. And I got no one else. I've been coming here every month for fifteen years. So fuck you if you forgot that."

Mickey receded into the metal chair and ran his palm through his short hair. Silver follicles caught the overhead lights as they flicked back into place. His face was angular, and his square chin pointed downward. He could have been an actor in another life. His blue eyes looked upwards from under his dark eyebrows. "Sorry. I'm not getting out of here. And I'm not getting my hopes up. It only makes it worse to be here after it doesn't happen."

"I got it. But we gotta try, Mick."

Maybe he recognized it meant more to me than him. "Ok, Will. I'll go along with it, but I'm not admitting shit I didn't do."

"Good. Cause I already paid Knuckles. In cash."

"That fucking crook." Mickey smiled again, finally.

After another quick hug, the guards buzzed Mickey back through the green door where he would be scanned and patted down for contraband. His greying hair personified the passage of time and the window for him to have any semblance of a normal life was closing rapidly. As soon as I was on the bus back to New York I cracked open my laptop. I spent the ride home researching the latest parole board decisions. There had to be a way.

CHAPTER SEVEN

Blinking Red Light

Ten hours on a bus in less than three days left a crick in my neck and I could barely turn my head to the right side. The last thing I wanted to do was spend my Monday in the Backwater, but I had to bill hours. After leaving the subway, my cellphone buzzed in my jacket. I dug it out of my pocket and "David Bell" was on the caller ID. It was already 11:17. Shit! Never once had I heard of anyone from the Backwater receiving a call from David with good news. I had a choice. Take the call and let him know I was on the street. Or run to the Backwater and act like I was just away from my desk. I let the phone ring and picked up my pace to Eighth Avenue.

When the elevator clanged open to the second floor I immediately saw Randall. "Will, where have you been?" His voice was harried. I was almost surprised he could put my name to my face so quickly. "Hurry, hurry! Didn't you get my emails? David wants to see you in his office!"

"When?"

"Hours ago!"

"About what?"

"About men from Mars! National Union! What else do you work on?"

The red light on my desk's telephone blinked at me. "You have two new messages. First message received this morning at 8:55. Beep. Bangkok Tailors will be in New York—" Christ! I was in no mood to have my inseam measured. "Message deleted. Message received this morning at 9:14. Will, it's David Bell. Call me at my desk when you get in." 9:14! No one gets in before 10:00 on Monday. Senator Galvin's call must've gotten someone's panties in a twist. I retraced my call and couldn't think of anything I fucked up.

A woman's voice appeared on the line after two rings. "David Bell's office. How may I help you?"

"June, it's Will Duggan."

"Oh, hi, Will. David's been trying to reach you. Hold on." Although he had been looking for me, it was jarring that David was about to take my call. "David asked if you could come to his office to see him." Shit.

"Of course. I'll be there in twenty minutes or so." Twenty minutes for every self-immolating thought to go through my mind while suffering the indignity of entering the Temple.

When I arrived, June ushered me into a large corner office with a view of Times Square. David was on the phone. His face was freshly tan from a weekend on the slopes and the color of his complexion contrasted stylishly against his slicked-back silver hair. His suit jacket was draped over the arm of a leather couch. June picked it up and hung it carefully on a thick cedar hanger in his coat closet as I took a seat.

David wore a fitted blue shirt with a subtle sheen offset by darker blue suspenders with two thin red stripes running their length. An even darker blue tie hung from his neck. He paced the office listening to a man's high-pitched voice over the speakerphone. He alternatively gazed out the window, checked his emails and looked at me. He finally clicked a button on the base of the phone.

"Sorry about that. Thanks for coming over." His tone was cordial, almost apologetic. My sense of unease increased. "Will, I asked you to come over because Chuck told me you received a call from John Galvin. Tell me what happened." I regurgitated the call in its entirety. "Why didn't you tell me about this last week? And why didn't I find out about a senator calling for four days?" My face turned beet red.

"Well, when something comes up I normally talk to Chuck because he's down the hall from me."

"Chuck said he told you I was away and to track me down." Whatever color was in my face dropped into my stomach and made my heart skip a beat on the way down. I raced through my memory. I was certain Chuck said he was going to tell David about Galvin's call. But if I threw Chuck under the bus, he was only going to think of some other way to sabotage me. Caught between two partners, there was no scenario where I was going to come out on top.

"I'm sorry, David. I must have misunderstood. I was trying to get my quarterly report out when the senator called." It was total bullshit, but I tried to act convincing.

"Next time a senator, the president or a police chief calls you, what are you going to do?"

"Call you."

"When?"

I wanted to kill Chuck. "Immediately."

He nodded his head. "Immediately. Good. Can I do anything to make myself clearer? Have I been clear?" I nodded affirmatively. Maybe I wasn't clear. "Anything else?" I shook my head.

As I pulled away from David's guest chair I had a thought. "David, before I go I have one other item. I submitted my quarterly report on Thursday, but didn't include anything about Galvin. Should I supplement it?"

David didn't hesitate. "Absolutely not. Listen, I'm working directly with Don Jones on our approach. And we don't want to put anything in the report that spooks the horses." I stared at David blankly. His squinting green eyes pierced mine. "You know what's happening with Don?"

I shook my head. "I haven't heard anything." David momentarily slumped into his leather desk chair. He scanned my face intensely. His expression did nothing to reduce my sense of being an outsider at the firm.

"This is top secret and you cannot tell anyone. Joel Weinberg is stepping down and National Union is going to appoint Don as general counsel at Thursday's quarterly meeting. The board of directors is onboard. Until that happens, we cannot present an overly negative outlook on the bank's litigation or anything else. We can't risk knocking Don's appointment off course."

Joel Weinberg was the longtime general counsel of the bank and oversaw all of its legal affairs. Don Jones had been associate general counsel for more than ten years under Joel. He was second in command in the legal department and as time went on began to wield increasing influence over decision-making, including the bank's selection of outside lawyers. David Bell and Smith Stevens had been the main beneficiaries of Don Jones' increased clout.

Law school roommates, David and Don remained close friends and I wouldn't have been surprised if Don was in Tahoe with David over the weekend. During the past ten years, Don had steered more and more legal work to David, and David had become increasingly wealthy and powerful within Smith Stevens because of it. If Don became general counsel he would be the final gatekeeper for all legal matters and dictate which law firms National Union hired and how much the bank would pay them. There were dollar signs in David's eyes.

"Do you understand?" I nodded. "Let's be clear. If you tell anyone about this. About Galvin's call. Even in passing or if it ends up in a report or I hear it from someone else, I'm going to find where you live and I'm going to burn the fucking place to the ground. Am I clear?"

"We're clear."

"About what?"

"If I fuck this up you're going to burn my apartment to the ground." I didn't own my apartment. In the back of my mind I thought the joke was on him.

"Good."

"David, one other thing. I owe Galvin a call."

"How long do you have?"

"I said I needed a few days and that was on Thursday."

"Call his office and buy some more time. Don knows what's going on. We'll handle it after the vote." David picked up his ringing phone and waved me out of his office.

CHAPTER EIGHT

A Toe

My desk phone seemed to increase in size when I returned to the Backwater. I dreaded calling Galvin, but didn't want to be surprised by him again. I punched the digits to his office feeling increased tension and anxiety with each touch. One ring, two rings, three rings. Please God, let it go to voicemail.

"This is the office of Senator John Galvin. How may I help you?" A woman's voice.

"Uh, this is Will Duggan calling for Senator Galvin."

"And what is this in regard to?"

"It's about National Union Bank & Trust. I spoke to the senator last week and told him I'd call him back. This is me calling him back."

"Ok. Please hold."

"Um-hmm."

"I'm sorry. The senator is unavailable right now. Can I have him return your call?"

"I'll be waiting by the phone."

The tension let me go and my body felt deflated. I had yet to accomplish anything, other than stress-eating three Snickers bars. The afternoon crawled by. Aaron was out of town at a client conference and I had no interaction with anyone in the Backwater. In his absence, I longed for some human contact, but wasn't going near Chuck. I didn't want to let him see that he got me or even that he got a reaction out of me.

Unfortunately, it wasn't unlike him to conveniently leave out details or to use his access to David to throw associates and paralegals he didn't like under the bus. The last time Chuck got me was a client black-tie charity fundraising dinner in Manhattan. He showed up at my cubicle at 5:45 looking polished in a freshly pressed tuxedo. He asked if I was ready to go.

"Ready to go where?," I responded.

"To the National Union Student-Athlete Scholarship Fund dinner."

"To the what?"

"Where's your tux?," Chuck responded.

"I don't have a tux."

"Well, we gotta go. C'mon!"

"I can't go. I don't have a tuxedo."

"You're better off going without one. David's going to be there along with everyone from the management committee. They're going to notice if you no-show."

Clearly Chuck had known about the dinner and conveniently "forgot" to let me know about it until fifteen minutes before it started. I went without a tuxedo and spent the evening trying to hide my blue suit and pink tie behind a Tanqueray and tonic and a plate full of finger food. It was embarrassing during the cocktail hour and mortifying when we were seated for dinner. David sat across the table from me and if his eyes were lasers I would've been reduced to a pile of ashes.

Six members of the firm's management committee sat at the table with us. Each one a senior partner of the firm. They were the people who decided who was hired, who was fired, who would become a partner and how much every attorney at the firm would be paid. And Chuck made sure I was dressed like a bumkin in comparison to them in their tuxedos and elegant evening dresses.

I stood out for all of the wrong reasons, and Chuck couldn't have seemed more pleased with himself. I survived that incident and others probably because I was a Smith Stevens nobody stationed in the Backwater with little prospect of a bright future at the firm. No one really cared and no one wanted to bother finding my replacement.

At 4:52 the area code 617 appeared on my desk phone's caller ID. My desire for human contact quickly receded. I tried to convince myself it was late. If I didn't pick up, maybe he'd think I went home. Bullshit. It was Manhattan and this was one of the biggest and baddest law firms in the country. He'd know I wouldn't get out of here before 8:00. It rang two more times and I snatched the handset off of its base before the call went to voicemail.

As I cleared my throat I heard, "Duggan, is that you? Are you choking? Quick, Andy, call 9-1-1!! I think Duggan's having a heart attack!! He can't believe I'm on the line . . ."

"Senator, it's me."

"Ah Will you're ok! Thank God! Andy, forget about 9-1-1. So where are we?"

"Well, I'm running it up the chain and waiting for my marching orders."

Senator Galvin muttered something I couldn't understand. "Should I call someone else?"

"No, no, no. I should have some news later in the week. The bank is in the middle of quarterly reporting and it's hard to get ahold of people. It should calm down in the next few days."

"Will, I'm not a patient man. And I don't like the runaround. The more you dance, the more something smells fishy. I don't have to tell you that. Don't make it stink if you know what I mean."

"I understand."

"Do you? You're in a tower in Manhattan and I'm on the street and people want answers. My constituents aren't happy. And I can't let them be unhappy with me. It's much better if they're unhappy with you. Got it?" Apparently Senator Galvin hadn't heard about the Backwater.

"I got it."

"I hope so."

The senator was ever present in the back of my mind as the week dragged on. The general counsel vote couldn't come fast enough and I hoped he wouldn't explode beforehand. If anything knocked Don's appointment off track, it would spell disaster for David. Don would leave National Union and then there would be a great unknown and the possibility that Smith Stevens' National Union business would dry up. Don would end up at another bank, but there would be no guarantee he could feed business to David at all, let alone at the volume he had done so at National Union.

At 6:36 on Thursday, Aaron texted. "Don is in." I could finally get Galvin off my plate and no longer had to worry about Don's vote crashing and burning. I expected a celebration was underway and snuck out of the office just after getting the news. When I arrived at my cubicle the next morning, the little red light was blinking on my desk phone once again. I picked up expecting an offer of tailoring services. "You have one fax message received this morning at 9:34."

It was rare to receive a fax and I immediately opened my laptop to read it. I found an email from the firm's electronic fax service. It was from the senator's office. I wasn't entirely surprised. At least it gave me something to flip to David and he could send it to the right people.

———— ——

"Dear Mr. Duggan,

I am writing to follow up with you in regard to our two recent telephone conversations about National Union Bank & Trust. As you are aware from our conversations, a number of my constituents have complained to this office regarding the closure of National Union Bank & Trust branches in their neighborhoods. The unavailability of traditional banking establishments in these neighborhoods presents a hardship to residents and makes them vulnerable to the predatory financial practices of non-traditional banking services, such as check-cashers.

My concern with the closure of National Union Bank & Trust branches in these communities is only heightened by the results of the litigation profile I shared with you last week. As I discussed with you, that profile shows National Union Bank & Trust has filed a significant amount of loan default lawsuits against its customers in urban areas, including the Boston neighborhoods of Dorchester, Roslindale, Roxbury, and South Boston. This profile further indicates that National Union Bank & Trust has seldom filed suits against customers in suburban areas such as Norfolk, Middlesex, Essex, and Plymouth counties, where the bank has numerous branches.

I requested information regarding the closures and the concentration of lawsuits within the Boston neighborhoods outlined above. To date, however, I have received no such information and it appears this office is being given the runaround. Please let this letter serve as a final informal request for information. I ask that you contact this office immediately to resolve this issue. Be advised that I reserve the right to seek the issuance of a legislative subpoena against National Union Bank & Trust to obtain this information directly. To facilitate compliance with this request, please note that I have copied Richard W. Chambers IV, the Chairman of the Board of Directors of National Union Bank & Trust.

Thank you for your attention to this letter. Please be guided accordingly.

Very truly yours,

John D. Galvin"

Fuck! A lightning bolt of panic coursed through my body. Barely anyone at National Union had any idea who I was. Now I would be on the lips of every single person in the bank's legal department and probably every member of the board of directors by lunchtime. I forwarded the email to David and Chuck as quickly as I could get it out. They would surely hear from someone at the bank within minutes of Dick Chambers receiving it. They had to be out in front of it before it was widely circulated. I kept telling myself David and Don were working on a strategy. It was now or never, and I would be glad to get away from this mess.

I hurried down to Chuck's office to see if he had read the letter. I wanted to get his reaction before I called David. His office was empty, but the lights were on and the golf game was up on his computer screen. I went to Randall's workstation to ask where he was. "He had to run out and won't be back for the rest of the day." I returned to my cubicle and called Chuck's cell. No answer. I texted and emailed him, but didn't receive a response.

I called David's office and no one picked up. It was strange that neither June nor her backup answered his line. I followed up on my email to David, but received no reply. I made the ritual pilgrimage to the Temple to see if he was around, but his lights were off. He and June were nowhere to be found. Chuck still hadn't read my text messages when I left the Temple.

He wasn't at GolfLand. I checked the bar at the Roosevelt, and he wasn't there either. Something was up, but there were a million places he could be hiding out in the city. There was still no reaction to Galvin's letter from either David or Chuck. I was becoming increasingly uneasy not knowing if they were ahead of the email or if they were about to be blindsided.

My cellphone vibrated in my hand. A text from Aaron, who still wasn't in the office. "Tripper just told me everyone at National Union is freaking out. What's going on? Call me." Jesus. My heart sank. I hit Aaron's contact in my cell.

"What's happening?"

"Tripper said some letter came into National Union addressed to you and the bank's legal department is flipping out about some investigation. He said they're being accused of redlining and the negotiation with Live Payday Check Loan might be called off. Is that true?"

"The letter is true, but I don't know anything about the deal. And they knew all about it. David said he was working on a response with Don Jones. I don't know why everyone's freaking out."

"Will, man, the lawyers at the bank are saying that they didn't know this was going on."

"That's fucking bullshit. David told me he was working on it with Don. Don knew."

"That's not what they're saying at the Temple."

I could feel my lower back locking up and stopped walking. "That's not true. He fucking knew!"

"I hope you have something in writing. I'm sorry to drop this on you, but I thought you should know you're on their radar."

"I've been trying to get David and Chuck on the phone all morning. They must've been out celebrating last night."

"I'm sure they'll straighten it out. But be ready just in case."

I was becoming less sure by the moment. And the reality dawned on me that I never exchanged emails with Chuck or David about my calls with Galvin. I violated the cardinal rule of practicing law—get it in writing. There were only my conversations with Chuck and then with David, and I hadn't told either of them about my last call with Galvin.

My guts were churning. I tried to convince myself David was taking care of it and there had to be some misunderstanding about what he and Don were doing to handle the situation. It was quiet when I returned to the Backwater.

My desk phone's red eye was blinking when I got to my cubicle. Maybe today would be the day I finally got fitted for a suit from Bangkok, Thailand.

Instead, it was David. "Will, call me as soon as you get this. I'm on my cell." I quickly punched the digits to his cellphone.

"Did you read that letter?"

"I did."

"What the fuck happened with the senator? Hold on." His voice sounded muffled as if his hand was covering the phone, but I thought I heard him ordering a cocktail. "Sorry. Where were we?"

"The senator."

"Oh, yeah. So what the fuck happened? I thought you had it under control."

"That's like saying I have control of a twelve-hundred-pound bull. He's going to do whatever he's going to do. I'm sorry."

"What are you sorry for?"

"For this blowing up."

"You didn't make it blow up. National Union did. Did you hear what happened last night?" I played dumb. "Don Jones is in. And he's going to feed us as much as we can eat. This is just more meat on the table and there'll be a lot more to come. I'm about to sit down with him right now. But I'm glad it was your name on the letter and not mine. I need you to be on standby. Frame up a skeleton to send to Galvin and hang by your phone. I'm going to call you and dictate the guts later on."

It was my first time working directly with David. I waited by my phone until he called me close to 7:30. He dictated a letter to Galvin promising full cooperation and requesting a time for a call. I grew more relieved with each keystroke and felt a glimmer of opportunity. I may have still been in the Backwater, but for the first time I had a toe in the Temple.

CHAPTER NINE

Virus

Early Monday morning I was seated in a large glass conference room overlooking Times Square. David stood in front of a table where several Smith Stevens attorneys were seated, but not another soul from the Backwater. "I have a call on Thursday with John Galvin and we need to prepare a robust response to his demands. Will, who works with you on the Massachusetts cases?"

"It's just me."

"That has to change. We're losing money if you're not spreading work around."

"It would take time to ramp someone up."

"Then you're going to find the time. A lot of what we're talking about is going to fall on you. So clear your schedule and pull in any resources you need. We have a lot of work to do. To begin with, I need a binder in my hands by lunchtime on Wednesday with spreadsheets breaking down all of our Massachusetts cases so I can understand what's happening. And you need to give me a memorandum discussing the claims National Union brings against customers in these cases. And that memo needs to describe the state of the law and identify any problem judges and jury pools. Have we responded to discovery? Do we send discovery requests?"

"We send discovery requests in every case."

"Good."

"But we don't receive discovery requests in a lot of cases. Most of the defendants represent themselves and don't know they can request information from National Union."

"Then let's not educate them. Get me examples of what we send and what we've received."

"What about documents? Have we sent documents to anyone?"

"We have, but it's piecemeal. The responses are tailored to the particular cases and only include bank statements and correspondence supporting the bank's default claims."

"What about corporate documents? Do we have a set?"

"We don't."

David grimaced. "Well, that's a problem. Get with Tripper and get what you need from him. Today." I looked at Tripper and he saluted me with two fingers against his forehead. "Will, you're my point person on this. I don't want to hear from anyone else. You got this?"

"I got it."

"Good. Time's a wasting. This is not the end of the line for this kind of investigation and I want everyone in this room to be ready for a storm. Got it?" He nodded as he looked around the group. "Good. Now get out of here." I stood up to go. "Not so fast." David told me to shut the door. "You understand this is a big opportunity?"

I nodded. "I know."

"This is something I'd normally give to Chuck because he's good at delegating." More like work-dodging. "But when I called him on Friday, he dropped the ball. He was supposed to be managing the litigation. He didn't even know how many cases we have. So you got the ball." Great. Now Chuck had a new reason to sabotage me. "Don't fuck it up. This is just a small part. You take it and run with it. This is going to move like a virus when word gets out about Galvin. And when it spreads to other states, you're going to do the same thing you're doing in Massachusetts."

"I'm not going to fuck it up."

"Good. Now go and bill!"

My head was spinning when I entered the Backwater. It was new territory for me and a lot to accomplish in forty-eight hours. Aaron left a sticky tab on my keyboard. "Shine?"

The red light was blinking ominously on my desk phone. "You have three new messages. First message received at 9:38. This is Noah Ericksen from the firm's *Pro Bono* Committee. Just wanted to thank you for volunteering. We approved Mr. Baines' case. No need to call me back. Let us know if you need anything." Oh, shit. I almost forgot I put the case through conflicts. It was even more unfamiliar territory to cover. I took a deep breath and added calling Desi to my rapidly expanding to-do list.

"Next message received at 11:22. Will, it's Charlene Parent. Hopefully you haven't jumped off a bridge. You looked a little pale at the end of that meeting. Don't worry. I'll handle the binder and the spreadsheets and start pulling stuff together. I've done it for David a million times. Call me and let me know where I can find the numbers and the case materials. But you're on your own with the memo." Thank God. Charlene was a career paralegal, who knew her stuff and had a record of saving associates' asses that would have made a doctor proud. And it looked like I was about to be added to her list.

"Last message received at 11:58. This is Jim Andersen. I just sent you an email. Please respond and let me know if you can meet me in conference room 42B at 1:00." Fuck. I flopped deeply against the back of my chair. The Grim Reaper. If he called it wasn't to tell you the firm was giving you a raise.

I immediately punched the number to Aaron's office line, which pushed me through to his cellphone. "Are you ever in the fucking office?"

"Some of my most important work happens on the streets. You know that. You're missing a pretty amazing shine. Tripper said you were in the Temple with David. Seems like someone is moving on up."

"Well, it was good while it lasted. I just got a voicemail from Jim Fucking Andersen."

"Maybe they're making you partner."

"Ha. More like they're about to throw me off the roof."

"Relax. You were just there with David. And according to Tripper you're the man now."

"Hopefully."

"On another note and I don't want to spook you, but Randall told me Chuck flipped out after talking to David on Friday. And then stormed out of the office." Now I knew why he wasn't around when I was looking for him.

"Between you and me, David told me I was on the case because Chuck didn't know anything about the default litigation."

"Who would've guessed Chuck didn't know shit? Such a legend." Aaron laughed. "Seriously, though, just watch your back. I guess that's business as usual with Chuck," he admonished.

"Great. I got so much shit to do by Wednesday and now I have another reason to watch out for Chuck."

"If I were you, I wouldn't let him have access to anything I was working on. Make all your documents private on the system. It wouldn't be the first time, you know?"

"You know I know. You don't think he already did something and that's why Jim called?"

"No way. It's too fast. And he's not that bright."

"I gotta make some calls, then I'm heading back over to the Temple."

"Twice in one day, Duggan. Impressive. Let me know what happens, partner. Peace out."

"Yeah, right." I laughed as I clicked off the call.

I marched back over to the Temple and again made the insulting trek through security and the firm's reception desk. At least this time the receptionists remembered me from my morning visit. I stepped into Conference Room 42B and Jim was seated between two women I had never seen before. Witnesses, shit.

"William, thanks for coming over on such short notice." As Jim spoke my heart thudded in my chest. "I have some good news." My head shifted sideways and my eyebrow raised involuntarily. "You're getting a new office." One of the women leaned in towards Jim's ear and whispered something I couldn't hear. "Strike that. You're getting an office that's new to you. All your stuff is being taken out of the Annex right now and will be brought over here this afternoon." Annex. I smiled. I was half-surprised he didn't call it the Backwater.

"H-here? To Times Square?"

"Yes. David Bell asked that you be relocated closer to him."

"Am I going to 50?"

"Yes you are." The "Money Floor." Every corner office occupied by a whale. And David was one of them and only rising. I couldn't help wondering what could happen if I hung onto his coattails long enough. Jim finished writing something on a piece of paper.

"All right. Let's take a look at your new digs."

As we walked from the elevator bank on the 50th floor towards my new office, my cell buzzed in my pocket.

"Dude, they just took your shit out of your cubicle! What the fuck happened?"

I quickly tapped a message back to Aaron. "I'm movin' on up!"

"What? To the Temple?!?! You fucking prick!!"

I couldn't help but smile as we walked to a large attorney office with bookcases lining the wall, a closet, and a large desk with two new computer monitors attached to one of the firm's latest model laptops. All of it illuminated by picture windows that stretched from the floor to just below the ceiling of the bright room.

Jim looked at me smiling, amused by my surprise. "Will this work?"

"Well, it's not exactly the Backwater, but I'll find a way." He giggled a little and seemed to blush, as if I had just said a dirty word.

"Your number has already been transferred over and IT will stop by in a little while to help you work out any bugs. Your new assistant is Amanda. You'll be sharing her with Bowdin Crowninshield, as she has capacity."

"Tripper."

"Yes. Tripper. So you know him?"

"I do."

"Do you need anything? Want me to introduce you to Amanda?"

"Thanks. I'm good."

"Email me if you have any questions or need anything." Jim then vanished from sight.

Members of the Offices Services staff appeared with boxes of my stuff from the Backwater. "No diplomas?" I shook my head. I had no desire to advertise my law school to my colleagues. "If you bring them in, we can hang them for you. This office was just painted, so that's the firm's preference. Do you want us to put this stuff in the shelves for you?"

"I got it, thanks."

After they left, I eased into a modern black office chair with knobs to adjust pressure on different body points. I spun around and looked down at Times Square more than 500 feet below. I could get used to this. I dialed Aaron.

"You son of a bitch! How did you pull that off? A goddamn nickelbagger in the Temple? You close to David?"

"Like three doors down."

"Dude, if you don't fuck this up, you might be a partner at this place. This is huge."

"I don't know about that."

"Nah, man. You're getting off the line. You can't work the line forever. You gotta get into management. And there you are."

"Seriously, this is just dumb luck."

"Don't be that way. You can make your bones. And even better, you're far from Chuck."

"He's probably on a roof across the street with a sniper rifle right now."

"Probably, but at least it's a tougher shot than it used to be. Anyway, congrats. And don't forget about us little folk in the Backwater."

"You're nuts. I gotta go. I'm already underwater here."

Aaron hung up and I clicked on my computer and scanned my emails. Maybe I was here simply to be close to David or maybe it was to keep me a safe distance from Chuck. Either way, it was an exciting and unexpected development. But I had no time to dwell on the reasoning. I clicked open a blank form on the firm's system and began tapping away at David's memorandum.

CHAPTER TEN

Smoke

I christened my new office by working on David's memorandum until after midnight. Charlene prepared spreadsheets and organized them in a white binder with numbered tabs along with an index making it as user-friendly as possible. She explained that the most important element of any binder delivered to David was that it be white. Any other color would be rejected and sent back to be fixed. If you entered Charlene's office, you couldn't help but notice the hundreds, if not thousands, of white binders filling her shelves. Each one dedicated to deals, cases, settlements, and other projects David brought into the firm.

I had no way of knowing if my current good luck would last, but I was determined to extend my stay in the Temple as long as I could. I had a massive black coffee in my hand as I passed through security at 7:15 on Tuesday morning for the first time without the insult of having to explain who I was. I seamlessly glided up the elevator and through the glass doors leading to the 50th floor from the elevator bank. I was greeted with the scent of a freshly cleaned office, as it had been vacuumed, dusted, and polished overnight. The overhead lights turned on automatically when I stepped in. I carefully set my coffee on a coaster on my desk and hung my overcoat in my closet.

The red light was blinking on my desk phone when I sat down to wake up my computer. I had been away for less than six hours. I clicked the button. "You have one new message. Message received at 7:08 this morning. Mr. Duggan. This is Daniel Tepper. I'm a reporter with the *Boston Post*. I'm calling because I wanted to discuss Senator Galvin's letter concerning National Union Bank & Trust with you. You can call me on my cell. I'm sending you an email with my contact info."

What the fuck? I wondered why Galvin would've sent his letter to the press. I tapped out an email to David. Just after I hit send a text from Aaron buzzed my attention away from my computer screen. "Dude, did you read the *New York Globe* today?" I couldn't remember the last time I actually touched a newspaper. I pulled it up on my computer, so I didn't seem completely uninformed, but couldn't figure out what Aaron was talking about.

I went down to the 42nd floor to see if there was a copy in the visitor's lobby. *The New York Times*, *The Financial Times* and *The Wall Street Journal* were all represented on a coffee table, but no *New York Globe*. I momentarily forgot I was at a white-shoe firm that wouldn't want to sully its reputation by associating itself with the paper's notorious Page Four.

I hustled into an elevator and stepped out into the chilly morning air without my overcoat. At the closest newsstand I distractedly passed five dollars to the attendant. Forgetting my change, I began leafing through the paper while slowly stepping back towards the office. I flipped through the greasy pages and on the sixth page there was a black and white photograph of John Galvin's bald head and famous scowl. "National Union Bank & Trust in Redlining Row."

I continued reading on. "Senior Massachusetts Senator John Galvin has accused National Union Bank & Trust, which maintains its headquarters in New York, of redlining its urban customers in Boston. In a letter to legal eagle William Duggan of the prestigious Manhattan office of international law firm Smith Stevens, Galvin accused National Union of discriminatory practices in shutting down branches and filing lawsuits against residents of minority and immigrant communities. The letter further accuses Mr. Duggan of playing hide-the-ball in response to the senator's request for information."

"Holy shit!"

Commuters trickled past me unaware of my panic. My cellphone was on my desk and I staggered back towards the Temple clutching the newspaper in my hand. Aaron beat me to the next text.

"Dude, are you ok?"

"Are you in the office?"

"Are you crazy? What time is it? Call my cell."

I sipped my rapidly cooling coffee, spread the paper across my desk and dialed the digits to Aaron's cell from my speakerphone.

"You're famous!" Aaron chuckled.

"What the fuck is this? It's not even what Galvin's letter says. It doesn't say anything about immigrant and minority communities."

"Relax, man. The client has the letter, right?"

"Yeah."

"So chill. It was going to get out anyway. On the bright side, just one day after leaving the Backwater you're a legal eagle. Not too bad for a kid from Boston." A smile cracked my lips. It wasn't how I planned on being associated with Smith Stevens, but there it was. Maybe it wasn't such a big deal. "If I were you, I wouldn't answer the phone today. Let communications handle it."

"Communications?"

"I love you, man, but how are you in the Temple and I'm still in the Backwater? Yes, Communications Office. You get called by the press, you send a message to them and they handle the response. And I wouldn't want to get ahead of David on any of this if you know what I mean. If you're quoted in the paper instead of him it might be a career-defining moment. Did you tell him?"

"Sending him an email right now. Do you think Galvin sent the letter to the *New York Globe*? Why wouldn't he send it to the *Boston Post*?"

"I don't know, man. Maybe he's playing hardball and wants to put pressure on National Union. The *New York Globe* is in the bank's backyard, after all."

"And the letter attacks me personally. It's so fucked up."

"Well, it did call you a legal eagle, so you have that going for you."

"Do you think David sent it to them?"

"I don't think so. That's not how he operates. He has no interest in seeing his name or the firm's in the *New York Globe* associated with redlining or playing hide and seek with a senator."

"Chuck?"

"Well, the article does go after you. I wouldn't put it past him to try to screw with you."

"If it was him, it's working. I came in early to get a jump on pulling stuff together for David and now I have this on my plate."

"That does have the hallmarks of a Chuck Special. I wouldn't worry about it, but I'll let you know if I hear anything. Look at you, you got a first-class office and now you have the first-class problems that come with it. I'd say this is a pretty impressive step up in your career since Friday."

"I guess that's one way to look at it. All right, man. I gotta grind."

"Peace out."

Minders, grinders, and finders. Those are the three basic kinds of attorneys that form any law firm's basic hierarchy. David was the classic large law firm finder. He was out developing new business for the firm by cultivating new client contacts, strengthening existing contacts and making sure he had his ear to the ground to catch any new case or deal that he might bring into the firm. Any finder that brought in new business would be credited with "generation" for generating new income for the firm. And even if the finder never billed an hour on the new business, he or she would receive a cut of whatever was billed to that matter by other attorneys.

While he was a litigator, technically, David fed work to a diverse group of attorneys at Smith Stevens, including other litigators, as well as deal attorneys, tax attorneys, class action and complex litigation attorneys and the firm's high-end estate practice. The only kinds of cases the firm didn't generally handle were criminal and divorce cases. Those were farmed out to a handful of fortunate firms not in direct competition with Smith Stevens in each state.

Chuck was a minder. Or at least he was supposed to be. Minders were tasked with overseeing the grinders so that the finders could continue to go out and find more work for the firm. Minders were intermediaries who made sure the firm's business was being handled. Successful minders could receive a cut of a finder's business, which could make the position highly lucrative. Many minders at Smith Stevens would never become finders because it was simply too difficult to bring in cases big enough for the firm to handle. Chuck was squarely in that boat, either because he didn't have the contacts to generate big business or because he was too lazy to go out and develop them.

And then there were the junior attorneys like me. The grinders. Almost all of us were newer to the practice of law and were trying to gain experience. The least experienced junior attorneys spent much of their days doing legal research, drafting memoranda answering specific legal questions and reviewing documents for their relevance to a case. Eventually they graduated to working on court filings, reviewing and summarizing depositions and preparing more complex memoranda for clients. Those lucky enough to survive the first few years at a large law firm took on greater responsibility and some eventually had direct contact with clients, made court appearances and took depositions.

Within that structure trust was earned gradually and with it came greater responsibility, increased recognition within the firm and, hopefully, financial incentives in the form of raises and bonuses. But there was always time pressure. The daily pressure came from making sure you were on track to meet your annual hours requirement. At Smith Stevens, that meant that associates like me had to bill a minimum of 2,400 hours per year to maintain their jobs and be bonus eligible. That averaged around two hundred hours per month. Or about fifty hours of billing per week—ten hours per day.

It might not seem terrible to an outsider, but the key word in the equation is "billable." Billable hours don't include lunches, bathroom breaks, personal calls, chatting with coworkers, administrative work, commuting or vacations. To bill ten hours on any given day would typically require you to be at the office between twelve to fourteen hours, unless you didn't pee, eat, or talk to anyone else the entire day. If you took national holidays off from work or went on vacation, you would need to make sure you billed the time you missed from the office on those days to ensure that you hit the 2,400-hour mark. And taking time away from the office would only increase your daily billable requirement or force you to work on the weekends to make up for it.

The other time pressure on grinders was advancement. It was unusual for someone to last as a grinder at Smith Stevens for more than seven years. Every grinder at the firm was an associate. Every minder was a junior partner, meaning they were technically a partner of the firm, but not an owner of the firm. And every finder was a full partner, meaning that they each had an ownership stake in the firm. If no finder nominated you for partnership by the time you had reached your seventh year of practicing law, you were likely out or on the way out of the firm.

Being a grinder at the Temple was a major step up from being a grinder in the Backwater. It was a sign of recognition and a hopeful indicator that I wouldn't be toiling away in anonymity in the Backwater until the firm ran me off after seven years of practice. With this new motivation I tried to put the distraction of the news behind me, as well as my suspicion that Chuck shared Galvin's letter with the *New York Globe*. But after 9:00, my telephone began to ring at a frequency that never occurred when I was a faceless peon in the Backwater. Taking Aaron's advice, I let every call go to voicemail. When Amanda arrived and checked in with me, I asked her to screen my calls and make a memo of them, rather than send me emails, to allow me to focus on my projects.

Just after 9:30 David responded to my emails. "Don't call him back. Tell Communications and let them handle. And keep your head down unless you want to end up in more newspapers." I was more than happy to comply.

"There have been some other calls. I'll send them all to Communications," I typed back.

"Good. I'll be in the office tomorrow. How's my binder?"

"It's coming along. I'll have it for you in the morning." I could feel my blood pressure rise as I sent the email. I still didn't have Tripper's documents and didn't want to overpromise.

I strolled down to Tripper's office and framed myself in his doorway. He looked up from his computer. "I was just thinking about you."

"Funny, I was thinking of you, too."

"I pulled together some materials that might be helpful. We're not giving these to the senator yet, are we?"

"Nah. Not yet, at least. Right now I just need to make sure David has what he needs at his fingertips."

"That's good news. First, I have the deal binder for National Union's takeover of Wampanoag." It was massive and appeared to be more than nine inches thick. "It has the contracts and all the exhibits related to the assets being transferred, such as financial holdings, loans, mortgages and so on. Pretty exciting, right?"

"Amazing." I flipped through the first few pages of the contract's "wherefore" clauses setting out the basics of the transaction.

"Next up is a deal binder for National Union's transfer of a few former Wampanoag branches to Norfolk Bank in Massachusetts. It has the contract with exhibits describing the assets transferred along with the physical branches. Those transfers included all of the branches' equipment, customers and any accounts they had with Wampanoag, excluding mortgages. Those remained with National Union. Even more exciting, huh?"

"Totally, but this is the kind of stuff that might help us. Just to confirm, there are no emails or communications in these binders, right?"

"Exactly. It's just the finished work product. No commentary or anything. Most of the communications and drafts are on the system. Pulling that stuff would be a mess. It's all over the place and includes work product from everyone who worked on the due diligence and various versions of the documents up to their final drafts. Please tell me we're not producing that stuff. Vetting it for attorney-client privilege alone would be a nightmare."

"Don't worry about it. Not at this stage. And hopefully not ever."

"Thank God. All right. Lastly, I have a binder for a mortgage deal National Union is trying to finalize. But it's a work in progress. Basically it's just drafts of the agreement and some of the schedules."

"Mortgage deal?"

"Yeah. National Union is selling a bunch of mortgages to a mortgage servicing company, BestRateLoan. It includes mortgages National Union took over in the Wampanoag deal. Is this interesting?"

"Maybe. Please tell me BestRateLoan is in a different league than Live Payday Check Loan?" Tripper grimaced and stuck out his hand parallel to the floor and titled it sideways a few times. "Great. And speaking of which, what's happening with that acquisition?"

"It's still in the works. Do you need that binder, too?"

"Probably. I want to arm David with anything he might need."

"I'll get Charlene to pull you a copy."

"Cool."

"Anything else?"

"God, I hope not. I think that should be about it, but I'll let you know."

I hauled the stack of deal binders back to my office. Before she left for the day, Amanda handed me a typed list of the calls she intercepted. I didn't have time to review the list, and had even less time to call anyone back before I handed David my work product. Instead, I spent the afternoon and evening pulling pages from the deal binders and revising my memorandum and the spreadsheets Charlotte prepared. Two nights in the Temple and two nights at work after midnight. The view was certainly better, but the same couldn't be said for the hours.

CHAPTER ELEVEN

Upward Trajectory

With my deadline looming, I arrived at the Temple before 7:00. A stack of call binders sat on my desk waiting to greet me. I opened the binders to check the contents and review my memorandum one last time. I glanced over at the list of calls. *New York Times, Daily News, Boston Herald,* and other names, including Desmond Baines. Shit. In all the excitement I forgot to call him. It would have to wait until later, as precious minutes were evaporating.

An email from David wooshed into my inbox with a red flag. "I'll be in the office in 45. Be ready for me."

With a binder under each arm I marched down towards his office with the list of calls dangling from my hand and brushing against my left thigh. I stationed myself next to a grey bank of secretary cubicles across from his corner office and waited for his arrival. My phone buzzed in my jacket pocket with a text from Aaron.

"Dude, you're even more famous today than you were yesterday. I trust you haven't seen the papers. No worries. I'm here for you. *New York Times,*

Wall Street Journal, Daily News. I can go on and on. Looks like you're not big on returning calls for comment. LOL."

"Awesome," I texted back.

Moments later David flew around the corner. He peeled off his cashmere overcoat and slung it over the ledge of June's workstation. He looked at me smiling and clapped his hands. "Whatcha got for me?"

He floated towards his office with me trailing in his wake. I handed him a copy of the binder as he sat down behind his desk. June soon appeared with his overcoat draped over her arm and hung it in his closet. She then stepped behind him and brought his computer to life. With a small notebook in her right hand and a pen in the other, she waited quietly for David's next move.

"So, June, did you know we have a celebrity in our midst?"

She smiled and in an exaggerated fashion said, "Oh, really? Maybe I can get an autograph."

"Time for that later. He's too busy today." He looked at me with a mischievous grin that made me nervous. I felt like I was becoming his new toy, but he had broken a few in the past. June vanished from the office. He cracked open the binder on his desk and leafed through my memorandum.

"How many cases do we have?" The number was right in front of him.

"Two hundred and thirty-five."

"Trial settings?"

"Twenty-seven."

"Worst County?"

"All of the trial settings are in Suffolk, but the ones in downtown Boston are the worst for us."

"Scariest judge?"

"That's easy. Judge Butler in Suffolk Superior Court. He likes settlements and doesn't like consumer loan cases. And if he sees me again on one of these cases, he's probably going to have me taken out and beaten with rubber mallets or worse."

"You won't be there for long. If you're supposed to be in here working on this stuff, I'm losing money if you're appearing in court. You need to spread the wealth. I want you to finish what you're handling in court. Otherwise, I want different boots on the ground and you need to keep on top of them. I make money by dealing with the clients, bringing in new business and farming out work. If I'm in court, I'm losing money. If you're in court, I'm also losing money. We have people and I'd rather not go there. Do you really want to be in state court grinding out shitty little cases? No, no you don't. Who's working for you?"

"Well, Charlene helped me pull the materials together. And Tripper pulled the deal binders."

David's complexion was the color of a tomato. "Maybe I wasn't clear. I told you to pull in everyone you needed. Who wrote the memo?"

"I did."

David exhaled heavily. "That's fucking bullshit. You don't draft the memo. If you're hoarding hours, you can go back down the street. Do you understand?"

"Sorry. Just the memo."

"If you want to go anywhere as a lawyer you have to manage people. Anyone can run a case. If you don't become a manager there's really no place to go here but out. I need you to drive the work down." I nodded my head. "There's a ton to do here. If you're doing first drafts of memos and research or putting binders together in a month, that's going to be a you problem. And it's not personal. Trust me. I don't care who's doing the work. But I can't have you losing money. Do you understand?"

"It won't happen again." I suddenly missed the Backwater.

"What do you know about the stuff outside of Boston?"

"There's not a lot of it. A dozen cases in Brockton and a few here and there, but nothing even close to what's happening in Boston."

"And what does that tell you?"

"It tells me there are more defaults in Boston than other places. It's just a numbers game. Population density is greater in Boston. There are more people and, hence, more lawsuits."

"Hmm. Think Galvin's going to buy that and walk away?"

"No. Galvin's a bull. He's not going to take our word for it."

"Exactly. We need data. We need an explanation supported by documents we can send to him. He has to see our proof and chew on it. We have to sell him our explanation. And he has to buy it. Do I have summaries of the deals? Did Tripper give you anything?"

"He gave me copies of the deal binders. He didn't do summaries."

"No, no, no. This isn't working." David looked towards the door. "Hey June, would you get Tripper for me?" My heart sank. "Will, I don't have time to read the agreements. I need bullets of the most important points. Something like that has to be in the can somewhere. I need you to think of these details."

"Ok." I looked at my shoes. I could feel my office in the Temple slipping away.

"Galvin's call is a big deal, but it's not the only thing I have cooking here today. And they're all big deals. So you have to break this stuff down for me. I have to be able to digest a lot of information in a short amount of time. And if I blank on the call, I need a quick touchstone to get back on track. I get it. This is our first time working on something together. But we have to get on the same page. If it happens again, I'm going to have to look somewhere else for what I need. Got me?"

"Uh huh."

"And if you don't want it and would rather work on the loan cases in state court, that's fine, but that work isn't going to carry you very far. You need to tell me if that's what you want." David's facial expression and voice were stern.

"That's not what I want. I want this opportunity. I'd rather be here than in the Backwater."

David cracked a smile when the word came out of my mouth. "Officially, we're supposed to call it the 'Annex.' But, good. I think we're on the same page. You're not getting fired, but you have to get up to speed."

Just as David finished speaking, Tripper walked in without knocking. "What's up?"

"What the fuck is this?" David held up one of the pages of wherefore clauses.

"What? You have all the deal points there."

"Wherefore? You want me to read fucking wherefore clauses? You gotta give me more than this. I need bullets. Somebody must've put together summaries of these agreements."

"We have summary memos."

"Then get them to Erika. I don't need the memos. I don't have time. I need bullets. Get me bullets. No more than ten and make them pithy. I want one page on each agreement. Got it?"

"Got it."

"And I need them this afternoon, so get hopping." With that Tripper spun on his heel and slipped out of view.

"Where were we?"

"The story for Galvin."

"Yeah. This is a giant bank, not the March of Dimes. Galvin isn't going to believe a word we say without documents to support it. We need a narrative that explains why the suits are loaded in Boston, but not in other areas. And we have to be able to back it up. Or we're fucked. What differentiates the bank's clients in the lawsuits from the bank's other clients?" I shook my head. "Lending standards. I worked through this with Don Jones."

"Lending Standards?"

"Yes. There's no way you would know this." I felt relieved that another strike wasn't about to blow past me. "National Union has different guidelines than those that were used by Wampanoag. Wampanoag took on risk that wouldn't be acceptable to National Union. As a result, there is a greater probability of default on Wampanoag accounts than there is with non-Wampanoag accounts. If those riskier Wampanoag clients had come to National Union directly, National Union wouldn't have loaned them money. And most of those Wampanoag accounts are located in the inner-city because that's where most of the Wampanoag branches were located.

"According to Don, when the deal happened National Union really only wanted the downtown Boston branches plus a handful of branches in the metro-West area, such as Newton, Weston and Wellesley. National Union wasn't looking to expand into urban neighborhoods like Dorchester, South Boston, or Roxbury. But Wampanoag wasn't looking to spin off branches. To prevent another large bank from swooping in and competing in the desirable neighborhoods, National Union took over the entire bank, including the undesirable branches and accounts. Then the plan was to break out the branches it didn't want to other banks or just fold them. You following me?"

"That makes sense. But are we going to produce documents to Galvin in the next couple of weeks? I don't know how we could pull all that together."

"No. I'm going to use the call to explore what he's looking for and buy us some more time, but we're not going to over-promise. Here's the thing and Don Jones is aware of it. Galvin isn't leaving National Union alone without a pound of flesh. We're going to give him that pound of flesh. But what we don't want to do is give him or anyone else reason to open up a probe and give National Union a full proctological.

"And it has to be coordinated. We don't want to resolve it with him and then have a bunch of other investigations at the state or federal level. We're going to work with Galvin and everyone else. We'll make a proffer of documents and other information with our side of the story and then work to enter into a settlement agreement with all of them and pay a fine or restitution. That's the goal, but it's going to take a massive and careful effort to get there."

"What about Live Payday Check Loan?"

David's eyebrows raised. "And what about it?"

"Are we going to proffer information about that deal?"

David looked at me for a long time. Finally, he broke the silence. "Maybe I wasn't making myself clear. This is a dance. We're going to dance with Galvin and anyone else. They want to look good and we want to look good. We're going to give a sufficient proffer of documents to satisfy their information requests, but we're not going to proffer information that triggers a full roto-rooter. We're only producing information that is relevant to their specific requests. Nothing more. Can I make myself any clearer? Do I need to?" By now David was questioning whether to send me back to the Backwater or just put me on the street.

"No. No, I get it. I've never worked on one of these, so I'm just trying to get my arms around what we'll need."

"So what do you need to do now?"

"I need to make sure Erika is pulling together the bullets and I'll put together a new binder. And I'll start figuring out how many of our defendants in the loan lawsuits were Wampanoag Bank customers."

"Good. But who's going to figure that out?"

"I'll pull together a team."

"That's right. Triage what information you have and figure out what you need. Then farm that down to the document review team in the Annex. Use Erika and anyone else you need for research and memos. I'm out of here at

7:00. I need a new binder in my briefcase before I leave for the elevator. Take out the Live Payday Check Loan stuff. Leave in everything else, but give me ten bullet points of the highlights of your memorandum. And give me anything you have about where our default defendants come from. Anything else?"

"That's all I have for you."

I returned to my desk and scanned my to-do list. It was loaded. I reordered the tasks by priority. If the opportunities for advancement in the Temple were greater than those in the Backwater, so were the chances of failure. If my first real meeting with David taught me anything, it was that I still had a lot to learn.

CHAPTER TWELVE

Big Guns

Just before noon on Thursday I pushed through the glass doors separating the elevator bank from the conference room floor. As I passed through the waiting area I was greeted by a half-dozen men in suits. They bowed slightly as I approached them and I reflexively bowed back before turning the corner. In the main conference room a crowd of attorneys endured a legal ethics seminar. Aaron was playing on his cellphone as I passed.

I entered 42D. Trays of penne and chicken parmesan sat on a credenza against an interior wall. It seemed like a lot of food for me and David. I sat down at a long conference table and opened up my call binder and waited for his arrival. The smell of the food gnawed at me, but I didn't want to be the first to dig in and have David enter while I was stuffing my face.

A few minutes after noon, he slipped into the room. "Clear your schedule. Today is off to a fast start. I've been on the phone all morning."

Before he could go further, Harry Josephson rounded the doorway into the conference room with his fingers lightly caressing the doorframe as he entered. In the neighborhood of 6'4" and easily 270 pounds, Harry had broad shoulders and a large belly that protruded over the belt of the fitted pants of his bright blue Armani suit.

Despite his physical presence, he walked lightly and almost gracefully with his heels only touching the ground when he stopped moving. Pigeon-toed, he never made a turn without touching a wall as he navigated the curve. He could have flattened me with a direct charge, but I could have pushed him over sideways with nothing more than a glancing blow. Rather than framing his face, his horned-rimmed glasses were dominated by thick black eyebrows contrasted against silver hair covering his tanned head.

The top class action attorney in the firm, Harry made more money than just about anyone else at Smith Stevens. He bounced from one white-shoe firm to another almost every three years and had a reputation for eventually wearing out his welcome everywhere he went. He also had a reputation for wearing out associates nearly as quickly, and left too many shattered careers in his wake to count.

"Harry, have you met Will Duggan?"

"I've never seen this guy before in my life."

"Well, that's probably because he was hiding out in the Annex until Monday."

"Then welcome to the firm." Two associates who trailed him into the room smirked when he said it.

"I was just about to tell Will the latest. He's been National Union's boots on the ground in Boston, but is now transitioning into overseeing locals, who will be covering the cases at the street level moving forward." The meaning of street level took on a new significance now that I was sitting fifty floors above Times Square.

"Our most famous associate." Harry smiled.

"Since we're all here, Harry, why don't you fill us in?"

"All right. Last night I got a courtesy call from Austin King. You know who he is?" Everyone knew who Austin King was. He was one of the most famous consumer class action attorneys in the United States. His firm in Galveston, Texas, was small, but powerful. He was known as the "King of Class Actions."

The only people who didn't like seeing Austin King coming were corporate officers. Everyone else in the system made money in his wake, especially class-action defense attorneys. He enlisted an army of researchers, who spent their days on the internet looking for potential class action claims that would form the basis of new lawsuits. Whoever sent Senator Galvin's letter to the *New York Globe* had inadvertently or intentionally triggered an avalanche.

"Austin told me he's representing a woman named Dorothea White. She's a former Wampanoag customer. National Union swallowed her branch then closed it. She lives in Roxbury and she's Black. And significantly, National Union gave Ms. White a car loan with a subprime interest rate. And it's a product that isn't offered outside of urban neighborhoods. Austin says he's been contacted by more than a dozen former National Union clients with similar stories. He said the product was only offered to minority customers. And he has documents to back it up."

David looked at me. "So what does this tell you?"

"I'd say things have gone from bad to worse."

"I'd say a lot fucking worse," Harry followed. "Austin's putting the finishing touches on a class action complaint he's filing by midnight tonight. He contacted me because he knew Smith Stevens represents National Union and wanted to give us a chance to get ahead of it with the bank and, hopefully, get retained on it. I've worked with him on a dozen cases and we have a good relationship.

"We trust each other. And we can work on this together in a way that limits the casualties. And hopefully everyone comes out of it looking as good as possible under the circumstances. That being said, the complaint is going to rough up National Union. It's going to have claims for unfair business practices and discrimination. He's going to claim redlining for shutting down inner-city branches and reverse redlining for targeting minorities with subprime financial products. The complaint is going to hit the bank on everything in every state where it has a presence. So our dear senator, what does he know about all this?"

Everyone in the room looked at me. I hoped David would chime in as the last person to have contact with him. "Well, he doesn't know about all that," I responded. "When he called me the first time, his only questions were about branch closures and pending lawsuits. He wanted information and threatened to issue a subpoena."

"That's a problem," Harry surmised. "But it's going to seem like a small problem soon. I'll bet you Austin's jet National Union gets a call from the Justice Department as soon as news of the complaint hits the internet. And you know this Galvin?"

"Not personally, but everyone in Massachusetts knows who he is. He's a fireball."

"Well, we don't want to set him off, but we can't be responding to requests for information in a piecemeal fashion, with dribs here and drabs there." Harry's associates wrote down every word he said on legal pads, but neither of them made a sound during the entire meeting. "We need to get with Don Jones as soon as possible and coordinate our efforts across the board."

"We can't give information to Galvin until we see Austin's complaint," Harry continued. "And even then, I don't think we're giving anything to him. We have to take a thoughtful approach and we don't want full-blown discovery. We need to settlement track this thing and agree on the information we're going to turn over. Just enough to satisfy the government, but not so much that we open up any other cans of worms. What do we have for time?"

"About ten minutes," I replied. Harry was ready to sink his teeth in, and David was only more than happy to spread billable hours his way.

Harry looked at me and his associates. "I'm not going to kick you out. This is a learning opportunity. But if any one of you opens your trap or so much as sneezes, I'll fucking kill you. We don't want Galvin to think we've assembled an army or are over-lawyering this already. Got me?" We all nodded.

"David, you introduce me. And then I'll tell him about the class action and that we don't want to get ahead of him or go behind his back. I'll ask him for some breathing room and will offer to send him the complaint once we get it. He'll get it once it's online anyway. The inside info should show him we're trying to work with him. Sound good?" Harry looked around the room as if he wanted approval from me and the other associates.

"Works for me," David responded.

"Good. Let's get him on the line."

"Senator Galvin, it's David Bell. I don't want to blindside you, but my partner Harry Josephson just joined me in the office. I have you on the box if that's ok."

"That's quite all right," Senator Galvin replied. I could feel a cough welling in my throat and did my best to muffle it, lest I forced Harry to fulfil his death threat. "I don't know if you know Harry, but he used to be an assistant attorney general in New Jersey. I'm going to let him step in, as there are some developments I think you'll find interesting."

"Senator, this is Harry Josephson. David asked me to be on this call because I have some news. Do you know Austin King?"

"Of course I know him."

"Well, Senator, a little bird told me he's filing a class action that alleges some of the same issues raised in your letter."

"Ok. Well, just so you know that's not how I operate. I didn't give that letter to the press and no one else here did, either."

"I appreciate that, Senator. I didn't mean to suggest anyone in your office did. Regardless, this complaint is about to come in and we're going to get a copy before it's on file. Once it's online it's going to blow up."

"I'm sure it will once the press gets its hands on it."

"What I'd like to do is send you a copy of it before anyone else outside of this firm has it. Then you can do with it what you may."

"But I'd also like to reschedule this call with you. I think our discussion will be more fruitful once we all have a chance to get our arms around it. Is that fair?"

"I think that's fair. When will I have a copy?"

"It'll be on file before midnight tonight and we should have a copy of it before then. We can get it to you as soon as it comes in. Would email work?"

"That works."

"Can you put us in the book for the same time next week?"

"I'll talk to you then." With that Senator Galvin hung up the phone.

Harry looked at all of us smiling. "What was it you said? 'Fireball?' Seemed liked a kitten to me. And he ate right out of the palm of my hand." Harry looked at me. "Will, you need to get that complaint to the senator as soon as it comes in. I'm emailing Austin right now to make sure you're copied on the email when he sends it."

I looked down at my cell and pushed the button. It was 1:14. The complaint was supposed to come in over the next ten hours and forty-six minutes. It looked like another night after midnight in the Temple was on the way.

David turned to me. "As soon as the email comes in, you need to start preparing a summary I can flip to Don Jones. This one's on you because you're birddogging the complaint tonight. I don't care how long it takes to complete it, but it has to go out to him first thing in the morning. And give me a one-page executive summary with bullets." I began to wonder if I would be leaving the Temple that night after all.

CHAPTER THIRTEEN

Storm Brewing

I returned to my desk on Friday morning four hours after I left it. It was 7:15. I carried a life-saving black coffee and a warm bagel from a coffee cart into the Temple. I pulled the executive summary from my briefcase. It was scarred with red handwriting from a set of hasty edits made while leaning against the silver door of an uptown 2 between Greenwich Village and Times Square.

The air conditioning in my office hummed along keeping the temperature at an arctic level. There was no other sign of life on the floor. I expected David would be in the office early and wanted to email the memorandum to him before he arrived. The week had been marked with some highs and some lows, and I couldn't afford another low. The learning curve was steep and I was barely hanging on.

I drained the steaming coffee as I tapped in my edits. I stepped away from my office with bagel in hand and pulled a copy of the draft off a large high-speed printer. The paper felt warm as I lifted it towards my face. I spent too much time in my office this week. I needed another point of view. As I looked for a place to sit I thought better of sitting at David's desk. I didn't want to risk dropping cream cheese on the carpet and defiling his fastidiously clean office.

I found an unused workstation and plopped down on a black padded chair. With a fresh perspective I lanced at the document with a red felt-tipped pen that had been resting behind my ear moments before. Short sentences with simple declarations. Run-ons were fatal. No five-dollar words. There was no need to try to impress with fancy vocabulary or risk pissing someone off with a word that had to be looked up.

I carved out words and revised my sentences to simplify them. My executive summary was short, sweet, and touched on all the highlights of the complaint. Harry hit it on the nose. It was brutal and alleged civil rights violations, discrimination, and unfair business practices. And it covered redlining and reverse redlining. National Union was going to go nuts when they saw it. I was glad David would be delivering the news, rather than me.

I returned to my office to enter my fresh edits. When I woke up my computer there was an email from David. It was 8:03.

"How's my summary coming?"

"Putting in my last edits now. Sending it within 15."

"Good. Put together a cover email to Don explaining what's happening. And attach a copy of the complaint with your summary. He knows what's going on, but he needs something to flip to the board of directors before the news goes public."

I finished entering my edits and gave the document a final readthrough. I typed out a brief cover email for Don and hit send to David. I exhaled deeply and walked swiftly to the elevator bank to head downstairs for another coffee. This time of the gourmet variety now that my rush to finish the summary was over. The streets around Times Square were bustling with commuters. After soaking it in, I headed back to my desk to play catch-up.

I ran into June on the way. "Is David coming in?"

"Not today. I think he's heading to his house in Sag Harbor."

"Nice." It was. For him and for me.

I sat at my desk and opened my inbox. An email from David immediately caught my eye. I braced myself. "Good work." Nothing more.

A phantom of stress exorcised itself from my body. I looked at the words for a long time with my chin resting on my palm. I wanted to tape it to my refrigerator, so seldom had I received any feedback, positive or negative, at the Backwater. As I scrolled through lines of unopened emails, my phone rang from a 718 area code. I let it ring a couple of times.

"Mr. Duggan? It's Desi Baines."

"Hey Mr. Baines!" I was so relieved by David's response I sounded like an overly-happy restaurant host welcoming back a favorite diner. "You got my message?"

"Yes, Mr. Duggan. Thank you for calling me. What's happening?"

"I have some good news. The firm said I could take on your case."

"That's great, Mr. Duggan! What do you need from me?"

"I don't need anything from you right now, other than a date to meet you in Mount Vernon. And we can go into court together."

"How about Tuesday? That would give me a couple of days to get prepared." Me, too. I could use the time since I had no idea what I was doing.

"Let's meet out front at 9:00. There's probably going to be a long line to get in, so that will give us time to get our story straight. Any questions?"

"I'm good. I have a letter from my therapist. I'm going to bring that."

"Sounds like a plan. I'll see you Tuesday."

I returned to my emails and became aware of the absolute silence on the floor. I got up from my chair and peered from inside of my doorway down the hall, but didn't see a soul. Only the tops of the heads of assistants working away in their workstations. None of them were close enough to speak to each other without raising their voices. Unlike the Backwater, there was no chatter or small-talk anywhere to be heard. The hallway was neat, but sterile, with dark carpeting offset by the grey workstations lining the interior of the floor. It felt like a hermetically sealed and lifeless spacecraft drifting through the abyss.

I sat back at my desk and ignored the silence. I continued working through my emails. After I finished I would try to figure out how to tie former Wampanoag clients to the default lawsuits. The Wampanoag deal binder sat on the edge of my desk. I hoped it would at least provide a start to figuring out where the defendants came from.

I looked back at my emails and thought better of wading through the defendants myself. David's admonition about spreading the wealth rattled through my mind. I clicked out of my emails and pulled up the firm's intranet. I started to type "Erik" in the search bar. The contact information for all of the employees of the firm with those four letters in either their first or last name appeared on my screen. "Erika Tavares" popped up and I tapped the six digit code to her office phone from the keypad on mine.

She picked up after one ring. "Hi, Will."

"Hey, you got some time to come down? I have another National Union project for you."

"Of course." Within a few minutes Erika was in my doorway. Her black curls tried to continue down the hallway after her body stopped moving. She must've run to my office.

"I have a bunch of stuff brewing with David and at the top of the list is trying to figure out where our defendants came from in National Union's loan default suits. National Union says they were previously Wampanoag customers and we need to see if we can back that up. Tripper gave me a copy of the Wampanoag deal binder. See if there's anything helpful in there."

"Ok. Do you need a memo?"

"Not yet, but if there's fruit, we're going to need an analysis. I also have this spreadsheet, which lists all of the National Union loan default lawsuits in Mass over the last five years. Maybe there's something to cross-check. And we'll figure out if the bank's story holds water."

"Ok."

"And there's this binder. It's a deal Tripper's working on where National Union is selling a bunch of mortgages to BestRateLoan. I skimmed it but don't know if it has anything good in it. Either way, we need to start with the default defendants."

"What's the deadline?"

"Nothing's set in stone, but the sooner the better just in case. Did you hear about the class action?"

"I did, but I haven't seen anything."

"I'll send you a summary with the complaint. David's sending it to Don Jones this morning, then it's going to the board of directors. I'm sure all hell's going to break loose once they read it. Let's plan to connect on Monday to see what you've found. And if it's too much, I can pull someone else in."

In a blink Erika vanished from my office and the only sound remaining in her wake was the quiet humming of the air conditioning system. I turned back to my emails and a familiar number from the 617 area code appeared on my cell.

"Kevin."

"Will? Can you hear me?" I heard the drone of Knuckles' old Mercedes convertible. Its best years were behind it, but he bought it just after he represented Tony Rings and would never get rid of it. More than once he had been seen driving on the highway soaking wet after the old beast's mechanical top refused to function during a rainstorm. "Hold on." It sounded like he was fumbling around with something. "You can hear me now?"

"I can hear you."

"Good. Sorry. I forgot to put my Bluetooth in my ear." Knuckles' voice was loud, but barely louder than the sound of the old car. "I'm on 95. I just left Cedar Junction a few minutes ago. I saw Mickey and was hoping I'd catch you before you left for the day. Is this a good time?"

"I'm good. What's up?"

"Have you talked to him?"

"Not since last weekend."

"All right. I told him to call you. I'll fill you in a little. He's ok . . ." My back immediately tensed. "He doesn't want you to worry. He's all right, but he got roughed up pretty hard. A couple of younger guys."

"Fuck. Is he ok?"

"He's ok, but he cracked a rib and chipped a tooth. He was moving pretty gingerly."

"What the fuck happened?" My voice raised involuntarily.

"Probably gang related. Some young guys showing out. You know Mickey. He's pretty much still a loner."

"Holy shit. Can we get him moved?"

"Already on it. They're putting him in another unit. At this point he's probably better off at Cedar Junction than being the new guy someplace else. He could end up at a real shithole. Like next level. I wouldn't. At least at Cedar Junction he's a known commodity to the guards . . ."

"Is there anything else we can do?"

"Yeah, you can talk to him again and try to put some sense into that hard head. I'm at a loss and he won't listen to me."

"He won't listen to me, either. You know I've tried. Is there anything else? Did the PI find anything?"

"Same shit as before. Nothing. No one is left in the neighborhood that would've seen anything. Unfortunately, we're shit out of luck. At this point we're just spinning our wheels and wasting money unless he changes his tune."

"There's gotta be something. What about the governor?" I was only half-kidding.

"Even if you had his direct dial, that's another waste of time. He's not dipping into a murder case." I felt deflated and leaned back and looked up at the ceiling as if there might be something up there that could help, but there was nothing. "The hearing is two weeks from Monday. You still want to go through with it?"

"I do."

"You're going to have to convince Mickey. He's pushing back. It's at least a chance for him to get out for the day."

"I'll do my best."

"That's all you can do. Oh, one other thing. I need you to replenish me. Can you do it?"

"Depends. What's my nut?"

"Same as last time."

"I can send a check today."

"Don't worry about it. Just give me an envelope when you see me." That went fast. I had already spent more than $100,000 trying to get Mickey out of jail.

"Thanks, Kevin. Anything else?"

"Nah, I think that covers it. Go out and get a beer. And please try to talk some sense into him."

"You know I will."

"All right. Talk to you—"

"Wait! Can I get your advice on something?"

"Yeah. Shoot."

"I got a *pro bono* case and I have to help a guy surrender on a warrant. He missed a court date a bunch of years ago and found out about the warrant when he applied for a job."

"In Boston? You working my territory?" Kevin chuckled.

"No, no. Down here in New York. It's in City Court in Mount Vernon. Next to the Bronx."

"It's pretty straightforward. Bring him inside the court and track down an assistant district attorney. Tell her you have a client who wants to surrender and she'll ask for his identification. Just give it to her and she'll get a printout of whatever's out there and take it from there. Depending on what it is, they might take him into custody. What's the charge?"

"Stealing a car and marijuana possession. And he can't go to jail. He's in a recovery program. He's bipolar. It would fuck him all up."

"Shit. Then tell him to bring a bunch of cash. They're not going to let him out of there without some money hanging in the balance."

"He doesn't have any. He's homeless."

"Then you better tell him to bring a toothbrush."

"Fuck. That's what he was told before."

"See, it's good advice."

"He's terrified. What the hell am I going to tell him?"

"You have to be straight with him. No matter what happens, you didn't do it. He made his bed and now he has to lay in it. That's life." Knuckles' advice did nothing to build my confidence. "When's this going down?"

"Tuesday."

"At least you don't have a lot of time to worry about it. Seriously, all you can do is come up with the best story you can based on the facts and pitch it to the judge. But don't puff. If you puff and can't back it up, you're toast. Maybe she's overloaded, maybe she's empathetic to someone in recovery. And then maybe you get lucky. And that's all you can do."

"Thanks, Kevin."

"All right then. Go get 'em." With that his phone went silent.

I was glad to have Knuckles' advice, but knowing the chances of Desi going to jail only brought home the gravity of the situation. Up to that moment it didn't seem real that a judge would lock him up. Now it didn't just seem possible, but probable. Tuesday's court date began to grow in size and menace. After going through the rest of my emails I checked the internet for Austin King's complaint. Still nothing available to the public and no word from David. It was 5:18 when I made a break from my office to the elevator bank and then down to the crowded streets below.

CHAPTER FOURTEEN

The Drill

I f the publication of Senator Galvin's letter in the *New York Globe* was a stick of dynamite exploding, the filing of Austin King's complaint was a nuclear blast. It landed with a thud at National Union over the weekend. Early Monday morning, before the bank could fully digest the news, the complaint went live on the internet. Within hours it was in the hands of court watchers and on the minds of class action attorneys around the country.

At 11:35 Harry's suit jacket was hanging from the back of a chair in a large conference room. The temperature was frigid, yet Harry was visibly hot while he stalked a large white board with a black marker. His blue silk tie swung wildly over his enormous belly. David watched the large man with palpable enjoyment that verged on wonder as he paced and oozed sweat.

The room was crowded with attorneys and paralegals, including Harry's associates and a document review team from the Backwater. By my calculation, the meeting was running National Union more than ten thousand dollars per hour. If David was looking to expand his mansion in Sag Harbor,

Austin King was going to make it possible. As I looked around, it struck me that Chuck was completely out of the picture.

"We're vectoring this case towards settlement. But to get there, we need to look like we're going to war. We have to take a coordinated approach to make it happen. National Union has urban branches in a dozen states." Harry picked a small black remote control off of the table and pressed it with his large, hairy thumb until it clicked audibly. A map highlighting the states with National Union branches appeared on a large screen. "What we can't have is the attorney general of each of these states subpoenaing documents from us, plus any other number of class action attorneys doing the same. And then have the Department of Justice seeking their own documents.

"So here's the deal. We're going to support Austin King's appointment as lead attorney in the class action. And I've worked with Sarah Moore before on complex discrimination cases. I called her on Friday and filled her in." Confusion betrayed my face. "For the uninitiated, Sarah is one of the big dogs in the Justice Department's Civil Rights Division. She carries a lot of weight and the state attorneys general will follow her lead. She's starting an investigation and will have a case on file before the end of the week. We'll be in business on that front as soon as it hits.

"So where does that leave us? With a ton of shit to do." Harry clicked the remote and another slide appeared on the screen. It read, "Control the Documents." "We have to get ready for a two-track process. On one track, we need to begin pulling together documents that support our defense. And as we do that, we need to identify our 'DGI's.'" I was lost again. "Our hot docs, our smoking guns. We call them our 'Documents of General Interest.' These are documents National Union doesn't want to share with anyone under any circumstances. And they'll make the bank want to settle to avoid disclosing them.

"We're going to red flag DGI's during our review. And if we can bring the class actions and the government cases to a sensible resolution, those documents will never see the light of day. No one is to set them aside as a 'hot doc' or a 'smoking gun.' No one does anything with them except flag them for now in case we need to use them."

Harry looked towards the team from the Backwater. "The document review team knows the drill. We need everything on branch acquisitions, branch closures, loan products, and lending standards over the last six years. Go big." Members of the team nodded at Harry. "David, can you get us a point person at the bank to work on pulling documents?"

"You got it."

"Once we get a first cut of documents from National Union, the Annex will do a deep dive for relevance. They'll flag attorney-client privileged and work-product documents. And they'll red-flag the DGI's. We're keeping all of the documents in-house until this thing is over. We're going to control the documents."

"Next up." Harry clicked the remote again and another slide appeared. "Control the Narrative." "This is the second track and it's the tricky part, but it's key. We have to tell a story that soft-shoes any perceived wrongdoing by National Union. We need to cultivate themes and support them with our documents. Control the narrative. We're not getting absolution for National Union, but we can get some wiggle room. We're going to settle, but not because we agree National Union committed wrongdoing or is a bad bank. Instead, we could see how it could be interpreted that National Union acted wrongfully in some circumstances. And maybe some customers fell through the cracks of its normal good business practices.

"The first theme is that National Union is a large bank with customers in twelve states. And by and large, most of its customers . . . or the vast majority of its customers never had a problem with National Union. So the starting theme is that nearly all of National Union's customer base is happy." He wrote "THEMES" in large letters on the white board. Next to a black dot, he wrote, "vast majority of NU customers happy." "Ok. That's the start."

"The Annex needs to find building blocks during the review. Satisfaction surveys, awards and the like. Then my team will get behind the numbers. Numbers of customers over the last six years. Numbers who have left. Numbers of new customers. And compare it all to the customers who have been sued. I guarantee you the number of customers sued looks tiny next to the number of customers overall." It wasn't even noon, and Harry's face was already sprouting a heavy shadow.

"Good. Moving on then. Hopefully everyone here read the complaint or at least Will's summary this morning. Let's examine that and what it says. In the macro, we have allegations of redlining and reverse redlining. We want to keep it in the macro and not get into the micro. We don't want the DOJ digging into individual customer stories or details about particular branches. The time and the cost would be devastating. And the longer all of this drags on, the more unhappy the bank's shareholders and board of directors are going to become.

"So let's start with the redlining allegation. Austin claims National Union is closing down urban branches across the country. But why is that? It's not because they're making money. It's because they aren't. It's natural selection. The strong survive and the weak don't make it." I wondered if Harry had any idea about Live Payday Check Loan. I glanced over at David, who was watching intently. "And it's a fact that National Union hasn't closed down all of its branches in the inner-city. And we can demonstrate both of these things.

"In terms of National Union picking on inner-city clients, there's more to the story. And there are reasons for it. Population density for one. There are simply more people in the inner-city than in the suburbs. And more people equals more lawsuits. And that's not all. David told me in Massachusetts, where all of this started, a lot of those clients were inherited when National Union took over another bank."

"Wampanoag," David added.

"Wampanoag. And National Union had different lending standards than Wampanoag. And most of those Wampanoag clients were based in the city. And we can point to the data. There were more suits from Wampanoag clients because the bar for them to get loans was lower than it would have been if they were National Union clients. I understand Will's on top of it?" Thank God. I stiffened in my seat.

"We've pulled all the materials we have on the Massachusetts suits and are tracking down our defendants and finding out who came from Wampanoag."

"Good, good," Harry replied. I felt a wave of relief pass through my body.

"Will, since you already have the roadmap for doing that in Mass, you're going to do it for the rest of our jurisdictions. We need to be ahead of the curve. I want you to get the info we need for all of the states. Same thing as in Mass. Pull together the background story on any bank closings and sales. Get us a story for each of them. Got it?"

"I'm on it."

"Good. Triage it with the docs we can get our hands on now. And we'll augment it after the Annex does its review. But let's see what you can turn around this week." I nodded pensively.

"Pull in anyone you need." David chimed in. "And lean on the attorneys handling National Union litigation in those jurisdictions." I had no choice, as there was too much going on for me to handle it alone.

"Will do."

Harry wrote, "Business Reasons Required Branch Closings" and "Default Suits Focused on Bad Risk Inherited Clients" on the white board. He moved on quickly. "So next up on the hitlist is the reverse redlining claim. This is, perhaps, trickier. But we can put together a fulsome response that will cast doubt on it." I could feel my anxiety rising, as the assignment appeared headed in my direction.

"This one's going to my team." The tension left me like air from an untied balloon. "We're going to explain the legitimate financial reasons for the alleged reverse redlining. We're going to explain that it wasn't reverse redlining *per se*. Instead, these products existed to service clients that couldn't qualify for traditional loan products under National Union's lending standards.

"The clients offered these products wouldn't have been able to obtain capital through traditional channels because of their risk. It could've been credit scores, bankruptcies, or a lack of assets. Whatever the reason, they would've had to turn to a predatory lender to obtain credit. And National Union was a better option and was trying to help out clients in a financial jam."

Maybe the explanation wasn't probable, but it was possible. That is to anyone who didn't know National Union was working behind the scenes to get into the predatory lending business itself. Harry scribbled, "NU Offered Subprime Products to Clients With No Access to Traditional Loans." He looked at his handywork with visible admiration.

"Once we have our themes firmed up and supported with documents, we're going to informally and voluntarily proffer documents with our explanation. What they need to see to settle and nothing more. No DGI's. We're going to do it before we get a subpoena. National Union has its hands full with this and we don't need anything else dumped on top. Everyone on the same page?" He looked around the room. "Good. Let's go get em!"

Harry's description of the proffer surprised me. When the federal government starts an investigation, the company being investigated has a duty to provide relevant information, even information that is painful to disclose. Yet it sounded like Harry was preparing to play hide-the-ball with Sarah Moore. And he was going to justify it by producing documents before National Union received a subpoena and the government could formally describe exactly what it wanted to see. I didn't want to find out what would happen if Harry's plan went sideways.

When I returned to my office, there was a note on my keyboard from Erika. I quickly dialed her.

"I went through the binders over the weekend and I think there's some interesting stuff. You got time to talk?"

"I'm slammed. How's your schedule this week?"

"For National Union, I have time." David could butter a lot of bread at Smith Stevens and this was a chance to impress.

"Can we connect tomorrow? And in the meantime, I have to do the same thing for all of the other states where National Union has branches by Friday. You game?"

"I'm in it to win it. Tomorrow works."

"Great," I sighed. "I'm going to send emails to everyone I need to get stuff from, then follow up with calls. I'll copy you and you can help me chase the stuff down. And tomorrow I'll fill you in on the details."

"Cool."

"I'm in court in the morning. I'll ping you as soon as I'm back."

CHAPTER FIFTEEN

Horse to Water

I arrived outside of Mount Vernon City Court just before 9:00 on Tuesday morning and picked a spot close to the front door to wait for Desi. Attorneys breezed into the courthouse and through security without waiting in line. Everyone else had to go through metal detectors. I had no idea what would happen once we were in court. I feared my last view of Desi would be the stare of an angry, upset, and frightened man being led off in handcuffs.

While my troubles were trivial next to Desi's, City Court was the last place I needed to be this morning. I had my work cut out for me when I returned to the office, but the firm's rules required that every client be treated equally. It was no excuse to push off Desi's case in favor of National Union simply because it was *pro bono* and there were other things going on. There would always be another emergency.

Around 9:30 the courthouse opened. The line of people waiting to get in snaked from the front door, down a walkway to the sidewalk and around the corner. And it kept growing. I hoped Desi would show up soon. His courage would be tested if he spent a long day watching defendants being led away in shackles. It wouldn't help my confidence, either. Watching experienced criminal attorneys would only show how far out of my depth I was in their court. If Desi's case went sideways, he would surely see I wasn't nearly as skilled or as capable as the attorneys representing other defendants. My heart pounded in my chest while my knees started to dance involuntarily.

I heard the heavy sound of a taxi door creaking open behind me. I swung around. It was an elderly man wearing a tweed scally cap and a brown corduroy blazer. A thin grey wool V-necked sweater framed his yellow button-down shirt with a thickly-knotted brown tie shielding his wrinkly Adam's apple. He unfolded a walker and worked his way to the front door of the courthouse. The court officers called to him. "Barney!" "Counselor!" "Mr. Gaynor!" I was horrified he would be sitting in the gallery while I made a fool of myself.

I took a walk around the building to calm my nerves. Desi was now over an hour late to meet me. I dialed the Vanderbilt Houses, but no one had seen him that morning. I began to worry something happened. Or maybe he finally realized he would be better off with an actual criminal attorney. I walked over to Gramatan Avenue to get a coffee and warm up. When I returned to the courthouse the line was gone. Occasional stragglers caught my jittery attention. I tried the Vanderbilt Houses again. I discarded the empty coffee cup and pulled open the front door.

I was late to church. Everyone looked at me as I walked down an aisle between old wooden benches in the courtroom. The air was stale and thick. Heavy winter coats made the room crowded and stuffy. Second-hand coffee leached from the breath of seated spectators and the aroma of the greasy spoons where they had breakfast lifted off of their clothing. My anxiety only added to the kaleidoscope of smell and tension in the air as I searched the courtroom.

I walked out and quietly shut the door behind me. I looked around the old marble hallway. I asked a court officer working the metal detector if anyone was looking for Will Duggan. "No one." I stepped back out into the cold and looked in every direction. I didn't want to waste four hours of my day in the middle of another client's emergency. After more calls to the Vanderbilt Houses and Amanda, resignation finally set in and I retreated.

The elevator doors opened to the 50th floor and I reentered the sterile world of litigation at Smith Stevens hundreds of feet above the real world problems on the streets below. It was a different universe than City Court, yet it was the same profession. As I strolled towards my office, Amanda stood up at her workstation.

"You got a call from Desi Baines."

"Shit. Don't tell me I missed him." I couldn't afford to turn around.

"No. Actually, he called to apologize. He said he couldn't make it today. And he was so sorry. He left a number."

I looked at a note she handed me. I was too relieved to be angry. "Anything else?"

"Erika stopped by to see if I knew when you'd be back."

"She's a gunner."

"You don't know the half of it. I told her you'd call her. So you better!"

"All right."

I sighed into my desk chair and clicked my computer to life. I dialed the number to the Vanderbilt Houses. "He's right here."

"Mr. Duggan?"

"It's me, but just Will please."

"I'm so sorry I didn't go. I just couldn't do it today. I'm not ready. I thought I was, but I'm not. I know you can fire me. And maybe you should. But I hope you won't. I want to go. I have to go. I have no choice. But I'm not ready. Can you forgive me? Can we do it another day?"

I exhaled heavily. I didn't need another thing on my plate right now and I had an out. I was frustrated he stood me up, but I thought of Mickey. Going to court wasn't easy. "It's ok. Stuff happens."

Desi sounded excited. "Really? Really? Thank you so much! It means the world to me. Can we do it another day?"

"Of course. But I'm getting slammed here with work right now. Can you give me a couple of weeks and call me when you're ready?"

"I will. I can use the time. Thank you so much, Mr. Duggan."

Just as I started to gather myself, Erika appeared in my doorway. "How was court? Did you win?"

"Nah, it didn't get that far. I got stood up."

"Oh. Sorry to hear that. Another day, I guess."

"Looks like it."

"Is now a good time?" She clutched white binders and a legal folder. A large engagement ring sparkled under my office lights. It was a Manhattan rock if I had ever seen one.

"Congratulations. Is that recent?" I pointed towards her finger.

"Saturday." She smiled widely as she said it.

"Holy cow. I hope you didn't work on this stuff all weekend."

"It's ok. It's my job." It was the life of an associate to squeeze personal events in between assignments, but it was jarring to me that I was now the one handing them out. "There'll be a lot of time to celebrate. But this is exciting stuff. Can I show you what I found?" I couldn't tell if she was happier about her engagement or her work product. "So I went through the Wampanoag binder. Take a look at Schedule D." I flipped through the binder. "If you weed through it, you'll see it has a list of all of the Wampanoag clients that became National Union clients after the deal.

"And if you look here, you'll see their names, addresses, account numbers and the last four digits of their social security numbers." There were hundreds of pages of account numbers and many thousands of clients listed on the schedule. "I found the live version of it on our system from when the deal was done. It's searchable. Then I took the list of cases you gave me and had Office Services turn it into a spreadsheet for me. I gave both documents to Charlene and she had the staff attorneys in the Annex go through them. They cross-checked the names and identified the defendants that came from Wampanoag."

I was impressed. As a graduate of the firm's summer associate program, Erika received training I never got as a transplant to the Backwater. It was a summer job that lasted for several weeks and paid significant salaries to students at top law schools. Smith Stevens extended offers to the program's stars and they committed to working at the firm before they graduated. Erika shined as a summer associate and was earmarked as a potential partner early on. She clearly had a better understanding of the firm's resources and how to use them than me, but she wasn't done yet.

"Then I had our analysts review the information, and they put together this chart for me." I didn't know the firm had a staff of analysts. Erika handed me a color document with a pie chart showing the number of former Wampanoag customers against the total number of suits. At the bottom of the chart was a bar graph, which showed the number of suits filed by the bank for the last six years, including before the Wampanoag acquisition. The tallest bars by far followed the takeover and showed National Union became much more litigious after acquiring Wampanoag customers.

"So what the review showed in Massachusetts, at least, is that almost eighty-five percent of the lawsuits filed by National Union were against former Wampanoag customers. And the vast majority of the lawsuits filed by National Union came after the Wampanoag acquisition. That's good, right?"

"It goes right along with National Union's story. If nothing else, it gives us some wiggle room for explaining why the majority of the suits are in the city. Do you think we can do the same thing with the other states? By Friday?"

"I'm already ahead of you. I spoke to Tripper and he pulled the deal binders for bank acquisitions in other states. Charlene's already coordinating with the Annex. The staff attorneys will do the same review as in Mass. Then I'll feed the data to the analysts and they'll give us more charts."

"That's amazing. Great work." I was more relieved than I could put into words. Without Erika, David would've returned me to the Backwater or worse by now.

"Any questions?"

"Nah, I think I get it."

"Cool. There's another thing. I don't think it's related, but I thought I'd let you know just in case." I could understand why Erika's desk was in the Temple and she never had even been inside of the Backwater.

"What's up?"

"Well, when I was reviewing the Wampanoag deal binder I took a look at the schedule of the mortgages that were transferred along with the branches and the customers. There were thousands of mortgages transferred from Wampanoag to National Union. A lot of the mortgages in the Wampanoag binder were rated as 'high-risk.' Actually, it looked like at least a third of them were high-risk. A bunch of them were listed as 'average-risk' and some were listed as 'low-risk.' I wondered if National Union was planning to cherry-pick the best assets and get rid of the rest.

"So I pulled the mortgage schedule from the BestRateLoan binder and lined it up with the Wampanoag schedule to see which mortgages are being sold to BestRateLoan and if they're all high-risk. The two schedules looked the same, just with some minor details changed. But both of them use the same mortgage numbers with a description of the property, the debtor, and some deed information. And each loan on both schedules has an assigned risk rating.

"You know what I found?" I shook my head. "When I was comparing the information on one of the mortgages that appeared on both schedules, I noticed the risk changed. On the Wampanoag version it was high-risk, and on the BestRateLoan version it was average-risk. It seemed strange."

"Hmm." These guys thought of everything.

"So I matched up another one. And found the same thing. High-risk to average-risk. And I became more curious. I kept looking and found even more. Some of the average-risk mortgages were changed to low-risk mortgages. It wasn't every mortgage, but a lot of them were changed. What do you think is going on? Is it a screw-up? Should I have the Annex do a review?"

I doubted it was an accident, but it was on Tripper's plate and mine was already full. "It's Tripper's deal. I'll find out what's going on from him. Let's not send it to the Annex just yet. I think they have enough to do for us right now. I don't want to abuse them more if there's a legitimate reason for the change. It's also a bit outside of what we're doing anyway."

"Ok."

"Let's touch base first thing tomorrow and go over where we are. I need to play some catchup on emails." I looked towards my screen as I said it. "Hold on. I just got an urgent email from Harry." I read it out loud. "'David and I met with Don Jones and National Union's Chairman, Dick Chambers, this afternoon. They have asked for a deeper dive into Austin King's claims and his likelihood of success on the merits to better evaluate the risks of National Union going to trial. To that end they have authorized us to engage in jury testing. I copied Patrick Cooley, who has graciously agreed to lend us his immense talent on this project. He is available for a video meeting at 2:00 New York time tomorrow. Please confirm your attendance. Thank you, H.'"

I turned to Erika. "Holy shit!" Patrick Cooley was one of the top trial attorneys in the United States. He was the top dog in the Smith Stevens trial practice hierarchy and a rock star among the firm's rock stars. Based in Los Angeles, he rarely stepped foot inside the office. Instead, he went from trial to trial in courtrooms across the country.

If more than ninety-five percent of the firm's litigation cases were settled rather than tried, Patrick Cooley was part of the reason. He was the boogeyman at the end of the nightmare that was litigating against Smith Stevens. The firm's massive resources and influence could make litigation against it brutal. And if you could withstand the onslaught and refused to settle, Patrick Cooley might be waiting for you at trial. While no trial attorney could win them all, he came pretty close and his presence alone was enough to spur settlement.

The chance of seeing him in action was a rare treat outside of his team, especially for associates in the New York office. Erika listened to the email with wide eyes and looked at me as if Santa Claus had just arrived unexpectedly. "Any interest?"

"Are you fucking kidding me?"

I hastily tapped out an email. "Harry, is there room for one more? Erika Tavares has been working hard on the National Union analysis and has been doing great work. We wouldn't be where we are without her."

Moments later Harry responded. "The more the merrier. Glad to have her on board. H."

"You're in. How about that?"

"Thanks, Will! I'm going to get back to it." She practically skipped out of my office. I turned back to my computer and began plowing through emails. Erika gave me confidence that we would be finished with our analysis on schedule and maybe even ahead of it.

I left the office before midnight, but my worries refused to let me sleep. I was scared for Mickey's safety and still couldn't convince him to say the magic words to get out of Cedar Junction. And although I caught a break today, I feared Desi was on the way to jail and I had no way of stopping it. I didn't want to think about what would happen to him once he was on the inside. The day of reckoning was coming for both of them. And for me.

"At least I'm doing something," I told myself out loud. "I'm doing what I can do. And that's all I can do."

CHAPTER SIXTEEN

Heavy Artillery

A large monitor revealed the inside of a conference room in Smith Stevens' Los Angeles Office. Patrick Cooley appeared on the screen just after 2:00. Erika sat next to me and scribbled anxiously on a legal pad. Harry peeled off a dark blue suit jacket. "Looks like everyone here is everyone that's going to be here. We've been working with Don Jones to convince the board of directors to authorize settlement discussions with Austin King and the DOJ.

"David and I met with Don along with the chairman of the board, Dick Chambers. Dick told us the board has misgivings about entering into settlement discussions so quickly. They don't like having a gun to their head. The board considers Austin King a corporate terrorist and would rather fight than negotiate with him. Everyone in this room . . ." He looked up at the screen quickly. "And on the teleprompter—sorry LA—knows the risks. Not the least of which is discovery and the unknown threats that lurk in the bank's documents and in the testimony of current and former employees. Unfortunately, the elements in the board that want to fight hold enough votes to prevent us from settling.

"That's their right. They can fight. And they have the financial resources to do it. But with what we're up against, I would be remiss as an attorney if I didn't counsel them on the risks of fighting to the best of my ability. I know I'm preaching to the choir here, and everyone knows the risks of a class action and a government investigation, so I won't go into the details. It's 'bet the company litigation,' yada yada and all that. But the long and the short of it is we agreed on a compromise. Don and Dick have authorized us to do jury research to help the bank decide if it should try to reach a settlement at this stage.

"For those of us who've done it before, we know how valuable a tool it can be in terms of counseling clients, shaping arguments, and preparing for trial. You've heard enough from me, though, so I'm going to cede the floor to Patrick, who has taken time from his busy trial schedule to help us out. Patrick . . ."

"Good morning, everyone. Or let me make that afternoon to my friends in New York." Patrick's tenor voice was soothing, but alert. His pronunciation was crisp, with a tinge of a Southern California lilt that bordered on straight Southern. He was tan and manicured.

I had little doubt that everything he wore had been scrutinized from color to fit by jury consultants to enhance his likeability. He was trim and clean-shaven. His salt and pepper hair leaned more towards pepper than salt on his fifty-five year-old head. His hair was curly, but kempt. Everything about him was pleasing to the eye and to the ear. Next to him on screen was his right arm: Barbara Hogan. The vast majority of the words Patrick spoke at trial came from her pen. Having her at the helm of his scripts and seated next to him in court gave him the confidence to jump from trial to trial.

"Thank you to Harry and David for bringing us in. We're excited to help out with this project." Barbara nodded. I wondered if he was always addressing a jury. "National Union is a new client to us. And we're getting up to speed as quickly as we can. We have about six weeks before our next trial. As a result, our goal is to have the jury research completed in thirty days.

"I don't know if everyone on this call has worked on jury research before. It's actually a lot of fun. It's not going to be a full trial with complete openings and closings. And we're not going to present witnesses or every exhibit. What we're going to do is test our themes against Austin King's themes, which will essentially be the same as Sarah Moore's themes. We want to find out what a jury would think of our themes and what they would think of Austin King's themes.

"How are we going to do that? Well, we have a method that has been an excellent predictor of jury behavior in the past. Each side is going to be given forty-five minutes to present their themes in the form of a truncated opening statement. During the opening each side will be allowed to show documents supporting their themes. And we need to show them the best of the best and the worst of the worst. Don't worry—we aren't handing out copies and all the test jurors sign confidentiality agreements. Then each side will have fifteen minutes to present closing statements.

"The entire mini-trial, if you want to call it that, will be recorded on video in advance of the jury testing. So our test juries won't be seeing live argument. Instead, they'll be watching the entire thing in a video presentation. I'll be doing the openings and closings for and against National Union. The reason is that we want each side to put its best foot forward. And also because we don't want bias—such as the jury likes one presenter more than another—to influence their decision. The only things we want tested are the themes.

"There will be three sets of test jurors and they'll all see the same exact video presentation. We're going to give the jurors sets of instructions and questionnaires. That part is going to be the most similar to an actual trial. And they'll be based on instructions and questionnaires we've actually used at trial. But they'll be customized to the facts of this case. And we're going to ask them to decide if National Union engaged in wrongdoing. And, if the bank was wrong, then we're going to ask if the bank should be forced to pay a monetary award. And if so, you guessed it, we're going to ask how much.

"The answers to the questionnaires at the end of the trial are an invaluable tool. I commend National Union for undertaking the expense at this early stage. Many clients wait to do jury research until after they've litigated an entire case. Doing it now will be helpful in deciding whether or not to settle or proceed towards trial. And if the answer is not to settle, then the results of the testing will be very valuable in steering National Union's defense moving forward.

"As I mentioned earlier, we have our next trial starting in six weeks. Normally Barbara takes care of every word of the scripts, and she's already getting ready for the next one. Missouri, right?"

Barbara looked up at Patrick. "Cleveland."

"Ohio. Excellent. Our next trial is in the Midwest and we're gearing up for that. Pharma case?" He looked at Barbara and she nodded approvingly. "Good." I didn't know if it was an act or for real, but they did have a reputation for taking their show from town to town. "Because of that trial, Barbara can't do what she normally does with our scripts for this jury testing. So we're going to enlist a couple of recruits to take the laboring oar."

Patrick paused and Harry cleared his throat. "Will has been working diligently on pulling together National Union's litigation data across the country. And no one knows what's happening in Massachusetts better than he does." Harry looked over at David, who nodded. "So I suggest that Will take the first cut of the defense scripts." I could feel the color wash out of my face as I turned completely pale. I had never tried a case and never prepared trial scripts, let alone trial scripts for one of the top trial attorneys in the country.

David closed the loop. "What do you say, Will?"

There was only one answer. "I'm in. I'm going to need someone to point me in the right direction on the format. It would helpful if I could see what they look like."

"Of course. We'll get you set up," Patrick replied.

Barbara perked up. "After the meeting, I'll walk you through the process and will send you some of our recent scripts to get you started."

"Thanks, Barbara," I responded.

"So the defense is shored up." Patrick looked in my direction. "National Union is in good hands. The next question is whether or not we have a worthy adversary in our ranks to put up against Will's legal prowess." He was teasing, as he didn't know me or my alleged legal prowess personally, but it made me smile.

"The adversary isn't in this room and isn't part of my group. Or David's or Harry's. We need someone in litigation, who is sharp and has some experience under his or her belt. And that person hasn't worked for National Union before. My personal belief is that someone who hasn't worked for the bank will be ruthless in his or her approach to preparing Austin King's script. We need someone who will attack. We have some feelers out. But if you know someone at the firm who you think will step in and do a bang-up job, please let us know. And do it ASAP."

One name immediately crossed my mind. I texted as quickly as I could. I was sure others in the room were hoping to score brownie points for doing nothing more than lining someone up. "911!! Dude, Patrick Cooley is looking for someone to do the plaintiff script for a National Union jury research project. Austin King and Sarah Moore involved. You interested?? I'm doing the defense. LMK STAT!!!"

Seconds later, Aaron texted me. "Are you fucking kidding me?? Where do I sign up??"

"Working on it now." I clicked from my text messages to the firm email on my smartphone and typed an email to Harry throwing Aaron's hat in the ring.

"Anyone have any questions?" Patrick looked around the conference room in Los Angeles and then to the camera. No one responded. "Good. Let's get to work. And send us names if you have them."

Minutes later Barbara answered the telephone with a raspy smoker's voice. "Get ready to see some hairy knees."

Erika looked at me and mouthed "hairy knees?"

I quietly giggled and mouthed "what the fuck?"

"You're going to see a lot of them."

I knew the words I was hearing, but felt completely lost. "Um, Barbara. I'm not sure if I got that right. Did you say 'hairy knees?'"

"Yeah, Patrick has very hairy knees." Erika and I looked at each other again and tried not to burst out laughing. "And you're going to see a lot of them." I looked at Erika with eyes bulging.

"When he's not on trial he spends most of his time at his racket club in LA. He stays away from the office. It's right across the street anyway. So when you send a draft, someone will run it over to him. He'll review it and make his edits. And then he'll text you a picture of any edits he makes. Usually they're on his knees and he's wearing tennis shorts. So you're going to get a ton of pictures of your script's pages on his hairy legs. Be prepared." Barbara giggled as the words left her mouth.

"Got it. Thanks for the heads-up."

"Anything you need, I'm here for you. I'm going to email you a couple of recent opening statements. You'll see the introductions are pretty formulaic."

"Cool."

"I'm also going to send you a jury research script from last year. It was a similar format to our current testing, but it was a case involving a medical device, so the facts don't really help. But you can see how we approached it.

When you get the research script, you'll see that it's a PowerPoint presentation with a bunch of slides. Every slide in the presentation has a couple of lines. And those lines talk about the image on the page. So, backing up for a moment, each page has an image. In your case, that's going to be documents, rather than pictures of a broken medical device and injuries. You might use the same document for multiple slides, but each slide will need to highlight a particular part of the document.

"And if there's information you can put in colorful charts, do that. The test jurors' eyes will glaze over if it's just boring banking documents. So you have to jazz it up where you can. Patrick is going to edit the hell out of whatever you give him. I'll take a look before you send it to him, but he's going to edit anyway. He always does it."

"Hairy knees?"

"Exactly. Who knows? Maybe you'll get to come to LA. Another thing. Be over-inclusive. You'd rather have him cut stuff out than ask where the rest of it is. So I'd prepare at least a hundred slides."

"Got it." Barbara disconnected and I turned to Erika. "Sounds like we have our work cut out for us. I'm a little concerned about those hairy knees."

"Me, too."

"When the slide deck comes in can you strip out whatever we don't need and get it ready for our documents?"

"I'll put in the state litigation charts the analysts are working on."

"Great. Let's talk later and see where we are."

"Sounds good."

She swiftly left my office. Erika was a force of nature and seemed energized to be working on a Patrick Cooley project. If I thought she was a Swiss Army Knife on the theme project, I was counting on her being a machete to get through the jury testing.

CHAPTER SEVENTEEN

Made His Bed

A fresh coat of green paint had been splashed across the door. The rusting metal was no longer visible, but the outlines of the chips were still there. As if someone had coated deep acne scars with makeup. The visiting room was pulsing with activity as Sunday visitors came and went. Squeals and hard "you're it's" surrounded me. Two adolescent boys scrambled around my chair. A woman barely acknowledged them as she stared at the door with her arms folded.

The door creaked open and a skeleton walked through wearing a baggy white tee shirt and green hospital pants. It took me a moment to recognize Mickey as he approached me. He had two black eyes and was fitted with handcuffs and shackles.

"What the fuck is this?"

Mickey shrugged. "Hi." I gave him a hug and he took a seat. He rested his hands on the cold metal table. His knuckles were raw and pink.

"Mick, what happened?"

His head tilted to the side and he lifted his palms towards the ceiling as he shrugged. "It's nothing."

"Nothing? Then why the fuck are you shackled?"

"There was a little dustup. It's fine. It's not permanent."

"How many times has this happened?"

"The cuffs? Just this time."

"No, Mick. Getting your ass kicked. How many times?"

"Seriously, Will. It's no big deal." Mickey looked agitated and bored at the same time. He was clearly not interested in talking about it, but I couldn't let it go. "And nobody kicked my ass." He looked over at an inmate visiting with his sons.

"Sorry, Mick." I didn't want to make it worse by saying the wrong thing. "Listen to me. You gotta get out of here. It doesn't matter what you say. They're just words to a bunch of strangers you'll never see again. It doesn't matter. It's your life, Mick. You really want to spend the rest of your life here."

"Will, I'm not doing it and I'm not talking about it again. I'm better off a murderer in here than a murderer out there." His face was red and his eyebrows hung low over his blue eyes.

"I'm not going to torture you. But would you fucking eat something at least? Jesus, you're starting to look like the Crypt Keeper."

"I'm trying, Will. The warden just had a hot tub installed for us. I was floating around in it last night with a plate of filet mignon on my chest. I got hit by a wave, though, and it slid right under the water. Tragic." He cracked a smile for the first time. My smile was tempered by the sight of the chipped tooth Knuckles told me about.

"Seriously, you had to break a front tooth? You're not as fast as you used to be." I bobbed my head side to side and took a couple of air jabs in his direction.

"That may be true, but I could still whup your ass. Even with these things on." He raised his cuffed wrists off of the table.

"You're probably right, you old bastard."

Mickey smiled wide, jagged chipped tooth and all. "So what about you? How's life in New York?"

"Same as Boston. Maybe a bit lonelier. Big city. More anonymity. I still don't really know anybody there."

"Then get the fuck outta there. You don't need that."

"I don't know. Work's going pretty good. I'm on a case with some big dick swingers."

"That's great, Will. You should be. You're the smartest guy I know. You can do anything." His blue eyes caught the light from overhead and beamed at me.

"Thanks, Mick." I felt embarrassed talking about work with Mickey, but he seemed interested. Even being stuck in Cedar Junction, he was my biggest cheerleader.

"Nah, I'm serious. Good on you. Not bad for a kid from Dorchester. Who would've thought it? If Alice heard you were a lawyer in a huge firm in Manhattan, she'd be choking on her menthol. Her ears are probably ringing somewhere right now. And she's rolling in her grave. Fucking A . . ." Mickey trailed off. His eyes looked away from me and towards the ground. We didn't talk about her often and when we did, there weren't a lot of happy times to reminisce over.

"So you coming tomorrow?"

"I wouldn't normally say I wouldn't miss it for the world, but right now I actually wouldn't miss it for the world. It's the only fresh air I'm going to get for a while."

"You—"

"Don't do it. I'm warning you."

"Nah, Mick. I wasn't going to nag. I just wanted to know if you needed anything."

His chin pointed outward as he grinned sheepishly. "I'm good. Thanks for reloading my card."

"No problem."

"Are you coming tomorrow? You're wasting your time. You should be at your office."

"You know I can't miss it. I'm Knuckles' co-counsel. I have to be there."

"Not bad," Mickey nodded his head. "I got a big shot Manhattan attorney on my case."

I laughed. "Yeah, right. I'll see you tomorrow. Please don't kill anyone tonight. Or get killed."

"Who me? I'm practically an altar boy."

"Then you look like a hell of an altar boy with your shiners and cracked tooth. What fucking church do you work at?"

"Latter Day Ass Kickers. I can sign you up." Mickey smiled.

The green door opened and a guard nodded my way. "Time."

"Tomorrow, Mick."

"Hey, Will. I know I'm a pain in the ass. And probably your worst client. But thanks."

"What the fuck else am I gonna do? You're my only blood left." He grinned. I hugged his bony shoulders, which were stuck in place by his hand-cuffs and watched his thin frame shuffle back through the freshly-painted green door.

It might have been Sunday, but Erika didn't seem to sleep or take a day off. She hammered away at the analysis of National Union's countrywide default litigation all week. As a result, we submitted our materials to Harry ahead of schedule. Erika turned to the jury research project as soon as the default analysis was complete. I was thankful for her work ethic, as she was providing me with a needed distraction.

Sunday afternoon and evening flew by as I worked on drafts of the script. Before I had completely woken up the next morning, I was in a cab from my hotel heading to the parole board hearing office in Natick. On the way I received a text from Aaron.

"Where are you?"

"I'm in Massachusetts. What's up?"

"I'm on the project. I owe you some beers. When are you back?"

"That's great news! I'll be in early tomorrow."

"Coolio. Peace out."

The taxi pulled to a squeaky halt in front of a small glass-paneled office building off of a main road in Natick. Knuckles was sitting in the last row of the gallery when I entered the hearing room. Royall Bay Rhum 57 Cologne greeted me before we shook hands. He looked serious and barely cracked a smile, which still revealed his bright white dentures behind his thin lips.

Knuckles spoke in hushed tones. "You see him yesterday? How'd he look?"

"I did. It wasn't good. Two shiners. And that chipped tooth. He looks like a junkie."

"I know, I know. Maybe it will garner him some sympathy. But if Mickey didn't change his mind overnight, this isn't going to go well."

"I know. But we gotta try." Knuckles nodded. "Hey, I got something for you." He looked puzzled until I took a thick white envelope out of my briefcase. Then he cracked a wide smile and the reflection of the bright fluorescent lights off of his fake teeth nearly left me snow blind.

"Thanks, Will. You're a good kid."

"I know you're not here for your health."

"There's no place I'd rather be."

"You're so full of shit." A silent chuckle shook Knuckles' chest.

He took a deep breath and sighed as the door from the hallway opened into the hearing room. A thirty-something woman entered followed by a middle-aged woman and finally a middle-aged man. Knuckles stopped smiling and took on a more serious mantle, as if he were at a funeral. The women and the man looked quickly in our direction and turned away while saying something in Vietnamese. I had hoped they would skip the hearing.

A court reporter set up her equipment and checked the microphones on the bench. The seats in the gallery steadily filled up with witnesses, observers, and participants for other hearings. And there were certainly reporters sitting along with them. A stout court officer in a dark uniform stepped into the room from a door behind the bench. "All rise!" Everyone in the room stood at attention as six hearing officers paraded through the door.

After they sat at the bench and collected themselves, the head hearing officer, Mary Deegan, a woman in her 60's with silvering hair in an antique-looking off-white blouse with a cropped collar, sat behind the gavel and tapped it against a tablet three times. It seemed unnecessary, as all eyes were on her anyway.

Ms. Deegan looked to the court reporter and asked, "are we ready?" The court reporter nodded her approval. "Then let's get started. On the record." She shuffled papers in front of her, held them with both hands and tapped them straight against the bench. "First on the list. Case Number W87561, in the matter of Michael D. Glynn."

Knuckles and I collected ourselves and hustled to the defense table. He placed a yellow legal pad with a series of handwritten notes on the tabletop. I took out a white binder, which included all of the filings and relevant materials from Mickey's case, and placed it on the table. The front of the binder said, "Michael Glynn Hearing Binder—March 18, 2019." Knuckles looked at the binder then looked at me. His forehead creased as his eyebrows lifted away from his eyes.

"I think Smith Stevens is leaving a mark on me."

Knuckles looked at his legal pad. "Could you make me one of those, but maybe in a color that's a little less tacky? I want to feel like a big shot."

If Knuckles was nervous, I couldn't tell. He was used to working alone, but didn't seem to mind the company. Legend had it that he once had a young attorney working with him years ago on a murder case. After three weeks of trial, the case went to a jury and it took them less than two hours to deliberate. When the jury foreman read "guilty" on the charge of first degree murder, the young attorney began to cry. As his chest heaved, Knuckles leaned over and asked in a whisper that could be heard by spectators in the gallery, "What the fuck are you crying about? He's the one going to jail." And that was the last time Knuckles worked with another lawyer.

Mickey was escorted into the courtroom by two court officers strategically positioned on either side of his body. He wore shackles on his ankles and handcuffs and a large white tee shirt and scrub pants similar to those he was wearing when I visited him the day before. He carefully sat between us at the defense table. Two prosecutors sat parallel to us at the Commonwealth's table and waited for the hearing to begin.

Knuckles leaned in. "How ya doin' Mick?" Mickey raised his eyebrows and pursed his lips tilting his head slightly downwards. "Great," Knuckles responded to his own question. "You change your mind?"

"About what?"

"About what you're going to say."

"No. I'm still innocent." Knuckles sighed and his shoulders lowered with resignation. "I know," Mickey responded.

"I know you know. Ok. Well, I didn't make the facts. I can only work with what I got. So we'll see how it goes. Unfortunately for you, the Tran family is here."

Mickey looked over his shoulder and winced. "Fuck," quietly breathed out of his lips. "Do we have to do this?"

"Well, we're all here. But if you don't do it, you're just getting back in the van to Cedar Junction."

Mickey digested the words for a moment. Before he could respond, Ms. Deegan interrupted. "Counselors, are we ready?"

"The Commonwealth is ready."

Knuckles looked intently at Mickey. Mickey nodded at him and Knuckles stood up and replied, "Michael Glynn is ready."

"Very well. Please introduce yourselves, and then we will entertain opening statements."

"Thank you, Ms. Deegan. Esteemed members of the panel. My name is Sandy Wilson and I'm an attorney for the Commonwealth of Massachusetts. I'll do my best to keep this short. Your Honors, in 2001 Michael Glynn pleaded guilty to second degree murder in connection with the October 17, 2000 armed robbery of the Lucky 88 Donut Shop in Dorchester and the murder of Van Nam Tran. Mr. Tran, who was known to his family and friends as 'Jimmy,' was just sixteen years old when he was shot to death. He was working at his family's business, which his parents opened with their savings after they emigrated to the United States from Vietnam.

"Christopher Higgins, now deceased, pulled the trigger of the gun that killed Mr. Tran. He fired four shots into the teenager's chest before fleeing with two hundred and eight dollars. Mr. Tran was alone and unarmed at the time of his death. Mr. Glynn, who is seated before you today, drove the getaway car. When he and Mr. Higgins were arrested following the robbery, the murder weapon was found in Mr. Glynn's car. Forensic examination established that it was the weapon used to kill Mr. Tran. After his arrest, Mr. Glynn admitted to police that he waited at the Lucky 88 Donut Shop for Mr. Higgins. And after Mr. Higgins entered his car, Mr. Glynn, at Mr.

Higgins' prompting, drove away, and I quote from the police record, 'like a bat out of hell.'

"After this confession, Mr. Glynn and Mr. Higgins were remanded to the custody of the Commonwealth pending trial. They were tried together and neither Mr. Glynn nor Mr. Higgins testified in their defense. After the close of the prosecution's case, and hearing the evidence against him and Mr. Higgins, Mr. Glynn, who was represented by counsel, accepted a deal offered by the Commonwealth. He pleaded guilty to second degree murder as an accessory in the murder of Mr. Tran and received a life sentence with the potential for parole after fifteen years. The case against Mr. Higgins continued and he was convicted of felony murder in the first degree with a mandatory life sentence.

"I respectfully submit to this esteemed panel that Mr. Glynn, despite his guilty plea, has never once on the record expressed regret for the killing of Mr. Tran and never once apologized to Mr. Tran's family for his murder." I could hear muffled weeping behind me. Without turning around I could feel the energy in the gallery, which was full of the families of other victims. Their eyes were on me, Knuckles and Mickey.

"The last time Mr. Glynn was before this body, he presented no adequate evidentiary justification for his brazen conduct or his request for parole. And I further respectfully submit to this panel that this hasn't changed. On behalf of the Commonwealth of Massachusetts, I respectfully request that Mr. Glynn's request for parole be denied. Thank you." With that, Sandy Wilson sat down.

Knuckles stood up. "Good morning, Your Honors. My name is Kevin Sullivan and I am here this morning on behalf of the parole applicant, Michael Glynn. It is true that Mr. Glynn has not apologized for the death of Mr. Tran. And it is also true that he has not expressed remorse for Mr. Tran's murder. The reason being is that Mr. Glynn has maintained his innocence since Mr. Tran's death on October 17, 2000. He has never once admitted that he was involved in the robbery of the Lucky 88 Donut Shop or the murder of Jimmy Tran.

"Mr. Glynn was nineteen years old on the day Mr. Tran was murdered. He had no serious criminal record prior to that day. He was simply in the wrong place at the wrong time. As he has maintained all along, including during his interview with the police on that fateful day, he was not involved in the murder of Mr. Tran. Mr. Glynn was not involved in the robbery. Mr. Higgins called Mr. Glynn and asked him for a ride and he obliged his friend. Little did he know Mr. Higgins had just committed a heinous crime before jumping in Mr. Glynn's car.

"Mr. Glynn was not represented by an attorney when he spoke to police that afternoon. He didn't believe he needed one because he knew he was innocent. He believed the truth he was telling would help the police with their investigation and he would be on his way. He didn't know about the robbery or Mr. Tran's tragic death until police told him during his interview. And never once has his story changed. Unfortunately, Mr. Glynn didn't walk out of the police station a free man that afternoon. And he hasn't been a free man since that day.

"And even more unfortunately, the one person that could exonerate Mr. Glynn is gone. Mr. Higgins, as you are aware, died in prison and never spoke to anyone other than his attorneys about the events of that afternoon. While Mr. Glynn hasn't admitted to the killing or apologized to Mr. Tran's family, it isn't because he's heartless or brazen. In fact, his heart goes out to them. It's because he is innocent and, as I said, was in the wrong place at the wrong time. Over the last eighteen years, Mr. Glynn has been an exemplary prisoner. He has been a participant in the many programs offered at Cedar Junction, including the culinary arts program and the computer skills program.

"I acknowledge that there are several disciplinary reports open against Mr. Glynn. However, I respectfully submit to this body that Mr. Glynn was not the aggressor in those matters. Instead, he has recently been targeted and I believe he will be exonerated when those reports are closed. As you can see from Mr. Glynn's appearance, he bears the marks of those incidents. And I submit that at the time of his last application for parole three years ago, his record at Cedar Junction was unblemished. In light of his time served, his good behavior, his participation in prison programming and his demonstrably tenuous connection to the death of Mr. Tran, on behalf of Mr. Glynn, I respectfully request that his application for parole be granted. Thank you."

After a pregnant pause Ms. Deegan looked up as she finished scribbling on a piece of paper. "Um, Mr. Sullivan. I caucused with the other board members about this case. We reviewed your current submission. And we reviewed your prior submission from three years ago. And, frankly, we don't see much difference between the two of them. I'm having trouble finding what has changed since your last submission and Mr. Glynn's last application that would warrant parole. Could you tell us what we're missing and what has changed?" I knew she was looking for an apology that wouldn't come.

"Your Honor. This is a tragic case for everyone involved. Obviously, none more so than Mr. Tran's family. I have nothing new to submit from an evidentiary perspective, as it appears that there were only three witnesses to the events of that day—Mr. Tran, Mr. Higgins, and Mr. Glynn. Unfortunately, Mr. Tran and Mr. Higgins aren't here and can't tell you what they saw. But Mr. Glynn's story has never changed. He was a teenager in the wrong place at the wrong time. And, without getting deep into issues of attorney-client privilege, he was advised by counsel to take a deal and he did. And like I said, he's never wavered from his story. It's the same one he's been telling since October 17, 2000.

"The only change is that Mr. Glynn is three years older. He is thirty-eight years old and has spent nearly half of his life in prison. He was never accused of pulling the trigger or being in the Lucky 88 Donut Shop when Mr. Tran was tragically killed. A friend called him for a ride and he did what friends do. He went and picked up 'Higgs,' as he was called. And minutes later Mr. Glynn's car was pulled over and soon after he found himself in a police station being questioned.

"Looking back, he wished he had asked for an attorney at that time. But that's water under the bridge. He's been a good prisoner. And he's done what has been asked of him. But he won't admit to something he didn't do. I ask for your consideration in this matter. Mr. Glynn turned twenty in prison. And if parole is denied, he will turn forty there. Thank you."

"Thank you, Mr. Sullivan. Your points are well expressed, but I am troubled by your statement that Mr. Glynn has contended he was innocent since the day of Mr. Tran's death. If I were accused of a heinous crime, I would shout my innocence from the mountain tops. But here Mr. Glynn pleaded guilty to second degree murder. This seems incredibly inconsistent to me. And I see from the record he claimed ineffective assistance of counsel, but that wasn't until after you took on his case. Am I wrong about that?"

"That is accurate, but he didn't have counsel prior to my engagement and was unaware of the issue until that time."

"And now it looks like he has developed a disciplinary problem. I see a half dozen incidents over the last several months. It seems to me that Mr. Glynn's rehabilitation is going in the wrong direction."

"May I interject?"

"Yes, Mr. Sullivan."

"It is true that there have been some recent incidents, but Mr. Glynn was not the instigator. As I mentioned, he has recently been targeted. I am certain he'll be cleared as soon as the reports are closed."

"I think we would like to hear from Mr. Glynn." She looked over each shoulder and the other panel members nodded in agreement.

After Mickey was sworn in, Ms. Deegan looked through him and then looked over to the Trans. "Do you have anything to say to the Tran family?"

Knuckles shot up from his seat. "Ms. Deegan, that question . . ."

"I'll ask it another way. Mr. Glynn, would you like to apologize to Mr. and Mrs. Tran for the death of their son?" Mickey stood up, looked at his feet and mumbled something inaudible.

"Is that a yes or a no?," Ms. Deegan asked sternly.

"I, I can't admit to something I didn't do." He didn't look up from his feet. "I feel real bad for the Tran family. But I can't apologize for something I didn't do. It was a tragedy, but it was Higgs, not me. I just gave him a ride."

Ms. Deegan cut him off before he could go further. "So the answer is still no. No apology. No remorse despite your guilty plea." Mickey shook his head. "You have to speak for the record."

"No," Mickey replied softly.

"Mr. Sullivan. Is there anything not included in your paper submission that you want to add?"

I knew where Ms. Deegan was heading and so did Knuckles. Instead of aggravating her further and possibly poisoning the well even more, he responded, "No, we have nothing further to add."

"Now that the parties have had an opportunity to be heard, this panel will respectfully give the floor to the Trans if they wish to make a statement." I looked over my shoulder and all eyes in the gallery were on them. Mr. Tran's eyes were bright red and Mrs. Tran held a white tissue to her nose. Their daughter stood up and began walking towards the bar. Her father touched her shoulder as she stepped away and she acknowledged his hand with hers. Her long black hair swayed over her navy blue suit jacket as she walked towards the podium in front of the panel.

"Good morning. My name is Lucy Tran. Jimmy Tran was my brother. My parents moved to the United States from Vietnam when Jimmy and I were children. They risked their lives and their savings to come here so we could have better lives. My parents opened a business similar to the one they had in Vietnam. A coffee shop. And for us growing up it was the center of our lives.

"My brother Jimmy was smart and funny and athletic. When he wasn't at school, studying in the library or practicing soccer, he was at the coffee shop. He was hardworking and loved to help my parents. He wanted to be a doctor and give back to our parents after all they had sacrificed for us.

"Jimmy was my hero growing up. I was born four years after him and I always looked up to him. Even though I was his annoying kid sister, he protected me and looked after me around Fields Corner. I was just twelve years old when he was killed. I was in our kitchen doing homework and waiting for him and my parents to come home. Instead, they were at the hospital hoping for a miracle. But the miracle never came. My aunt came over and watched me. And when they finally came home they broke the news to me." Lucy sniffled as the words came out of her mouth and she dabbed her eyes with a tissue. As she spoke I remembered that same night. But instead of my parents coming home to tell me my brother was dead, it was the police telling me he was in jail.

"Chris Higgins pulled the trigger that killed Jimmy and Michael Glynn pleaded guilty to driving the getaway car. And never once has he told me or my parents he was sorry." Mickey looked down at the table as Lucy spoke. "While he never asked for my forgiveness, I forgive him. But I don't believe he should be allowed out of jail.

"Jimmy wanted to be a doctor, but didn't get to live to see his dream come true. To honor his memory I followed the path he chose for himself. I became a doctor and his memory inspires me every day. On my behalf, and on behalf of my parents, I respectfully request that Mr. Glynn's application for parole be denied." Lucy stepped away from the podium and walked quickly back to her parents. They huddled, hugged, and sobbed.

Ms. Deegan looked at each table. "Thank you, Ms. Tran. Are there any other statements?"

Sandy Wilson stood up. "No. The Commonwealth rests on the papers it submitted. I reiterate the request that Mr. Glynn's application for parole be denied."

"Mr. Sullivan, anything to add?"

"No. Thank you for your consideration."

Ms. Deegan nodded. "This concludes the hearing on this matter. The panel will issue a decision as quickly as time permits. Thank you. You are dismissed."

I hugged Mickey quickly before he was led away by court officers. "Thanks, Will," he whispered in my ear.

"You got it. I'll visit soon."

Knuckles and I walked out of the hearing room together. "What do you think?"

"You know what I think. The same thing. I wish I had a brother like you. You're a good kid. But I'm sorry, he ain't going anywhere."

"I know. Thanks. I had to try."

"Well, maybe you can get him to change his mind one of these days."

"Hmm."

"Grab a beer?"

I was tempted even though it wasn't even 11:00. "I wish I could. But I gotta get back to New York. Crazy busy in the office right now and being here didn't help."

"You big shot lawyers. Must be nice."

"It pays the bills."

Knuckles smiled wide. He loved to hear about money, especially when lawyers were making it. "I bet it does."

Several emails from Erika were waiting for me when I connected my laptop to the internet on the bus. She had been hard at work on the script and kept me busy during the ride back home. If nothing else, the work kept me from thinking too deeply or feeling too darkly about the events of the morning.

CHAPTER EIGHTEEN

Setting the Stage

My cellphone buzzed on my desk and there was a text message from the 310 area code. It was a photograph of a page from my draft jury script covered in barely legible red scribbles. The page was framed by a set of hairy knees and short white tennis shorts. The text message was followed by another and another until dozens of images crowded my phone.

I saved the images and forwarded them to my firm email account. Afterwards, I printed them out on one of Smith Stevens' high-speed color printers. It was a process that had been going on for days. Erika and I studied the pages and tried to interpret the meaning of the scribbles. A comma that had previously been removed had now returned. Periods were changed to exclamation points. And the sentences continued to shrink to punchier and more powerful blurbs of information.

We arrived at the office early by Manhattan standards each morning and stayed late into each night. Patrick's process was painstaking and thorough. He was clearly examining every word and every detail. While it was a grind for me and Erika, it was the same for him. He was fiercely protective of his reputation and would never agree to associate himself with work product that was anything less than perfect. His dedication paid off, as his rate recently hit $1,500 per hour.

While we worked on the scripts, the document review team in the Backwater churned through hundreds of banker's boxes filled with copies of National Union's policy manuals, training materials, internal memoranda, emails, and communications to the outside world. They green-flagged the good and red-flagged the bad. As green-flagged documents rolled in, Erika and I used the best of them in the script.

Our presentation was data-focused. It hit satisfaction surveys, lending standards and strategies and National Union's generally low rate of defaults across all of the states where it had branches. We included information about National Union's community outreach and the availability of sub-prime lending products aimed at individuals with low credit scores and other obstacles to obtaining capital.

We had pictures of community events, including National Union employees volunteering at park clean-ups, fun runs and soup kitchens. There were excerpts from the bank's hiring manuals and internal diversity education materials. We could demonstrate based on data and statistics that National Union loaned money to people in the inner city, including in marginalized communities, at a rate that was higher than most national and regional banks. And most people were satisfied with the bank according to independent customer satisfaction surveys.

While there were loan default lawsuits across the country, similar to what Erika discovered in Massachusetts, many of those suits arose from loans National Union inherited when it acquired other banks and their branches and clients. We could show that more than sixty percent of the suits arose from loans that wouldn't meet National Union's traditional lending standards.

And very few of the suits involved the sub-prime loan products that National Union offered.

Ten days before the mock trial, Erika sat next to me at my desk and we both watched the speaker on my phone expectantly. While Erika and I sat in space-station quiet, on the other end of the line activity buzzed around Aaron. I heard Chuck's voice in the background. "Christ, couldn't you get a conference room? Or come to my office?"

"I thought about coming to your office to see the look on your face, but then I thought better of it. There's nothing worse than seeing a grown man cry. And trust me, you're gonna cry when you hear what I wrote." Aaron chuckled.

Patrick strictly forbade us from sharing our scripts with each other. He didn't want the presentations to sound like a play. Instead, similar to a real trial, he wanted us to go for the jugular and explained that the element of surprise would drive competition. As we sat on opposite ends of the line, neither side knew what the other had written or included as exhibits, but it was clear Aaron took Patrick's direction to heart.

"Yeah, right. Big bank. Big bore," I replied.

"Just wait, dude. You're gonna shit your pants." Erika looked as if she had just been greeted with an offensive smell. I looked at her and repeated the words.

"He's fucking with us," I commented. Erika shrugged.

"Trust me. You're dead. I know why they didn't want you or another National Union lawyer working on this."

"Why's that?"

"Because some things can't be unseen. And no one at National Union would want to work with you again if you wrote the things I put in the script."

"Jesus . . ." I sighed.

"Just wait."

Moments later Patrick's assistant connected him to the call. "Good morning. Ah, good afternoon. Guys, I wanted to say thank you for all your hard work on this. We have a way to go, but I think things are progressing nicely. I usually like to step away from my scripts and let another voice take over. I can better gauge my response and how a juror might respond. So what I'd like to do is have you each read your script to me over the phone. Then we can talk about them. And then tweak and fine-tune. Let's be natural and do it in order. Aaron, will you start things off?"

"Sure."

"Before we begin, can you share your screen so we can follow along with what you're looking at?" My computer chimed and a view of Aaron's desktop with his script appeared on my screen.

"Ready."

"Same here," Aaron followed.

"Good. Let's do it," Patrick responded.

"I'm just going to read it straight through. Right?"

"Exactly. Pretend you're me pretending to be Austin King."

"Ok." Aaron cleared his throat. "Good morning. My name is Austin King. I'm a lawyer from Galveston, Texas, and I represent people who have been wronged. You may be wondering to yourself right now, 'why's a lawyer from Galveston, Texas, here in a courtroom in Boston, Massachusetts?' And I'll tell you why. It's because I represent people in cases that are so small it doesn't make sense to file a lawsuit. But when a lot of people have been wronged the same way, I can represent all of their interests in one case. And that case is called a 'class action.' And that's why I'm honored to be in your presence today. In this class action a lot of people have been wronged by a bank." Erika and I watched Aaron's slides flip past on my computer screen.

"Aaron, slow it down a little for me."

"Ok, Patrick." Aaron audibly shuffled paper on his desk. "That bank is National Union. If you watch television you've seen the commercials and you've probably seen the branches." A picture of National Union's logo appeared on the screen.

"It's one of the largest banks in the country with branches in a dozen states. And it has offices in the suburbs and cities." Pictures of an urban and a suburban branch appeared. "And over the last several years it has aggressively expanded its footprint." A map of the United States with red dots flashed up. "This map represents the places where National Union had branches five years ago. And this map shows where National Union has branches this year." Another map with more red dots appeared.

"To expand its footprint, National Union has taken over banks in states around the country." A slide showing the logos of more than a dozen defunct banks, including Wampanoag, appeared on the screen. "And that's what some banks do to expand. They acquire other banks. And take over their branches and inherit their customers." Aaron's presentation was organized, but it didn't exactly have me shaking in my boots.

"The problem for National Union has been that it didn't want all of the customers or the branches. And it has closed down branches. And has left its customers with no local bank branch in their neighborhood." The text Aaron read was accompanied by a picture of a former National Union branch in a city neighborhood. There was litter on the sidewalk and the windows of the branch, which was located on a corner of an old brick building, were boarded up. The dirty outline of the words "National Union Bank & Trust" remained.

It was getting a little juicier, but I still didn't feel alarmed. On the next page was a picture of a middle-aged woman. She wore a pink wool sport coat over a white button-down shirt. Her cheekbones were sharp and angular and her eyes, which were framed by horned-rim glasses, looked kind, yet weary.

"This is Dorothea White. She's my client and she is the plaintiff in this case. And she was wronged by National Union. And she represents the interests of every other person who was wronged by National Union. But I'll get to that in a few moments. Ms. White is fifty-four. She's the mother of an adult son and an adult daughter. And she was the loving wife to her husband, Fred, who sadly died a couple of years ago after twenty-six years of marriage."

A picture of the White family at their twenty-fifth wedding anniversary accompanied the text. Mr. White looked frail, but happy. Tubes ran from his nose to a green tank on the floor next to him. Aaron had mined the social media accounts of Ms. White and her family and struck gold. I was beginning to feel uneasy. I looked at Erika and a scowl was beginning to creep across her face.

"Dorothea is loyal. So loyal that she still wears her wedding ring. And she told me she'll never take it off and will wear it to her grave. And she's loyal to her church, and loyal to her neighborhood. She has lived in Roxbury, Massachusetts, her entire life. And she tells me she'll never leave. She has seen good times and bad times there." Images of Roxbury flashed across the screen.

"Through thick and thin, she has built relationships and is considered by many to be a pillar of her community. If you were to walk through Roxbury with her, you'd remark at how slowly it goes. And that's because it seems everyone knows her and wants to say 'hi.' If you're her friend in Roxbury, you'll soon have many other friends. And Dorothea's loyalty extends to the businesses in the area. She's been going to the same hair salon, the same supermarket and the same restaurants for decades." Pictures of the salon and the supermarket supported the text. I was beginning to feel anxiety about the impersonal graphs and documents we relied on in National Union's defense.

"Dorothea was even loyal to her bank." A picture of a Wampanoag branch appeared on the screen. It was on a corner of an old brick building. There were trees lining the street and the sidewalk looked like it had just been broom cleaned. As I studied it I realized it was the same building that housed the now-abandoned National Union branch. Erika and I quickly made eye contact and looked back at the presentation. "Her bank was Wampanoag Bank. And like every other business she relied on in the area, she went there for decades."

The picture of the abandoned branch appeared on the screen. "That is until National Union took over Wampanoag. Wampanoag was the only bank in Dorothea's neighborhood for more than fifty years. It was a pillar and helped maintain stability in the area. Then National Union came in. Almost immediately, National Union replaced all of the Wampanoag employees. Dorothea went from knowing everyone in the branch to being a stranger overnight. And almost as quickly the bank's services changed. First the hours shrank. Then the Saturday hours disappeared. Then tellers began to disappear. From four to two. And on some days there was only one." Erika and I quickly made eye contact.

"The cash machine in the entrance was moved inside. And then customers could only use it when the bank was open. Despite the difficulties of doing business with National Union, Dorothea kept going there. In reality, she had no other place to go, as it was the only bank in her neighborhood." A picture of a long avenue highlighted the text, and there was no bank in sight, only the abandoned National Union branch. "Dorothea has always had a car. She relies on it to get back and forth to her job in South Boston, where she works as the director of the Shawmut House." A picture of the Shawmut House appeared on the screen.

"If you don't know what the Shawmut House is, it's a transitional homeless shelter. It helps adults receive treatment and transition from homelessness to employment and stable housing." Austin King must've fed information to Harry. "Dorothea could've done anything she wanted with her life." A picture of her in a suit with a group of well-dressed women appeared on the screen. "This is her at her twenty-fifth anniversary from Vassar College. Yet she chose to give back to her community. And she has worked at Shawmut House since her graduation. First as a social worker, and now, as I mentioned, she's the Director. And that took a lot of work and dedication."

The National Union logo appeared back on screen. "When Dorothea needed a new car, she went to National Union for a loan. But she was told she didn't qualify. She asked herself, 'how could this be?' When she told me I asked the same question." A copy of Ms. White's credit score appeared. 805. "This is Dorothea's credit score. It's one of the best in the country. She owns her home. She's an executive and has worked at the same place for decades. It didn't make sense."

An internal memorandum on National Union's letterhead appeared. It was addressed to the manager of the National Union branch in Roxbury. Highlighted on the screen were the words, "redirect clients towards special loan products designed to ameliorate credit risk." Aaron read the words. "And that's just what the loan officer at the branch did. He offered Dorothea a subprime loan to finance her car purchase. Instead of four percent, which was the rate of her prior loan, she was offered a loan at sixteen percent.

"That rate was off the charts. But she's an organized person and preferred to keep all of her financial business with one institution. And she had a history of paying off debt early. So she took it. But what happened next surprised her. Just months after securing the loan from National Union, National Union sold it to a loan servicing company called eFinance Auto Loans. And eFinance Auto Loans took over the loan and her payments. Dorothea wasn't alone. National Union has sold thousands of car loans to eFinance Auto Loans. The bank will tell you it has a low rate of default on its subprime loans, like the one it gave to Dorothea. And it's true. But it's only true because it typically sells those loans to other financial institutions for a profit right after the paperwork is signed. And those financial institutions do the dirty work.

"And months after the loan was sold, Dorothea received a letter from National Union saying the branch in her neighborhood was being closed with the address of the next closest National Union branch. It was more than three miles away in downtown Boston. And there was no easy way of getting there from her neighborhood in Roxbury. Soon after, a notice of the closing appeared on the window of the branch." The shuttered branch appeared again on the screen. "And why would National Union shutter a branch that had been in service for decades—first as Wampanoag Bank and then as National Union?

"Because it deemed the inhabitants of the neighborhood as undesirable and as vulnerable." Another internal memorandum appeared on the screen next to a picture of a white middle-aged man with silver hair and a pale complexion in a dark suit. "This is a picture of Davis Richards III. He's an Executive Vice President of Planning and Strategy for National Union." Language from the memorandum was highlighted on the screen. It was entitled "Branch Closing Policy and Strategy" and was marked "Confidential—Do Not Disseminate."

Aaron read from the document. "'Interstate banks may close branches upon appropriate notice to customers and the Federal Reserve Board. In instances where a bank is located in a low-income or moderate-income area, the notice to customers must provide the address of the Federal Reserve Board, which may receive comments from affected bank customers.

"'Experience in these areas indicates that it is rare for affected bank customers to correspond with the Federal Reserve Board regarding branch closures. Significantly, neither federal law nor the Federal Reserve Board's policies provide financial institutions with required forms or content for the notification of bank closures. Rather, the financial institutions may determine the content of such letters at their own discretion. As a consequence, the content of such letters is critical in limiting correspondence to the Federal Reserve Board from aggrieved branch customers.

"'In addition, in instances where the maintenance of banking products, including loan products, has been transferred to outside financial institutions, the likelihood of such correspondence is further reduced.'" It was a mouthful, but just an excerpt from what was a mind-numbingly long memorandum. "So what does all that mumbo jumbo mean? It means that a bank can close a branch by simply telling federal regulators and its customers that it's closing the branch. But it has to tell its customers they can complain. And how does it limit that? By making the letter as confusing as possible. And by getting rid of as many customers as it can before sending the letter.

"And that's just what National Union did in Roxbury. It sent loans to other financial institutions. And it sent this letter to Dorothea." The letter appeared on the screen. At the bottom was a block paragraph in small print. At the beginning of the paragraph was boilerplate explaining National Union was insured by the Federal Deposit Insurance Corporation along with several legal disclaimers. Imbedded within that paragraph was a sentence stating, "Comments regarding the closure may be transmitted by regular mail to the Federal Reserve Board at 20th Street and Constitution Avenue N.W., Washington, D.C. 20551."

"Look at that. In small print. Even the address is confusing. And how many people complained to the Federal Reserve Board about the branch closing? Not a single person. And I think you can see why." Aaron moved on to the next page of his script, which showed pictures of two white middle-aged men with silvering hair. "This is a picture of Steven Powell. He's another Executive Vice President of National Union. He specializes in closing branches. And that is Francis Yost. He's also an Executive Vice President. His specialty is in acquisitions and planning. Mr. Powell works in New York and Mr. Yost works in Cleveland." My unease began to climb.

"This is an email from Mr. Powell to Mr. Yost, entitled, 'Roxbury Branch Closure—Confidential.'" The email appeared on the next page of the script with sentences highlighted in yellow and enlarged above the rest of the text. The pictures of the two executives sat at the top corners of the screen. "Roxbury location closure progressing smoothly. Letters are out. Do not anticipate pushback. Neighborhood ripe for alternative financial services vendor. High population density. Dark and underrepresented. Several vacant storefronts in proximity to branch and no other branches within half mile. Please advise."

I looked at Erika and hit the mute button on my phone. "'Dark and underrepresented?' What the fuck?" Her face transitioned into a full scowl.

Aaron continued. "According to National Union, Dorothea's neighborhood is 'dark and underrepresented.' National Union is going to tell you Mr. Powell was referring to empty storefronts when he wrote that phrase. But anyone who knows anything about that neighborhood knows what Mr. Powell meant."

A pie chart appeared on the next slide. "This chart breaks down the population of Roxbury by ethnicity. As you can see from the data, over sixty-one percent of the population is Black. Nearly seventeen percent of the population is Latino and under fifteen percent of the population is white. And I submit to you that those numbers don't reflect the ethnicity in Dorothea's neighborhood, where an even higher percentage of her neighbors are Black."

The script flipped to the next page and a picture of Dorothea in her pink sweater and glasses appeared on the screen. "Dorothea reflects her community. She is hardworking and she is stable. She is Black. And National Union targeted her and her neighbors because of the color of their skin. You may be wondering about the benefit of driving customers away with bank closures and high-interest loans."

"I'll tell you the answer. Greed." Above the words on the script was a large image of the bright yellow logo of Live Payday Check Loan. Aaron was going for the jugular. "This next document is entitled, 'National Union Bank & Trust Reports Fourth Quarter Results—Report to Shareholders.' This is

National Union's quarterly report, which is available on the internet." The front page of the report flashed onscreen.

"On page sixty-two of the report you'll find a section entitled, 'Note 11: Significant or Pending Acquisitions.'" The section and its text were highlighted in yellow. "It reads, 'On November 30, 2018, the Bank announced its support for the acquisition of LPCL LLC by NUBT Holdings Ltd., a wholly-owned subsidiary of the Bank. The transaction is expected to close in the second half of calendar 2019, subject to all applicable closing conditions having been satisfied. Refer to Note 37 of the Bank's 2018 Annual Consolidated Financial Statements for a discussion of the announced transaction.'" It was a minor note most people wouldn't notice in a seventy-five page quarterly report, but Aaron knew exactly what he was looking for. And Austin King and Sarah Moore with all of their resources would certainly discover it before long.

"And what's interesting about this fact? LPCL LLC?" On the next page was a printout from the Office of the Secretary of the State of Ohio. It showed the registered trade name of LPCL LLC. "What's interesting is that it operates under a name you might have heard before. 'Live Payday Check Loan.' You may have seen the ads on television. Or if you've spent time in certain neighborhoods in Cleveland, St. Louis or Detroit and some other places, you may have seen its locations there.

"It's a check cashing business. And National Union is taking it over through its subsidiary. And it is why National Union shut down Dorothea's branch and is shutting down other urban branches around the country. Because they are located in neighborhoods that National Union considers 'dark and underrepresented.'" The email between Steven Powell and Francis Yost appeared back on the screen. "And once the deal is closed and National Union controls Live Payday Check Loan, those closed branches won't be replaced by branches of other banks. They'll be replaced with predatory check cashers.

"And National Union is betting no one will complain. And no one will stand up for Roxbury and other neighborhoods. Because it believes they're underrepresented. But National Union's wrong." The next page of the script had a different picture of Ms. White. She was wearing a dark suit and looked serious. "Dorothea White is here to stand up against National Union. She's here to protect her friends and neighbors from predatory lending practices. And she's willing to put her name on the line for anyone across the country that has been wronged by National Union."

"Aaron, hold up for a moment," Patrick interrupted. "That is excellent, excellent, excellent work." I could feel the energy beaming off of him from across the country. "This is exactly why we do these exercises. Why jury testing is important. And why it's good to bring an outside set of eyes to a project.

"Will and Erika, you did an excellent job, as well. But, unfortunately, as lawyers, we don't make the facts. We can only try the cases. And in all candor among us girls, I'm not trying this case. I'll quit the firm before I try this case. If National Union doesn't settle, that's on National Union. I guarantee you if Austin King and Sarah Moore subpoena documents and witnesses they'll put the same story together.

"Please spend some time responding to Aaron's material in your script and get something to me by noon tomorrow. I know the document review is still going on. If they mine anything good, fit it in. We have more than a week, so there's time to get this in top shape. Good work, everyone." I clicked off the speakerphone and Erika and I sat in silence and digested what just happened.

I thought back to sitting in Judge Butler's courtroom with Catherine Corcoran and my first discussion with Tripper about National Union's takeover of Live Payday Check Loan. I realized Ms. Corcoran was just collateral damage to National Union's campaign targeting branches in minority neighborhoods. Senator Galvin had hit the nail on the head months before. The neighborhoods losing branches and being targeted with lawsuits were full of "immigrants and minorities." His words rang in my head.

"We're dead."

"Yup," Erika replied. Disappointment creased both of our faces.

"Dark and underrepresented? Fucking seriously?"

"And this is who we've been working for night and day," Erika added fuming. I sighed as the realization continued to sink in and shook my head.

"There aren't enough charts and surveys in the world . . ." My mouth twisted. Erika and I tried to put our shock and disappointment aside, but it refused to dissipate.

CHAPTER NINETEEN

We Bad

My eyes felt like they had been fried overnight on the low heat of a gas burner. I looked pale and vampiric as I stood in front of Mount Vernon City Court on four hours of sleep. Erika and I continued to hammer away on the defense script and Patrick's voluminous edits overnight. It was just before 9:00 and I told Desi I would wait for him until 9:30. If I didn't see him, I was going back to Manhattan.

I shuffled around anxiously as the line to the courthouse began to snake around the corner. I had until noon before Patrick got to his club and began to barrage us with more edits. Erika would hold down the fort in my absence. At 9:15 on the nose, I saw Desi crossing the street. I walked towards the crosswalk and he spotted me.

"I'm ready, Mr. Duggan. Let's do this. And wherever the cards fall, that's where they fall." He had courage or was at least putting on a strong front. I didn't want him to see how nervous I was out of fear that it would put a crack in his armor.

"You got this." He gave me a hug.

"Nah, I got you. I know you got this." My heart tightened in my chest.

I looked down at my shoes. I didn't want him to see my eyes or my fear that I was about to send him to jail and destroy his recovery and progress. I took a deep breath and let it out slowly.

"Let's get in line and do this." I said it loudly and as confidently as I could muster. I hoped the sound of it would awaken some untapped inner-strength.

The line quickly carried us through the courthouse doors. We walked into the criminal courtroom, which was filling with attorneys, the accused and their friends and families. I told Desi to sit down on one of the benches in the gallery of the large courtroom and to save some space for me. I caught the attention of a court officer on the other side of the bar. He waved me through and I approached the empty bench where the judge would soon sit.

"I'm here with a client who wants to surrender on a warrant."

"The ADA is right there." He pointed towards a man in a light grey suit with jet black hair.

I walked towards him and waited close by as he finished a conversation with another lawyer. "Hi. I have a client that wants to surrender on an old warrant."

"Is he here?"

"Yeah, he's back there." I pointed in Desi's direction. The young assistant district attorney didn't seem enthusiastic about having another case thrown on his plate.

"Do you have his ID?"

"Hold on. I'll get it." As I walked back towards Desi, I noticed the ancient Barney Gaynor sitting in the gallery waiting to be heard.

Desi retrieved his ID from his pocket and I dutifully delivered it to the ADA. "Are you representing him?"

"I am."

"I need a copy of your notice of appearance." Shit. I had been so burrowed into the script project I forgot to put one together.

"Are there forms here?"

"Hmmf," slipped from between his lips. He arched his eyebrows and scanned the room, as if he wanted me to follow his gaze. The courtroom was teaming with people and smelled like body odor and stale peanut butter and jelly sandwiches. It was full of criminals and their lawyers. Anything not bolted down on this side of the bar would disappear before the day was over. "Just scribble one out and give it to me. And do one for the judge unless you want to be here all day."

I sat down next to Desi and began quickly drafting two notices of appearance on my yellow legal pad. Desi didn't seem to notice or maybe he didn't care that I was such a hack. While we sat in the gallery, vans pulled up to the courthouse from the street and began to unload prisoners from different jailhouses. The Honorable Mark Bailey would decide their fate. Some inmates were here for arraignments, others for hearings and some to schedule a trial date. Some would walk out on their own recognizance, while others would be remanded to the custody of the State.

Just before 10:00, Judge Bailey sat down at his bench after the court officer bellowed "all rise" towards the back of the long room. Maybe it was age, experience, or both, but Barney Gaynor was the first attorney to have a case called. He gradually entered the bar from the first row of the gallery. His white and black walker nearly rammed the entrance at slow speed. Another lawyer leapt from the gallery in a nick of time to swing open the gate for the aged counselor to pass through. My anxiety rose from my heart to my throat and I wondered if I would even be able to get a word out by the time Desi's case was called. At the speed Mr. Gaynor was moving, I feared we'd be in the courthouse until the next morning.

At least there was no need for introductions as the judge cheerfully quipped, "Good morning, Mr. Gaynor." Two court officers led a young man to the defense table where Mr. Gaynor was standing. The old attorney's bent and crooked frame could barely support his torso. He leaned over to look at his papers and it appeared his forehead would touch the defense table.

"Good morning, Your Honor. I'm appearing today on behalf of Stanlee Coven."

"One moment, Mr. Gaynor. I'm going to let the State begin first."

"Ok, Judge."

"Good morning, Your Honor. Seth Heller on behalf of the State of New York in the matter of Stanlee Coven. You're honor, Mr. Coven was denied bail at his arraignment, has retained counsel, and now has requested that he be released on $2,500 bail. The State vehemently opposes the request. He has been charged with receiving stolen property and as Your Honor can see Mr. Coven has a lengthy arrest record. He's originally from Rhode Island and represents a significant flight risk."

"Thank you, Mr. Heller. Mr. Gaynor, what sayeth you?"

Mr. Gaynor stood up slowly from his chair and remained hunched over the table. "Your Honor, Mr. Coven has, indeed, been arrested before. But as you can see from his record, he has never jumped bail and has no history of defaulting on court appearances. Mr. Heller's comment that Mr. Coven is from Rhode Island and represents a flight risk shouldn't carry any water, Your Honor. He moved here when he was five and has lived in the State of New York for more than two decades. This is his home. As he doesn't represent a true flight risk, I ask for bail in the amount of $2,500, which I believe is reasonable under the circumstances. And is consistent with Your Honor's prior decisions."

The last line hit me like a punch in the stomach. I had never appeared in this court before and had no idea what Judge Bailey's prior decisions were or what he would think of Desi or my arguments. The judge scanned the file in front of him, took out his pen and signed a paper. He looked up quickly. "Bail granted at $2,500."

The court officer took the paper and handed it to Mr. Gaynor. I felt relieved that the first case was a minor victory for the defense. At least the deck wasn't completely stacked against Desi. As the morning wore on, dozens of defendants passed through the courtroom. I watched intently for any guidance on how I should handle myself. Around 12:45 Judge Bailey announced he would break for lunch at 1:00 and resume proceedings at 2:00.

"Do I have time for one more?," he asked to no one in particular.

His law clerk's face was buried in a pile of disheveled paper. She sprang up quickly and looked at a large clock hanging on the wall opposite the bench. "It's going to be tight, Judge."

As the words left her mouth, a young man in a brown tweed jacket and tan khaki pants crossed through the bar. He handed her a few sheets of paper loosely held together with a staple. Before crossing the bar back into the gallery, he handed a copy of the papers to Seth Heller, who studied them.

"What's that?," Judge Bailey asked. "It looks thin. Think we can do it?"

"It's a surrender, Judge," the law clerk replied. My spine stiffened and my stomach churned and let out an audible gurgle that caused Desi to look down at my belt.

"Let's see," Judge Bailey coaxed. She handed him the papers. Judge Bailey looked up at the clock. "If we run over, we'll just come back late. But this shouldn't take too long."

"Ok, Judge."

"Call it for me."

"People of the State of New York against Desmond Baines. Case number 06-42138. All parties and counsel."

I looked at Desi and tried to sound confident. "It's go time. Come with me." He nodded and I couldn't tell who was more terrified. The moment of truth was finally here for both of us.

We hastily made our way to the defense table. Before I could put down my briefcase, Judge Bailey quipped, "2006. An oldie, but a goodie. Mr. Heller, could you enlighten me?"

"Yes, Your Honor. The defendant has appeared today to surrender on a warrant for his arrest that has been outstanding since 2006. The defendant was charged with grand larceny of a vehicle and criminal possession of a controlled substance, which charges are still pending. Following his arraignment, the defendant posted bail and failed to appear for a status conference in his case on September 18, 2006. To my knowledge, Your Honor, this is the defendant's first attempt to surrender on the outstanding warrant that was issued following his default. In light of his default and failure to appear for more than a decade, as well as the seriousness of the charges pending against him, the State submits that defendant remains a flight risk and requests that he be remanded to the custody of the State pending trial."

"Thank you, Mr. Heller. And what sayeth you . . ." Judge Bailey looked at the papers on his bench, then at me and Desi. "And you are? Who is the defendant?"

"Your Honor, my name is Will Duggan and I am the attorney for Desi, er, Desmond Baines."

"Counselor, did you file a notice of appearance?" I realized I had returned the scribbled pages attached to my legal pad to my briefcase.

"Sorry, Your Honor. I prepared notices this morning."

I took my yellow legal pad out of my briefcase and removed two sheets from the binding. I handed one to Seth Heller and began to walk towards the judge with the other in my hand until the court officer said, "not so fast." In my panic I had lost track of protocol. I stopped on my heel and handed the document to the court officer, who looked at it quickly before walking it to the judge. It was amateur night and I was exposing myself as the rankest of amateurs. If Desi tried to flee for the exit or requested the assistance of effective counsel I wouldn't have blamed him.

"It's ok," Judge Bailey smiled at me. He had never seen me appear in his courtroom before, and I appreciated the act of mercy. I tried to calm myself and took another deep breath. "So, Mr. Duggan, thank you for the notice of appearance. Let's start again. What sayeth you?" Desi looked down at his shoes. We stood close together and I could feel his left leg trembling against my pant leg. Or maybe it was mine.

"Good morning, Your Honor. My name is Will Duggan and I'm counsel for Desmond Baines, who is standing to my right." It dawned on me that it was the first time I had represented an individual in court. I had never once introduced myself as anything other than as counsel for a bank, first Wampanoag and then National Union. It felt good saying it and my posture straightened.

"Your Honor, Mr. Baines has voluntarily appeared here today to surrender on the warrant that is outstanding for his arrest." Judge Bailey nodded with approval as I spoke, as if he were a schoolteacher and I was a kindergartener he was trying to conjure the alphabet out of. He showed me none of the contempt that I frequently experienced from the judiciary when appearing on behalf of National Union. "Mr. Baines is in the transitional program at the Vanderbilt Houses in the Bronx."

"The homeless shelter?"

"Yes, Your Honor. Mr. Baines has been homeless and currently is homeless. But he is working to turn his life around." Desi looked up as I spoke and I noticed the judge acknowledge him with a nod. "As part of that process at the Vanderbilt Houses, Mr. Baines has received counseling for drug and alcohol addiction and has succeeded in being clean for over a year now. He has received job training and applied for a job in a kitchen.

"And that's when Mr. Baines discovered there was a warrant outstanding for his arrest. He obtained his criminal record and saw it for himself. He came here today. And it wasn't easy. It was very scary. But he came here because he wants to move on with his recovery and move on with his life. And he is dedicated to that no matter the consequences in this Court." Judge Bailey nodded as I spoke.

"He will continue to receive treatment and will continue to work on his recovery. I ask Your Honor to deny the State's request to remand him to its custody. I ask that you remand him to my custody and if he doesn't appear for trial, I'll answer to the Court." I wasn't even sure what the words meant, and was surprised when they left my mouth. Judge Bailey seemed surprised, too. They were either the product of my panic over keeping Desi out of jail or my growing confidence, as Judge Bailey seemed to be chewing on every word I was saying.

"That's an extraordinary offer, counselor." Judge Bailey looked at Desi. "Mr. Baines, your attorney clearly believes in your recovery and trusts you're not going to disappear again."

"Well, I'm not," Desi replied suddenly. I cleared my throat and quickly tapped Desi on the shoulder. He looked at me over his thin frame.

I leaned over close to his ear and whispered, "you don't have to talk to the judge. You have a right not to talk to the judge."

"I don't care. I want to. I want to tell him myself. Can I?"

"Ok. I'll ask. But you're sure?" Desi nodded. It was uncharted territory and the fact that I didn't shut him down immediately was probably further evidence of my incompetence. "Your Honor. Mr. Baines would like to address the Court. I advised him of his rights and he has waived those rights."

"Mr. Baines, you may speak."

Desi looked to me and I nodded. "My name is Desmond Baines, but everyone calls me 'Desi.'"

"Good morning, Mr. Baines."

"Judge, you can call me Desi."

"Thank you, but I prefer to keep things formal for the record."

"Ok. I wouldn't be here today if it wasn't for Mr. Duggan. He came to the Vanderbilt Houses and my counselor said I could trust him. And I trust him. It was hard for me to come here and he helped me. And I won't burn him."

Judge Bailey nodded attentively as Desi spoke. "I've had problems. Problems with drugs and alcohol. I was addicted. But I got counseling and treatment. And I learned I have bipolar disorder. And I learned since then that I was self-treating my bipolar with drugs and alcohol. And I stopped drinking and drugging and won't do it again. I want to continue my treatment. I want to keep getting better. I want a job and an apartment. I'm working on my relationship with my daughter. I haven't seen her in years. She lives in North Carolina. But we spoke." Desi began to get teary-eyed and I felt my eyes getting glassy.

"I made mistakes. Lots of them. I know that. When I was arrested, I was on drugs and alcohol. I wasn't myself. I wasn't the way I should have been. I wasn't the way I am now. But I'm trying to move forward. And to move forward, I have to take responsibility for my past. I have to reconcile my life now with my life then. And that's why I'm here. I have the best lawyer. He helped me get to this courtroom."

My feet shuffled involuntarily when he said I was the "best lawyer" in front of a room full of better lawyers. I felt my eyes getting glassier as he spoke to the judge. I looked down at my feet and tried to keep my composure. The moment of judgment was coming fast and I wasn't prepared for bad news.

"How long have you been in recovery?"

"More than a year with no alcohol and no drugs."

"And you get treatment every week?"

"Yes, Judge. Every week. One on one and in group." My heart felt like it would burst as Desi described his progress. Then it felt as though a knife pierced it.

"Mr. Heller, in light of Mr. Baines' statement and Mr. Duggan's offer, what sayeth you?"

"Your Honor, I appreciate the defendant's efforts and his lawyer's offer, but the fact remains that serious charges are pending against him. He defaulted and disappeared for more than a decade. The State stands by its position that defendant remains a flight risk and requests that he be remanded to the custody of the State pending trial."

"Counselors, this is an extraordinary set of facts. On the one hand, the charges pending against Mr. Baines are serious and he has a history of default. On the other hand, Mr. Baines appeared here today on his own to answer those charges and to reconcile them with his sobriety. As a judge of the State of New York, it is my duty to dispense justice." My throat tightened and my heart thumped heavily in my chest. Desi's knees began to shake rapidly and sent tremors through his entire body.

"In light of the information presented here today, including Mr. Baines' statement regarding his recovery and Mr. Duggan's offer to accept custody of Mr. Baines pending trial, the Court is moving *sua sponte*..." His words trailed off as he fumbled with some papers in front of him on his bench. He looked to his law secretary. "Can you give me a blank order?"

"Sue what?," Desi whispered to me. "Is that bad?"

"*Sua sponte*. It means the court is moving to do something on its own without being asked by a lawyer to do it." I was too nervous to say another word.

"Ok. I'm going to read this into the record as I write it down. On the Court's own motion, it is ordered that the charges pending against Defendant

Desmond Baines in the above-captioned matter are hereby dismissed with prejudice." Judge Bailey signed the piece of paper and my heart nearly jumped out of my chest.

"It's over? Is it over?," Desi asked.

"It's over," I replied excitedly. "Thank you, thank you, thank you, Your Honor," sputtered out of my mouth in the direction of his bench.

"Thank you, Judge," Desi followed.

Judge Bailey looked at him and smiled. "You're welcome, Desi. Good luck to you. And let's stay out of here, alright?"

"You got it. I won't be here again."

The judge rose and the court officer shouted, "all rise!" He then disappeared through a door behind his bench and I retrieved two copies of his order from the law clerk.

"Let's get out of here." After we worked our way out of the courtroom and through the courthouse's busy hallways, we found ourselves standing outside of the building's front door. All of my anxiety and fear about this day spun through my mind and began to well in my eyes.

We stood quietly for a moment and Desi broke the silence. "We bad! I told you you're the best." He strutted in place as the words left his mouth.

"No. You're the best. You got yourself out of there. I was just window dressing."

"Nah, Mr. Duggan. I wouldn't have done it without you."

My mind drifted as his words washed over me for a few moments. I couldn't believe what had just happened. Maybe I had given up on criminal law too easily. A cab honked loudly in front of us and I quickly returned to reality. And my relief receded back to fear. "Desi, let's get the fuck out of here before they change their mind. Run!"

We began to run away from the courthouse through Roosevelt Square across the street like a couple of bandits. Eyes followed us with curiosity as tears began to roll down my cheeks. I didn't care if Desi's popsicle-stick legs broke on the way. I would have carried him on my back if I had to. I just didn't want him to ever go back into that courthouse again.

CHAPTER TWENTY

Hard Truth

Barbara coughed heavily through the speakerphone. I imagined clumps of nicotine forcing their way up the back of her throat. "I looked at the scripts again. We're dead. Patrick's ready to quit the project. Don't let him. Call Harry if he tells you he quit. Nerves. But he isn't trying this case in a million years." I didn't relish the thought of talking the firm's top trial attorney off a ledge.

"We need a magic bullet," Barbara continued. "But I think it would've turned up by now. Patrick asked me to work on enhancing the defense script with you. Is there anything you can think of that might buff up the defense? Something that isn't in there? Or maybe a new angle?"

"There's not much," I replied. "The only thing that comes to mind is strengthening the argument that National Union found better homes for its loans with other lenders. A lot of old Wampanoag loans ended up elsewhere. And I think the same can be said with the mortgages. Or at least can soon be said for the mortgages."

"That's thin. And is that even true?"

"That's National Union's position according to legal."

"Thin. Listen, unless they're idiots, they're going to settle. 'Cuz like I said, we're going to get killed. No one has warm feelings about banks. And 'dark and underrepresented?' In writing? What the fuck is that? I guarantee you they don't want to see Steve Powell or Frank Yost questioned under oath about what that meant. And if Austin King and Sarah Moore get a copy of it, they're going to want a trial."

"We need to have the scripts in final by Friday. Patrick is going to try to give you edits until the moment he goes on camera. But he can't do that. And he knows it, but you're going to have to stop him. Let's connect again on Wednesday. In the meantime, let me know if you find the magic bullet or a silver bullet. Or something. Anything. We're dead."

The phone clicked off and Erika parroted, "we're dead."

"I know. But it's going to settle. We're just going to get this to where it needs to go."

"Nice guys," she remarked sharply.

"Yep."

"How long have you worked for them?"

"Not that long. Most of the time I worked for Wampanoag. That was before it was eaten. It wasn't like this before. Any of it."

"I hope they get killed. I wish it would go to trial and the world could see."

"Me, too. But that's not going to happen."

"Maybe we could send the email to the press after it's over."

"I wouldn't even think that thought, let alone say it out loud. I'm going to see if Aaron has any bright ideas."

"Cool. I'll take another look through the green tabs and see if there's anything inspiring."

"Sounds good."

I deflated heavily into my chair and punched the digits to Aaron's office. He was still an inmate at the Backwater, but after the draft script he put together his star was on the rise.

"Look who it is? Hiding from me? Scared to look victory in the eyes? Like Icarus, you flew too high too fast and now it's all going to come crashing down. It's nothing to be ashamed of."

"What? I'm confused."

"I texted you twenty minutes ago. I was about to find a replacement. We're heading out for a shine. You coming?"

"I'm in."

"That's more like it. He's back. Can't keep a good man down. Grab that blonde bastard and meet me downstairs in twenty. Much to discuss."

I was glad to have an excuse to get out of the Temple and wandered down the hall to Tripper's office. I stepped into his doorway.

"Think fast!"

He passed a foam basketball to me. I immediately shot at a small net hanging off the door of his closet. It bounced off of a little white backboard, lipped off of an orange rim and fell to the floor.

"Never going to make the team like that," he commented and shook his head.

"You ready?" Tripper nodded and slid his long legs sideways, removing his shiny tassel loafers off of his desk in a graceful motion.

The doors to the elevator whooshed shut. "Thanks again for the deal binders. We'd be lost without them."

"No problem."

"There was one thing with the BestRateLoan binder."

"Oh yeah?"

"Yeah. A bunch of the loans being sold were from Wampanoag."

"Mm-huh."

"It looks like a lot of ratings changed. Like from high-risk to average-risk and from average-risk to low-risk." His shoulders lifted towards his ears. "Seems like a lot of change in a few years. Bad loans becoming good ones."

"What can I tell you? National Union." He raised his eyebrows and blew a gust from between his lips.

"Isn't that a problem?"

"For whom?"

"National Union?"

"No. That's BestRateLoan's problem. They can do due diligence. There are thousands of mortgages. No one's getting into it. BestRateLoan wants the debt and National Union wants to get rid of it. Everyone wins."

"What about regulators?"

"Nobody cares. National Union is insured. BestRateLoan is insured. It's an apples-to-apples-transaction. BestRateLoan is a sophisticated purchaser. No one's going to scrutinize the deal. It's not like they're being sent to the mafia. Anyway, I hear National Union has other problems to deal with right now." Tripper chuckled as a chime rang and the door to the elevator opened to the lobby.

Aaron stood in Times Square beaming. He wore a dark grey wool suit with heavy white pin stripes contrasted against light tan wingtips. His tan face framed by a pink checkered shirt with a blue tie hanging from a thick knot under his collar. As always, a silky pocket square dangled from his jacket pocket. This one was blue and pink and played off of his shirt and tie. Tripper and I inspected ourselves in our drab office wear then each other and both of us smiled as we looked back at Aaron. We pushed through the glass doors onto the sidewalk followed by a blast of air as the building's hermetic seal was broken.

The shine was a relaxing and welcome break from looking at Patrick's hairy knees. A greasy towel slapped against Aaron's wingtips. "Where we grabbing a beer? Ya'know, to *stratergize*." He said it with an exaggerated Texas accent. "And this time it's billable!"

"I don't know," I said weakly.

"Well, he does have a point," Tripper offered. "We're all working for National Union and there is a lot to discuss about jury research."

As a corporate guy, I wasn't sure what Tripper's role was in the jury testing at that point, but I didn't need any further prodding. "St. Pat's?"

"Is the beer wet?," Aaron asked. "Is it cold? Does it taste like el pipi del diablo?," he continued.

"Yes, yes and it could if you want it to."

"Good enough for me. Let's do it."

I didn't have a lot of time left to find a magic bullet, but hoped Aaron could think of something. And I also hoped he would share it now that he had Patrick's stamp of approval and his star was shooting. We sat around a small high-top table dominated by a large pitcher.

I sipped the bitter yellow lager and looked at Aaron. "Why aren't you rushing to get back to the office? Aren't you under the gun for Friday?"

"Nah, I'm good. Just moving some commas back and forth, but that's about it. Patrick said the heavy lifting is over."

I nearly spit out my beer. "You fucker! I'm still looking at hairy knees all day and night. And Barbara told us to try to find a magic bullet for the script before Friday."

"Wait, hairy knees?" Tripper's entire face pursed as the words left his mouth.

"Yeah, hairy knees. Every day Patrick sends us pictures of the marked-up script taken with his hairy knees as the easel."

"No, you maniac. Patrick sends *you* pictures of his hairy knees. I don't look at his hairy knees."

"Then who looks at his hairy knees?"

"No one. What's wrong with you? Hairy knees? Tiny red scribbles on texted pictures from a cellphone? Are you crazy?"

"What else should I do?"

"You do what I did. I called Office Services in LA and told a guy there that I was working with Patrick. And I incented him to run over to Patrick's club every time he had edits and get them. He then scans them in color and emails them to me. Piece of cake." As lost as I was navigating the firm's resources, Aaron always seemed to have it figured out.

"How'd you incentivize him?"

"I dropped a couple of hundies to him in the inter-office mail and a couple of times a day I'd get an email with a fat attachment with all of Patrick's edits."

I shook my head in disbelief. "You paid someone in LA hundreds of dollars to scan the edits to you?"

"Don't tell me you forwarded hundreds of pictures of his hairy knees to your email from your cell every day? You're insane. You must have been in the office night and day." It was true, but I wasn't about to admit it out loud. It was embarrassing enough just thinking about it.

"So you're done?"

Aaron nodded. "Except for minor edits. But I'm done. And National Union is deader than fried chicken. And the script I read to you and Patrick was watered down. If we used the original, I don't know what National Union would be deader than."

"Watered down? All the pictures of Dorothea White? The abandoned branch? 'Dark' and fucking 'underrepresented?' That's watered down?" My face felt purple.

"Yeah. Watered down. 'Dark and underrepresented' was the tip of the iceberg. You have no idea what was red-flagged in National Union's boxes. I had at least fifty emails and text messages to choose from. Not just those knuckleheads."

"Yost and Powell?"

"Yeah, and one of their bosses. It was bad."

"Holy shit."

"Yeah, holy shit. I threw everything that would fit into my original draft. Patrick couldn't believe what he was reading. Yost said the 'n-word' in a text message to Powell. After Patrick read the whole thing he told me he was quitting the project. David talked him down and asked me for a copy. A couple of days later Chuck came to my door and said, 'here's the new draft. Make sure these are the only pages in the next version and save it as a new document. Then destroy every version from before, delete every email attaching a prior version and shred every printed copy in existence. And confirm it to me in person when you're done.'"

"Jesus Christ. What happened?"

"I did what Chuck told me to do. What else could I do?"

"Yeah, but what happened with your first draft?"

"I don't know if David ran it up the chain and sent it to Don Jones, but someone sanitized it. 'Dark and underrepresented' is bad, but there was so much worse."

"Shit. We're toast."

"But that's a good thing. If Sarah Moore or Austin King got their hands on that stuff, she'd ride it to a judicial appointment and he'd buy . . . What hasn't he bought yet? A jumbo jet? A country? Shit . . . I'm just glad I don't work for National Union. I think you and Erika would quit if you saw what I saw."

"Maybe that's why they put a stranger on it."

"Perhaps. But if the case doesn't settle, you're going to see all of that stuff anyway."

"They'd be crazy to go into litigation and let Powell and Yost testify."

"It's never going to happen," Aaron replied.

"I was hoping you'd have an idea for a magic bullet, but I'm guessing not."

Aaron rested his chin on his palm and thought for a couple of moments. The volume of the jukebox seemed to increase during the silence. There was no magic bullet, but maybe the jury testing would teach National Union a lesson. We all looked at an empty pitcher of beer on the small tabletop then at each other.

"I can't do it," I blurted. "I gotta get back to the office. Maybe Erika found some silver and we can smelt a bullet."

"Not happening," Aaron taunted. "You gonna use some charts? Some customer satisfaction surveys? Dead as fucking fried chicken. You're wasting your time." He was right.

I got back to my desk and buzzed Erika. "I just saw Aaron. We should talk."

Moments later she popped into my doorway. "What happened?"

"Dude, this is bad. Like real bad." Her eyes grew wide. "Aaron said his original script was sanitized and there is worse stuff in the boxes National Union sent to us. 'Dark and underrepresented' is the least bad thing that was in his script. And there's no denying what it means. He gave it to Patrick and then to David. And it came back with a bunch of pages removed. And he was told it was the new draft moving forward."

"Jesus." Disappointment creased Erika's forehead and her eyes flashed with anger as she shook her head. "This isn't what I signed up for. Any of it. I want to bolt."

"You can't just bolt. Firms only want you if you have another job. It's career suicide. They're a bunch of fucking assholes, but you can't light yourself on fire because of it. It's not going to make anything better."

"Then I'm out of here as soon as I can find something else."

As a junior associate with only one firm on her resume and sterling academic credentials, she would probably land quickly at another firm. My situation was more complex, and little did Erika know I was using my salary to fund the pursuit of Mickey's freedom.

I sighed, "I'm with you. I'm gone as soon as I can go. I didn't sign up for this, either."

My cellphone began to buzz on my desk. "Why don't you get that? And I'll start tuning up my resume. I mean, I'll get back to finding a magic bullet."

I picked the slim black phone off the desk. "Kevin. It's Will."

"How's tricks?"

"Can't complain. Living the dream. How are you?"

"I'd be better if they let your brother out of jail."

I expected news and had little hope of it being good news. "That good?"

"Good isn't the word that comes to mind. I received the decision from the parole board this morning. You want some highlights? And I use that word loosely."

"Ok."

"'During the hearing, Mr. Glynn failed to show remorse for the death of Van Nam Tran. Furthermore, despite his guilty plea, Mr. Glynn fails to take any responsibility for his role in Mr. Tran's death. When presented with the opportunity to apologize to Mr. Tran's family, Mr. Glynn refused.' You can imagine where this is going."

"I don't think you'd need to be a brain surgeon to figure it out."

"'After careful consideration of all relevant facts, including the nature of the underlying offense, the age of the inmate at the time of the offense, criminal record, institutional record, the inmate's testimony at the hearing, and the views of the public as expressed at the hearing or in written statements to the board, we conclude by unanimous vote that the inmate is not a suitable candidate for parole.

"'The board is of the opinion that Michael Glynn has not demonstrated a level of rehabilitative progress that would make his release compatible with the welfare of society. Mr. Glynn is serving his second state commitment and has a criminal history as a juvenile. It is the opinion of the board that he would benefit from additional treatment and programming to address his causative factors. Parole is denied with a review scheduled three years from the date of the hearing.'"

"Great. Those are the highlights?"

"Just a taste. There's more, but I think you get it."

"So what's next?"

"We have to wait another three years until he comes up for parole again. But, there's another thing?"

"Yeah?"

Knuckles exhaled heavily. "When I connected through to tell Mickey about the decision this morning my contact told me he got tuned up again."

"Fuck."

"He didn't say anything to me about it and I didn't ask. But I was told he was in a common area when it happened. And it happened fast. Three on one."

I squeezed the back of my neck with my left palm to try to relieve the tension. "And that's not enough to get him out? When's it going to stop? When they kill him?"

"Hey, I know. I know. They're moving him to a different unit and they're keeping an extra eye on him, but it's a full house. If it keeps up, he's going to get moved to the Disciplinary Unit. Trust me, no one wants to be there. We can request a transfer, but I doubt we can get him into a lower security prison. Like we've talked about, he could end up in a worse situation. We're going to need to think on that one."

"Jesus . . ."

"Will, you're trying, but Mickey has to play ball, too. Can you talk to him again?"

My entire back was locked. "It's pointless."

"Just try. At least you're trying. In the meantime, he should be ok."

"I'm back in town next week. I'll see him when I come up."

"Butler?"

"Yeah, and I'm not looking forward to it."

"Works in Manhattan, but comes back to Boston to pick up dog shit." Knuckles chuckled a couple of times. "I don't know, but I don't see that as the right fit for you. By the way, what happened with your big criminal case?"

"He walked."

"He walked! You're kidding. Congrats! How'd you do that?"

"He told his story and the judge bought it."

"Bullshit. Don't sell yourself short. That's great. Your first one, right? Batting a thousand. Not bad for a rookie." A smile creased across my lips. "Let me buy you a beer to celebrate when you're up. And maybe you can also tell me how you got Mickey to change his mind."

"I can only hope."

"Me, too, Will. Me, too."

CHAPTER TWENTY-ONE

Circus

On Saturday afternoon Erika and I watched a large flat-screen television in a small conference room like two scouts sitting around a campfire. It was a live feed from a hotel ballroom in Boston, where the first test jury was watching Patrick forcefully argue Austin King's case against National Union. On one side of the screen Patrick orated in front of the exhibits Aaron prepared. On the other side the jury watched with rapt attention.

Patrick's voice was crisp and he rarely blinked his eyes throughout his presentation. A white collared shirt with a red tie framed his tan face, while a simple blue suit with no pocket square made him seem common and accessible, rather than one of the wealthiest and most successful defense attorneys in the country. Patrick wouldn't risk doing anything that would alienate a jury. He was friendly and spoke in his customary short sentences. There were no big words and nothing to leave anyone with more than an eighth-grade education wondering what he was talking about. Every gesture and movement was practiced and his near-constant eye contact transfixed the jury.

We listened and watched the jurors' faces. Heads shook and brows furrowed as he discussed Ms. White's connection to Roxbury and National Union's treatment of her community. My back tensed as he prepared to drop the nuclear bomb. As the words "dark and underrepresented" left Patrick's lips, the entire jury appeared angry and taken aback. Several jurors began to scribble furiously on notepads.

"Holy shit. If my family knew about this, I'd never be able to go home again. My father would make me quit."

"Hopefully this is settled soon and we can move on."

"I already sent out resumes."

My eyebrows arched. "Really?"

"Yeah. I didn't sign up for this. I'm outta here as soon as I land something else."

Following the video presentations, each of the test juries deliberated on camera. Before a single vote was cast it was clear National Union was in deep trouble. They were tasked with compensating Dorothea White for the loss of her bank branch and for National Union putting her in a subprime car loan. The first jury awarded her $10,000. The next $25,000. And the third $80,000. The amounts were small potatoes for National Union when it came to paying one person, but in a class action it was an unmitigated disaster. If National Union lost at trial and had to pay damages to thousands of people, its losses could easily exceed one billion dollars.

Even worse for National Union, the test jurors were also tasked with determining if the bank should be punished for its conduct. As the forepersons read their verdicts, we couldn't take our eyes off the screen. "Five hundred million. Holy shit!," Erika squealed. "One billion!" By the time the last foreperson announced, "ten billion," we were both giggling.

"I can't fucking believe it. Those fucking assholes are going to lose their minds."

"This has to settle, right?," Erika asked.

"If that was the cleanest red-flagged document and there are more out there and they're much worse, they have to settle."

"How much will it go for?"

"I have no idea. Five hundred million. A billion. More maybe? I guess it depends on what Austin King and Sarah Moore see."

National Union didn't react to the research over the weekend. David and June were out when I arrived back at the Temple on Monday morning. I decided to lay low and catch up on emails with the goal of leaving at a normal hour. Midway through the afternoon a call from Aaron broke the silence.

"I told you National Union was dead. You're lucky I took it easy on you. It could have been much worse. You should thank me. And you better be around on Wednesday."

"Why's that?"

"Because the King, and I do mean the King, is going to be in the Temple in person."

"Austin King?"

"Yes, the King of Class Actions, my man! In the office with Sarah Moore."

"Holy shit! Legal royalty."

"You'll know he's in the office because you'll smell the money when he enters the building."

"Why?"

"Do I have to explain everything to you? Because he's so rich, dumbass."

"No. Fuck you. Why's he coming into the office?"

"To negotiate a settlement of the claims against National Union. And you couldn't see it when I said 'negotiate,' but I was making little air quotes with my fingers when I said it."

"What do you mean?"

"I mean Harry and Austin picked out a number they could live with weeks ago. Harry just needed to get the board to approve and Austin would get Sarah to sign off. David and Harry were with Don Jones and the board all morning and spent the weekend talking them off the ledge. Jury testing scared the shit out of them. They authorized Harry to settle for two-fifty."

"We're going to settle for two hundred and fifty million dollars?"

Aaron responded with a disgusted "uhh."

"What?"

"Are you serious right now? He asked for two-fifty and is going to settle for two-fifty? Think about it. Where are the heroes in that story?"

"Ok, so how much?"

"One hundred. National Union gets killed in testing to the tune of billions. Harry and David ask for two-fifty from the board to settle with Don Jones' blessing. It's settled for a hundred and Harry, David and Don come out looking like geniuses. They just saved the bank hundreds of millions, if not billions, of dollars."

"Jesus Christ. And Sarah Moore's on board with that?"

"Hell yeah. Harry and Austin have done it before with her and everyone wins. Sarah gets the state AG's in line and she gets credit for punishing National Union for a hundred million dollars. She doesn't have to do anything else. The King of Class Actions puts a cool twenty-five million bucks in his pocket for filing a class-action complaint and gets to play the role of sugar daddy doling out the remaining seventy-five million to thousands of former National Union customers. The board pats itself on the back for saving the bank. And, like I said, Harry, David and Don are heroes. And you know what the best part is?"

"What's that?"

"Smith Stevens is billing millions and millions to National Union and the spigot is only going to get opened wider because of this. We're going to get paid."

"What about 'dark and underrepresented' and all the other red flags?"

"What about them?"

"The DOJ isn't going to react to them?"

"Buddy, do I have to teach you everything? Sarah Moore and the DOJ are never going to see them. If they did, do you think this would settle for a hundred? National Union is going to admit to some missteps but deny redlining and reverse redlining. Harry is going to proffer a set of documents cleared by Smith Stevens and National Union as proof and that's all she wrote."

"I need a shower."

"Oh, cut the shit. This happens all the time. Things settle. A number is taken out of the air. And a hundred million is a lot of money. How do you quantify damages in something like this?"

"I don't know, but the test juries figured it out. If people knew, they'd go crazy. And maybe it would be more and National Union's customers would go elsewhere."

"And what? Put a ton of people at National Union out of work? People who had nothing to do with anything? Seems like a hundred million going to pay victims and their lawyers and not putting good people out of work is a good result."

"Maybe you're right. I don't know. It feels so slimy."

"Of course I'm right. This is how it always happens. It's just a game. And this is how it's played. The court will approve Austin as counsel for the class and approve the settlement after a hearing. Anyone who doesn't like it can tell it to the court. And if the court agrees with them, then so be it. And if the court doesn't agree, then so be it also. There's no reason to get it twisted."

"I guess."

"You *know*, dude. You know. This is how it works. You're not going to jump out the window, are you?"

"Nah. I'm cool. I'm just spent."

"Alright. Get some rest. I'll see you on Wednesday. Peace out."

There was little for me to do before Austin and Sarah appeared in the office. Harry's team prepared the settlement agreement and the proffer of documents and information on its own. When Wednesday morning arrived, Aaron nonchalantly wandered by my doorway.

"So this is how the other half lives. Not bad for a nickelbagger. C'mon, I heard Austin's downstairs. Let's go before it's too late."

When we passed through the glass doors on the 42nd floor, the atmosphere felt light. Normally it was staid and serious and the receptionists had the humor of undertakers. But today they were both smiling and we followed a trail of a musky cologne down the hall. We heard loud laughter as we rounded a corner and saw Austin King in all his glory. He was tall and stout and wore a grey pinstripe suit with cowboy boots and a cowboy hat.

Harry walked next to Austin and the contrast was stark. Austin walked assuredly with the heels of his boots striking the floor forcefully with each step. A slight swagger in his hips titled his head towards his right shoulder with each strike of the heel of his right foot. His large cowboy hat exaggerated the effect, and he looked more like a character from a movie than a real person.

Next to Austin, Harry looked like a Russian circus bear trained to dance ballet. He was also tall, but rounder. His pigeon-toed gait pushed him onto his forefeet, and he looked as though he was tiptoeing through the office, trying not to draw attention to himself. If Harry became aware of the contrast, I wondered if he would ever walk next to Austin again.

They disappeared through the doorway of a conference room, and, as usual, Harry's fingers lightly brushed the doorway as he made the turn. We hurried our pace, as we didn't want our window to meet Austin to close. As soon as we stepped through the doorway, Harry greeted us like old friends.

"Aaron and Will, great to see you!" He shook both of our hands, which was unusual between attorneys inside of Smith Stevens. "Sarah and Austin, I'd like to introduce you to two of our attorneys, who have put a lot of work into this case. Aaron Goldberg and Will Duggan."

"Aaron and Will. I'm pleased to introduce you to Sarah Moore." Sarah stood up and was tall and wore a dark suit with a skirt and a light blue buttoned-down shirt. She was athletic and her handshake was firmer than mine. She looked like she had been a collegiate swimmer. Intelligence shined through her bright blue eyes, and her presence was intense and intimidating. After shaking our hands, she returned to her seated position at the conference table and resumed tapping out words on her government laptop.

"And gentlemen, this is Austin King." Austin smiled widely. His handshake nearly pulled my right arm out of the socket. He towered over both of us.

"Nice to meet you, boys." His twang bounced off the windows of the conference room. "So you keepin' this guy in line?" His voice was as big as he was and friendly. He aimed his thumb over his right forearm towards Harry as he said the words. "Count your fingers if you shake his hand!" Austin laughed hard as if he had just coined the stale line himself.

He looked like he was ready for a celebration, but Sarah didn't seem interested in joining the party. I wondered if she didn't appreciate the old boys' club act. Or maybe she didn't know the fix was in and was steeling herself for battle. Either way, I couldn't imagine her out celebrating with them if the case settled. Her demeanor gave me some hope that the class-action circus wouldn't have as easy a ride as Aaron described.

"Boys, you sticking around for the arm-wrastlin'?," Austin asked loudly, almost yelling.

"Unfortunately, these guys have to get back to work. National Union can't afford to have so many attorneys in one room. And we need to keep the lights on here."

"You better not be goin' cheap on me, Harry! Otherwise, I'm going to take you to try-all!"

Austin looked towards the ceiling as the words left his mouth with an exaggerated drawl. He laughed hard, but the "yee-hah" I wanted to hear failed to launch from his immense belly. His large white teeth shined through his wide smile and he looked at me and Aaron and gave us an exaggerated wink. I stared at him for a long time. I realized it was all a show. The King of Class Actions never had any intention of taking Harry or National Union to "try-all."

CHAPTER TWENTY-TWO

Chum

I found an empty spot in the front row of the gallery of Judge Butler's courtroom far from where Catherine Corcoran was sitting. Even though Austin King filed a class action against National Union, the federal court in Boston, where the class action was pending, had yet to stay National Union's default cases and it was uncertain if it would. As a result, National Union's lawsuit against Ms. Corcoran continued to move forward and I still had to make appearances.

As I sat waiting for Judge Butler to take a seat behind his bench, I could feel hatred burning against the back of my neck. Each time I turned my head I caught a glimpse of Ms. Corcoran staring at me in my peripheral vision. It was a departure from the last time I saw her when she could barely look at my shoes. The crowd in the gallery continued to grow as Judge Butler's clerk, Debbie, organized a large stack of papers on his bench. Without explanation, she had cancelled the mediation I requested and replaced it with another status conference.

Negotiations between Austin, Sarah and Harry ran all day on Wednesday and were ongoing when I left the office Thursday afternoon to travel to Boston. My marching orders remained the same. No compromising on amounts, only on payment terms. At 9:30 on the nose Judge Butler stepped out of a door behind his bench. The court officer dutifully yelled "all rise" and everyone in attendance stood at rigid attention. A crisp white collar rose from behind his robe and framed a handsome purple tie which boasted a thick Windsor knot. As usual, his bald head was polished to a blinding shine.

As he sat down relieving everyone in the room of their duty to stand, he leaned over to Debbie and said something that was inaudible to anyone in the gallery. Moments later to my surprise she called out, "National Union Bank & Trust versus Catherine Corcoran, case number 18-26732. All parties and counsel." My heart skipped a beat. It was the first case called that morning. To my further surprise, when Ms. Corcoran stood up she was accompanied by a man in a dark blue suit.

Before I could enter my appearance, Judge Butler looked at the man and said, "Good morning, Mr. Johnson." Shit. I was about to get hometowned in my own hometown.

Debbie loudly blurted out, "appearances," after the judge and Mr. Johnson exchanged niceties.

"Good morning, Your Honor. Will Duggan on behalf of Plaintiff National Union Bank & Trust."

"Good morning, Mr. Duggan," Judge Butler replied.

"Your Honor, for the record, Bryan Johnson on behalf of defendant Catherine Corcoran."

"Good morning again, Mr. Johnson. I'm looking at the notes here." Judge Butler scanned a long blue legal-sized folder, which contained copies of all of the documents filed in the case. "Ok. So the last time the parties were here, they were directed to discuss the terms of a settlement. Could someone give me an update on those discussions?"

Mr. Johnson stood up at the defense table faster than I could rise from my seat. "Your Honor, I was recently retained in this case and was not privy to any discussions with National Union or its counsel. And, further, I am unaware of any substantive discussions that moved the ball forward. My understanding is that National Union is firm on the amount and would only discuss payment terms."

Judge Butler looked in my direction. "Ok. Mr. Duggan, where are we?"

"Your Honor, National Union's position is that it would rather try the case on the merits than accept a compromise."

"Hmm," Judge Butler sighed. "We talked about this the last time you were here. You're going to spend more money taking this case to trial than it's worth. What is it? Twenty-six thousand dollars? That's bad business. And it sends a message to me. That National Union is unreasonable. And don't think I don't know what's going on with National Union these days. I read the newspapers. Austin King. The Department of Justice." If he only knew what was really happening. "So with all that action. Everything that is going on, National Union wants to fight over twenty-six thousand dollars? And go to trial, no less?"

Bryan Johnson stood up. "Your Honor, if I may?"

"Go ahead, counselor."

"I'm new to this case and am getting up to speed. I think Ms. Corcoran has done a great job, but she's not a lawyer." He looked down at his client, who smiled when she looked up at him and nodded her approval. "She didn't understand all of her rights, but now she does. I'm fine with breaking off settlement talks if National Union wants a trial. But if National Union wants a trial, I want discovery. I need depositions of corporate officers and I need the opportunity to request documents.

"I also want leave to file counterclaims, including for National Union's unfair business practices. And I know how busy Your Honor is and that a trial date won't be next week. I respectfully submit that there wouldn't be any unfair prejudice to National Union if we proceed with discovery and counterclaims." Austin King had chummed the waters with his class-action complaint and it was attracting other sharks.

"This Court's docket is packed," Judge Butler commented. "And a trial date wouldn't be for many months, which would afford National Union ample time to respond to discovery and Ms. Corcoran's counterclaims. It is the policy of this Commonwealth to have trials on the merits. And the discovery of evidence is necessary for a trial on the merits. I can see no unfair prejudice to National Union. Mr. Duggan, do you have any objection?"

"Your Honor, I do object. This case has been pending for more than a year and this is the first time discovery or counterclaims have been raised."

"Are you suggesting National Union would be unfairly prejudiced? And if so, how so?" There was no unfair prejudice and no valid reason for Ms. Corcoran not to have a fair day in court if National Union didn't want to settle.

"No, Your Honor," I replied weakly.

"Good. Then I'm going to set this case for a final scheduling conference in twelve months. We'll set a trial date at that time if the parties can't reach an agreement. You two work out the dates and submit a proposed discovery schedule. Anything else?"

"Yes, Your Honor. One more thing." Bryan Johnson stood up. "I wanted to advise the Court that I intend to file a motion to consolidate all of National Union's loan default cases for coordinated proceedings before Your Honor." Judge Butler's ears perked up. Consolidation would mean he would hear all of National Union's cases in Massachusetts. Managing a large litigation involving many parties could be a steppingstone to a higher court or even a lucrative career as a mediator if he chose to retire from the judiciary.

"Consolidation?" Judge Butler seemed to welcome the motion. My body felt like a deflated balloon.

"Yes, Your Honor. There's been quite a bit of press lately regarding National Union's litigation practices. And, as Your Honor has already alluded to, Austin King recently filed a class action against National Union for its business practices."

"So why consolidate if there's a class action pending? Wouldn't this be a matter in the purview of the federal court? Perhaps vis-à-vis a motion to stay this case with an opportunity to be heard in that case?"

"Well, Your Honor, Austin King's class action seems to be focused on redlining and reverse redlining in predominantly minority neighborhoods and his class action, as I understand it, is focused on minorities who were allegedly targeted and discriminated against by National Union. As you can see, not to be too blunt about it, but my client doesn't fit into Mr. King's class action. Yet, based on articles I've read and docket information I've reviewed from courts around the Commonwealth, there may be hundreds of defendants like my client, who have also been victimized by National Union.

"And from what I have reviewed, many of those people don't have representation. But I'm willing to bet, if betting were legal of course, Your Honor, that a lot of those folks are going to lawyer up as information about the class action continues to trickle out. And similar to this case, a lot of those cases haven't had discovery. And once attorneys get involved, they're going to want to get documents and sworn testimony from National Union.

"So what I intend to move for . . . Well, the purpose of my motion is to consolidate the cases before you. I would submit that this Court is uniquely suited for consolidation. Consolidation would save a lot of resources if all of the cases are overseen by one judge, rather than numerous judges around the Commonwealth. And many of the cases are in Suffolk County anyway. And at this point, we don't know what's going to happen with the class action. If there's going to be a trial. If the class itself will be approved. If Austin King will be appointed class counsel. Or if the case will eventually settle."

Neither Judge Butler nor Bryan Johnson had any idea that the fix was in and that it had been for weeks. It wasn't my place to divulge that information, and I had no idea how broad the settlement was going to be and if it would include people like Catherine Corcoran.

"Mr. Duggan, do you have any comment or objection?," Judge Butler asked.

I stiffened quickly from my slouch and stood at attention. "Your Honor, there are cases in different counties with different defendants and different circumstances for each case. I respectfully submit, without having all of the relevant information in front of me, that those differences would be too great to warrant consolidation. This isn't like a hip replacement litigation where everyone had the same defective hip device."

"Mr. Duggan, the cases all involve National Union, do they not? And they all involve loan products issued by National Union? And there can't be that many loan products. So all we're really talking about are details like the amount owed and the default dates as being the differences. Am I wrong about that?"

"Your Honor, I would need more time to respond, as this is the first I'm hearing about it. I need time to educate myself."

"Good. You'll have time to educate yourself. Rule 42, which governs consolidation, gives me broad discretion to consolidate cases involving a common question of fact or of law. I'm going to give Mr. Johnson leave to file his motion. And you'll have a chance to educate yourself and respond. Is thirty days with two weeks to respond fair?"

"That sounds fair to me."

"Yes, Your Honor," I followed.

"Excellent. I look forward to seeing your papers." They were words I never expected to hear. "Anything else?" No one replied verbally. "Good.

Don't forget my scheduling stipulation." He looked down at the papers on his bench and scribbled something.

It was just a conference, but it felt like a loss. Or multiple losses, actually. And we weren't even close to trial. If the case proceeded into heavy discovery and if Judge Butler oversaw all of National Union's default cases, National Union was going to have a rough ride. In the universe of bad things I imagined would happen following National Union's new approach to the default suits, consolidation in front of Judge Butler wasn't one of them. At least the conference was over early.

My head was pounding when I passed through security at Cedar Junction. "Jesus Christ, Mick." I gave him a gentle hug as he gingerly approached the table. He still wore shackles and handcuffs. And if his appearance was an indication of his activities lately, he wouldn't be coming out of them anytime soon. A large bruise creeped out from underneath a bandage over his left eyebrow and his right hand was encased in a fresh white cast. "What? Did you fall off the fence trying to escape?"

"I wish. It wasn't quite that heroic."

"What the fuck happened?"

"It's just bullshit. No big deal. It happens."

"What happens?" The family next to me looked over as the words left my mouth. I tried to regain my composure and lowered the volume of my voice. "Mickey, what the fuck? What's going on in here? Every time I visit you look like an old punching bag."

He tilted his head and furrowed his eyebrows as he whispered close to me. "Shit happens. I've been lucky. But it happens. It will pass. They'll move on."

"Mick, this doesn't look like moving on. What next? Your leg? They smash your fucking head in? Who did this?"

"No one. It's no big deal."

"It is a big deal, Mick. I'm trying to get you out of here before this escalates any further. But you're not making it easy on me."

"Listen, Will. I never fucking asked you. I appreciate it, but I never asked. Alright. But if I do what you want, I might as well be dead out there. At least in here I die with dignity."

"Dignity? Did you say dignity? There's not a dignified fucking thing about dying in here. You'll die a fucking murderer. And that's all anyone will ever think. You get out and at least you get a chance to live."

"That's no life, Will. I'm thirty-eight and haven't had a job since I was a teenager. You're my only family member. You and Kevin are the only people that visit me. There's no life for me out there."

"But you'll be alive. And you won't be dead in here. A fucking murderer." Mickey shook his head in disgust. My heart was pounding underneath the pocket of my dress shirt. If Mickey's hands were out of the cuffs, he would've hit me. "Give me a bone. Give me something. Just something to work with. You gotta get out of here. You're a walking corpse." My face was flush and my eyes were getting glassy.

After a long pause, Mickey bowed the index finger on his unbroken hand. I leaned in towards him. "It's Thánh Den."

"Fuck. Thánh Den is doing this to you?," I whispered.

Thánh Den was a relatively new, but already notorious, gang operating out of East Boston with members filtering into every correctional institution in Massachusetts. They were also nearly exclusively Vietnamese and probably didn't appreciate Mickey's role in the death of Jimmy Tran or his claims of innocence.

"Yeah."

"And you haven't told anyone?"

"Will, if I told anyone, they would've cut me into ribbons by now. But everyone knows."

"Mick, if you don't tell someone for real, they're going to cut you into ribbons. We gotta get you the fuck out of here."

Mickey's calloused exterior momentarily wavered. It was the first time his life had been threatened inside of Cedar Junction. If the life sentence handed down by the Commonwealth of Massachusetts didn't mean death for Mickey, Thánh Den's vengeance certainly would sooner or later.

"Yeah," he swallowed hard.

"I'm seeing Kevin this afternoon. I'll find out what I can do. Sorry about the decision."

"It's not your fault. That was on me." I looked down at the table and nodded. It was true, but hearing Mickey say it made me feel worse than the decision did. "We'll get them next time, right?," Mickey added. Three years was a long way off and I worried there wouldn't be a next time.

"Yeah. We'll get 'em," I responded weakly. I knew Mickey would die in here if he didn't change his story.

"Will, I'm sorry about before. I'm tired. But I appreciate you. And . . . thanks. It means a lot to me."

"You got it. What else am I gonna do?"

"Meet a girl. Start a family maybe."

"You are my family, Mick. We'll figure out how to get you out of here. I'll get Knuckles to work on it. He's the best. He'll figure something out. But we're going to need you to play along."

"Um-hum." Although Mickey seemed resigned to his fate, I still would've been surprised if he finally said the things he needed to say to get out.

A guard walked into the visiting area. "Time, fellas."

Mickey got up slowly. I went in for another gentle hug and, unable to hug me in handcuffs, he pushed his body deeply into mine. The short silver hair on the side of his head bristled against my ear. "Thanks, Will. For everything."

CHAPTER TWENTY-THREE

The Exception

When I pushed through the blue wooden door I immediately saw Knuckles holding court with a group of younger attorneys. Two pieces of ice held on for dear life as he punctuated his sentences with a glass of brown liquid. I was amazed he hadn't already doused everyone in the front row of his lecture. He noticed me approaching out of the side of his eye and became more animated.

"Now this, ladies and gentlemen, is the rarest animal you will ever see in this esteemed tavern. A big-shot New York lawyer. From Smith Stevens, no less. Can you believe that? I think he wants to be my associate, but I'm going to have to let him down easy. He's too soft for criminal law." He looked at me. "Jesus, you gotta get out of the office more. You look like a cadaver." I laughed, and as soon as the ice was broken, Knuckles' minions laughed with us.

"All right, all. We have business to discuss. I'll catch up with you later." The group disappeared back into the mass of patrons crowding around us. Knuckles lifted his old attorney case off of the chair next to him and hung it from a hook hidden under the bar. "Slumming again today? How was Butler?"

"I don't want to talk about it."

"That good?"

"Let's just say all of my cases might be in his courtroom in the near future."

Knuckles grimaced. "Ouch. How'd you make that happen?"

"Wasn't me. My defendant lawyered up and retained some guy named Bryan Johnson."

"Get ready for some action. He's a consumer guy and is going to turn the screws."

"Great. I was kind of feeling like I needed another headache."

"Better you than me." Knuckles chuckled as he downed his brown drink with a violent backwards thrust of his head. "Petey! Harpoon and another one of these!" He then looked at me. "Harpoon, right?"

"Yeah."

"So what's the latest and greatest?"

"Well, in the not-so-great department, I saw Mickey this afternoon."

"Hanging in there?"

"Barely. He's still a punching bag. Between the chipped tooth . . . and now he has a broken hand and a welt on his head, he'll be on the cover of *GQ* any day now."

"Fuck," Knuckles muttered. For the first time in a while his pearly teeth were sealed behind his lips. "I didn't know he busted his hand."

"It gets worse. Thánh Den."

Knuckles winced. "Thánh Den?" I nodded. "Well, now we know why." Our drinks arrived and we took deep sips at the same time.

"Is there anything we can do?"

"Same stuff. Get him moved to another unit and away from them. But there's a risk he'll be stuck in disciplinary. And that'll be miserable. We could appeal to the Department of Corrections. But then he's just going to get moved to another facility. And he could be in a worse situation. At least they know him at Cedar Junction and are working with us."

"What if Mickey changes his story?"

"That would be a miracle, but he has three more years."

"How about an emergency petition to the parole board?"

"That's iffy and probably won't be well-received. He was just there. Is he going to tell them he found Jesus, too? In less than three months?"

"We gotta try something."

"Kevin Sullivan!" A booming voice interrupted our discussion and a thick hand audibly slapped Knuckles' shoulder. Knuckles playfully spun around with his fists up.

"Tim Molloy, you crazy bastard. What? They took your ankle bracelet off?"

Tim lifted his foot off the ground and pulled his pantleg away from his ankle. "Nothing to see here."

As they chortled, I sipped my beer and unlocked my phone. An email from Harry with a red flag landed in my inbox. "Great News! National Union Team, I wanted to thank you for all of your hard work on the document review, jury testing and settlement agreement projects! I am pleased to announce we reached a settlement of all of the claims pending against National Union this afternoon. That includes the class action claims filed by Austin King and the governmental claims, including those filed by the Department of Justice and the various state attorneys general.

"As part of the deal, National Union will pay $100,000,000 as a fine to the relevant government agencies. This agreement is unique among financial institutions, however, as that amount will be used to fund the compensation to class members, attorneys' fees for class counsel and the administration of settlement payments. While this is great news, there is work to be done. Austin King will be seeking appointment as class counsel and moving to certify the class. And we'll be moving for approval of the settlement. There will be a video meeting at 2:00 New York time on Monday. Please confirm your attendance. Thank you, H."

Moments later my phone buzzed with a text from Aaron. "You owe me a beer, you nickelbagger. Actually, I'm changing that to a Scotch. And a good one. Did I call it or did I call it?"

I shook my head and sighed. "You called it. So the King of Class Actions did it again. Think he'll take us out on his yacht?"

"Definitely! We exchanged cell numbers. I'll get you an invite." I wasn't sure if he was joking. Knowing Aaron, they probably did. "St. Pat's in twenty?"

"Dude, I'm in Boston. I need a rain check."

"Nice try. I'm not forgetting. I will kick your ass if I don't have my Scotch by Thursday. Understood?"

"You wish."

A kissing emoji popped up on my cellphone's screen. "Anyhoo, I'm out. It's total chaos here."

"What's up?"

"Shredding party. A truck is pulling up tonight and all of the National Union stuff is toast this weekend now that they've settled."

"What?"

"The boxes are being stacked to go."

"Wow."

"That's how they do. We certainly aren't keeping them. Aight. Brown stuff on you next week! Peace out!"

I read Aaron's texts again. "Shredding party." All of the evidence in Smith Steven's possession would be destroyed. Every racist and discriminatory email and text message would reside solely in the possession of National Union. And that's only if the bank hadn't already destroyed its copies. I never saw the emails Aaron saw and never would. Neither would any partners at the firm beyond David, Harry, Patrick, and Chuck. They'd never find their way to Austin King or Sarah Moore. The entire ugly affair would disappear from physical existence and eventually from memory.

As Knuckles and Tim continued to chortle, a seed began to germinate in my mind. What would happen if Sarah Moore saw the emails and text messages Aaron saw? Maybe she'd see National Union and Smith Stevens pulled a fast one with the King of Class Actions. I had no idea if she knew the fix was in, but I had my doubts.

"Will, I want you to meet the fifty-third best criminal lawyer in Boston." I turned to see Tim Molloy smiling in my direction. He seemed to be feeling good.

"Fuck you, Knuckles. I'm at least the forty-sixth best." He laughed hardily as the words floated through the air. "Good to meet you, Will. How'd you get tied up with this guy."

"Personal and confidential," Knuckles blurted. "No trying to poach my clients. It's tacky."

Tim smiled. "All kidding aside, you're in good hands with this guy. He's the best criminal lawyer in town. He'll take care of you."

"Jesus," Knuckles replied. "You're giving me a case of the feels. If you want me to buy another round, just ask. It's less embarrassing."

"I hate to turn down a free drink from a legend, but I have to roll out. Good to meet you." Knuckles and Tim shook hard.

"He's one of the best," Knuckles commented as Tim parted our company. "Sorry about that. So, where were we?"

"Cedar Junction, the Department of Corrections and an emergency petition to the parole board."

"Oh yeah. I love taking your money, but I hate that you're wasting it. I could put together emergency papers for the parole board, but I think they'll be a nonstarter. And you'll just be burning cash."

"You could do it *pro bono*."

Knuckles feigned spitting out his drink. "*P-pro bono?*" He looked at me aghast. "Only a masochist would do this *pro bono.*" My head tilted slightly and Knuckles smiled. "And you. And you, of course. You're not a masochist. Not at all. Cheers to your big criminal court win!" We clinked glasses and sipped our drinks. "That took some stones to go in there your first time. Good stuff. No moving in on my turf, though." He elbowed me in the ribs as he said it and smiled. "Seriously, though. That's great. And I bet it felt good."

"I still think about it at night. The consequences . . . It keeps me awake."

"I get it, but he was responsible for the consequences. Not you. Anything you did for him made the situation better, not worse. Am I right?"

"I guess so."

"Of course I'm right. What if he was stopped by the cops and arrested somewhere? It's a much different story and a much different outcome."

"Probably."

"Definitely, but that's not what happened. And now he's free because of you. You should be proud of that. You did good."

"Thanks, Kevin." I felt myself sitting a little more upright in my barstool. "Kevin, remember you said something about clemency from the governor? Like if he owed me a favor?"

"Wait, you're rich? And you've been holding back on me all this time? I think I need to adjust my rates."

"Oh yeah, Mick and I are trust fund babies. I totally forgot. I'm going to call in a distribution." Knuckles chewed on a piece of ice as he listened and smiled. His supernaturally white teeth seemed to glow in the dark atmosphere of the bar. "But what if we could trade something to win Mickey's release?"

"Like information?"

"Yeah."

"Like Mickey knows something and I'm just finding out now?"

"No. What if I know something? And it's big?"

"That depends how big and how useful it is."

"It's pretty big and pretty useful."

"Pray tell, Master William, what is this big and useful information? Please tell me it's not that National Union's a terrible bank. I think we all know that." My eyebrows raised. "What? I'm not a total caveman. I read the newspaper. It was kind of hard to miss your name in the *Boston Post*. You're famous. Who knows? Maybe it'll help."

"It is National Union. Can I tell you in confidence?"

"Private and confidential?"

"More like attorney-client privilege confidential."

Knuckles paused for a moment of seemingly deep thought. "Scout's honor." He buttoned his lips with an imaginary key and threw it over his shoulder.

"Ok. National Union is settling a class action and a government investigation into its discriminatory business practices."

"The Austin King class action?"

"Exactly. It's totally confidential. And no one knows publicly."

"Ok." Knuckles listened intently.

"To make the settlement happen, National Union turned over some documents in a proffer to Austin King and the DOJ and denied any major wrongdoing. But before it did that, Austin King and Harry Josephson, a partner at Smith Stevens, agreed on the settlement amount and the mechanics of how the settlement would go down."

Knuckles nodded along as I spoke. "Ok. I'm not really seeing a major red flag here."

"I don't think the government was in on the deal between Austin and Harry. I don't think the DOJ's lead attorney, Sarah Moore, had any idea there was a deal in place before she met with them for settlement discussions."

"But if the government agreed to it . . . What am I missing?"

"The government only saw the proffered documents and not the universe of relevant documents. And there was some really bad shit there. The documents proffered were sanitized by National Union and Smith Stevens before they were given to the DOJ. We did jury testing and I saw an email between two executives that referred to a neighborhood in Roxbury as 'dark and underrepresented.'" Knuckles' cheek twitched.

"Another attorney told me it was the tip of the iceberg and he saw text messages between the same executives with the 'n-word' in them. And those executives were responsible for shutting down branches in Black neighborhoods."

Knuckles' eyebrows raised sharply and a "whoo" whooshed from between his lips.

"But I don't think the government ever saw them. I don't think Smith Stevens or National Union was truthful with the DOJ about the existence of bad documents or the validity of the discrimination claims."

"That's pretty fucked up, Will."

"I don't know what Austin King knows, but I doubt he'd care. He's getting paid. I was told that he, Harry, and Sarah did a deal before, so he and Harry may have used her trust to push this deal through. I saw Austin at the office with Sarah when the settlement discussions began. He seemed like he was there for a party, but she was all business. I think the whole negotiation and the proffer were orchestrated by Harry and Austin. It was easy money for Austin, and National Union avoided a huge problem. If the DOJ knew about the n-word text messages, I have trouble believing it would be settling without real discovery. Or settling for the amount it's settling for."

"How much is that?"

"A hundred million."

"Shit. That's not painless."

"True, but, in reality, it's a blip on the radar for National Union. National Union's board authorized up to two hundred and fifty to make it go away."

"Two-fifty?"

"Yeah, and they probably would have gone higher. The board was scared about what might happen. A test jury awarded Austin King billions in punitive damages. And the test jurors only saw the 'dark and underrepresented' email. And none of the other racist stuff."

"Ok." Knuckles' mouth pursed and twisted to the side and his eyes drifted away from me. He then took a slow sip of brown liquid. "So you want to tell the government that National Union and Smith Stevens lied about the existence of bad documents?"

"In exchange for Mickey's release."

"I don't think I have to tell you, but that's a pretty big ask. You're trying to exchange a murder for a fraud. State to federal. It's not exactly apples to apples . . ."

"There has to be something I can do."

Knuckles exhaled heavily. The wheels were spinning behind his eyes. "If National Union and Smith Stevens lied about the existence of bad documents to the DOJ it's a crime."

"That's what I thought."

"Under 18 U.S.C. 1001 you can't make a false statement to the government. The law casts a big net and it has teeth. People have gone away for years for it, including executives. It might give you a window, but you'd have to tread very, very carefully. You have the attorney-client privilege in your way. You'll be accused of divulging client confidences and Smith Stevens and National Union are going to come after you with a vengeance. You're going to be sacrificing your career if it goes wrong and blows up. Maybe worse. And there's no guarantee it would work."

"I'll do whatever it takes. I don't care. Mickey's a dead man if he doesn't get out of Cedar Junction soon."

"Jeez. I wish I had a brother like you. You're a good kid and I don't want to see you crash and burn. If you're going to report National Union and Smith Stevens for lying about the existence of bad documents, your statements to the DOJ have to be limited to the wrongdoing. You know what I'm talking about?" I shook my head.

"Crime fraud."

"Crime fraud?"

"Yeah. The crime-fraud exception." He waited for a light to turn on in my head that didn't click. "To the attorney-client privilege," he added after a pause. It still didn't click. Knuckles knew I was lost. "Hopefully, you'd never come across it during your career. An attorney can't participate in a crime or a fraud with a client. As a result, the attorney-client privilege doesn't apply to communications between an attorney and a client made in furtherance of a crime or a fraud. Some have even argued that an attorney is obligated to disclose those communications to law enforcement to prevent crimes from happening."

I watched Knuckles intently as the words hung in the air. "That makes sense. Unfortunately, the proffer was handled by the firm's class action team and I wasn't a part of it. So I don't know what was discussed."

"I think we can get around that. If National Union gave its bad documents to Smith Stevens and the government never saw them, there must've been discussions between the firm and the bank about hiding them. If there wasn't a legal reason for hiding them, those discussions wouldn't be protected by the attorney-client privilege. And that's where your window would open, but the bad documents are the key to opening it. And you haven't seen them?"

"No."

"That's a problem. If you don't have first-hand knowledge of the documents' contents, you can't be a witness. You'd be testifying about what you heard from someone else and that won't stand up in court. It's hearsay. And if the person you heard it from doesn't stick to his story, Smith Stevens and National Union are going to flatten you." Knuckles held a piece of ice with his teeth.

"On top of all that, there's no guarantee Sarah would be interested," Knuckles continued. "She could end up with mud on her face for failing to do a thorough investigation and cover her ass. And even if she bites, she might not offer a deal and still go after National Union and Smith Stevens for violating Section 1001. Mickey will stay in jail and you'll have gained nothing for your trouble. This is a huge gamble that could go wrong in a lot more ways than it could go right."

"If there's a shot it could work, I have to try it. Mickey's running out of time."

"Honestly, it's more like a Hail Mary. Are you sure about this?"

"I'm as sure about it as anything."

"At this point, it's your word against National Union and Smith Stevens. And they're already playing hide-the-ball. Can you get your hands on the documents so you can back up what you're saying?"

"They're at Smith Stevens, but they're going to be shredded. A truck is coming tonight." Knuckles' face was pained with concern.

"I think this is crazy. But if you're going to have a chance to do it, then you better get your ass to New York before those documents get destroyed. Otherwise, this is over before it began. And we'll deal with how you got them when we figure out how we're going to approach Sarah." He looked at my half-empty pint glass. "I got these. You can buy next time and finish your drink then. But you better get going."

"Thanks, Kevin. I'll let you know what happens."

"You got it."

I bolted from the bar and ran in my wingtips with briefcase flailing to the closest rental car agency nearly half a mile away in Government Center.

Finally seated behind the wheel of the last car available—a tiny blue subcompact—I raced from Boston towards New York hoping to beat the shredding truck to the Backwater. Afternoon turned to evening as the small car sped down Route 95.

CHAPTER TWENTY-FOUR

Blue Peanut

T he tiny car's engine wailed as I rounded the corner from 52nd Street onto Eighth Avenue. It was a longshot, but if there was a car small enough to fit into any space, the Blue Peanut was it. A large panel truck with a "Shred & Pulp" logo sat in front of the Backwater. I circled onto 53rd Street. There was no spot. Instead, there was a long line of traffic. A red light changed to green and back to red again without any traffic moving. Fuck! I punched the top of the steering wheel, probably fortunate to not trigger the airbag. My window was closing. I pulled the Blue Peanut into a bus stop, clicked the lock button on the keyless remote and ran for the corner of 53rd and Eighth Avenue.

As I rounded the corner, the shredding truck was quiet. I was too late. My heart sank and frustration welled in the corners of my eyes. I walked by the truck and its crew to the front door of the Backwater. I pushed the familiar front door open and quietly peered my head into the building. There was no sound and no sign of life. I walked through the empty lobby. More silence.

Instead of taking the building's noisy old industrial elevator and risk blowing my cover, I stepped up heavy metal stairs.

I pushed through an old metal door to enter the Backwater and was reminded of Mickey walking through the old green metal door to meet me in the visiting room at Cedar Junction. I peered to the right then to the left. There was neither a sound nor a soul. The lights were on, but the entire floor was quiet. I passed blocks of cubicles on my way to the Pit. My heart began to thud. Hundreds of brown banker's boxes stood in lines stacked four boxes high waiting to be shredded. There was still a chance. I quickly pulled a box from the stack and put it on a review table. I lifted the lid to thousands of pages of documents neatly packed inside. No green flags. No red flags.

Maybe it was a box of duds. I pulled another one and found the same thing. And another and another. I began to worry that the tabs had been pulled off after the project was over. Then I would be more likely to win the lottery than find a smoking gun. I began ripping the lids off of every box on the top row in a vain effort to find red flags. The shredding crew and whoever was monitoring them would ride up the elevator at any moment. I feverishly took down boxes one after another and scanned the contents. I stacked the useless boxes back in an increasingly disorganized row.

I found nothing. Hopelessness descended. I pulled off a lid. Dozens of little red sticky tabs standing on end. A rush of adrenaline coursed through my body. My heart pounded and I pulled red-flagged documents out of the thick stack of papers packed into the box. I quickly reviewed one. An email between Steve Powell and Frank Yost. Motherload! Before I could pull more, the old industrial elevator kick into gear and there were heavy footfalls on the metal stairs. The elevator's ancient gears gnashed together as it approached the Backwater.

"Fuck!," I yelled quietly through my breath.

I quickly restacked the boxes and put the box with the red flags at the end of the row. I ran as far from them as I could get before the elevator doors opened. A chime rang at a ridiculously loud volume and I heard one of the doors separating the elevator bank from the floor groan agape. I prayed it was the overnight cleaning crew. I sheltered in Aaron's cubicle to discretely catch a glimpse of whoever was cutting through the office.

Moments later I heard squeaky wheels rolling into the Backwater along with laughter and men's voices. "They're in the middle. Roll the dollies over there. Let's stack everything we can fit and make as few trips as we can. I don't like that elevator."

I looked up to see who from Smith Stevens was babysitting. It would be against firm policy to allow a work crew into the Backwater without supervision. I didn't see anyone, just a half dozen Shred & Pulp employees evaluating the boxes. If there was a moment alone, I would run over and pull as many red-flagged documents as I could and head for the stairwell away from the shredding crew. And no one would ever know they were missing.

Dollies squeaked towards the elevator bank one after another. The men's voices echoed until the elevator's large doors shut. Then the mechanical whine of old gears. The floor was silent. I looked up from the cubicle. I was alone again. I jogged on my tiptoes trying to be quiet. Then the side door closest to the stairs opened and clanged shut. I couldn't see who walked through the door, but hoped it was no one I knew. I was stranded in the middle of the Pit and began to walk past rows of workstations back to Aaron's cubicle as naturally as I could. My heart throbbed behind my shirt pocket and anxiety surged through the veins in my neck into my skull. The minutes were running out and every interruption cost me.

As I approached Aaron's desk a voice called out to me from across the floor. "Will Duggan, is that you?" Fuck! It was the absolute last person I wanted or expected to see in the Backwater on a Friday night.

"Will, what a pleasant surprise!," Chuck offered seemingly without irony. "Missing the old place?" He walked in my direction and I decided against being trapped in Aaron's workspace.

As his body came into view, I noticed he was carrying a six-pack of beer in each hand. "Stocking up?"

"I'm making sure all of this stuff goes tonight." He nodded over towards the boxes.

"What's that?"

"Those are the documents pulled from National Union. The bank asked us to shred them, rather than send them back."

"Wow. That's a lot of boxes. I had no idea."

"Well, that was a big review, but it sounds like Harry has it covered. So all of it has a date with the shredder. Did you see the truck?"

"I did, but I didn't know what was going on."

"That was me. I was running late. I had to take care of something out of the office." It didn't take a lot of deep thinking to imagine what Chuck was doing instead of being where he was supposed to be on a Friday evening.

"What are you doing here?"

I stammered momentarily. "Uh. I was stopping by Aaron's cubicle because . . ." I looked over towards his desk and noticed a Washington Nationals pennant hanging next to his computer. "He said he was going to leave some tickets for me. I didn't see them, so I'm going to have to connect with him this weekend."

"Late night, huh?"

I looked at my phone and saw that it was after 9:00. "Yeah." Chuck nodded. I couldn't tell if he was buying my story.

He looked at me with an air of expectation. "So, what are you doing now?" His question hung in the air uncomfortably and I wondered if he saw me going through the boxes and was letting me paint myself into a corner.

"What do you mean?"

"Tonight. What are you doing?"

I felt a wave of relief. "Nothing. Tonight. Nothing. Just going home to crash. That's it." In my clumsy mental panic I forgot I was standing in front of a man holding a dozen beers with time to kill.

"Good news. For me at least. Take one of these." I took one of the six-packs and realized I had just made plans for the evening. "Let's put them in my fridge. I'll put the game on."

Of all the things that could've gone wrong, spending the evening watching the Yankees with Chuck never entered my mind. We sat in front of a flat-screen television in Chuck's office. I watched helplessly as the shredding crew rolled load after load of boxes out of the Backwater and onto the old elevator.

Chuck caught me gazing. "Want to go watch? The truck can shred seven thousand pounds of paper an hour. With four hundred boxes weighing about fifty pounds each it should take less than four hours."

Mickey's chances of freedom dimmed further with each delivery to the shredding truck. When Chuck went to the men's room, I stood up and gauged whether or not I could make it to the boxes, retrieve some red-flagged documents and stash them somewhere before he came back. The crew streamed in and out of the Pit with empty then full dollies and the opportunity never materialized.

After more than three hours of torture, the shredding crew's supervisor appeared at Chuck's door. "All done."

"All done?," Chuck asked. "Holy shit. That was fast!"

"Want to see the carnage?" The man held a metal clipboard in his heavy hands. I expected a cigar would be firmly planted between his lips as soon as he left the Backwater.

"Want a beer?," Chuck asked.

"Don't mind if I do." We walked over to the now-empty space. The man looked at the clipboard in his left hand and read between sips. "Four hundred and thirteen boxes. Cross-shredded in the truck out front. Boxes and all. When the remnants get to New Jersey tonight they're going to be pulped." There were small indents in the carpet where the stacks of boxes previously sat. Otherwise, there was no sign the documents were ever in the Backwater.

"Pulped?," I asked. "Like pulp?"

"Exactly. Pulping. It's next level. Even with cross-shredding, there's still a risk someone can reassemble the documents." I nodded as he spoke. "Some clients pulp their documents. It's basically a bleaching process. Between the cross-shredding and the bleaching, no one should be able to piece the documents back together." I had no intention of dumpster diving for National Union's shredded documents, but the bank wasn't taking any chances.

"There must've been some bad stuff in there."

"I don't ask questions. I just shred. They tell me what to shred and I shred. Alright gentlemen. Thanks for the beer. Next stop Jersey." The supervisor headed for the elevator bank and into the Manhattan night.

"I gotta get out of here. I had a long day in Boston."

Chuck smirked for a moment and looked over towards the television hanging from his wall. "I almost forgot. You're a Red Sox fan. Why didn't you say anything?"

"I don't care. Beers sounded good. Thanks, Chuck." I wondered if my explanation sounded as hollow to him as it did to me, but he didn't react.

I staggered out of the Backwater more from the weight of disappointment than the beers. After crossing 53rd Street I remembered the Blue Peanut. Shit. I turned on my heel from Eighth Avenue in the direction of Ninth. I arrived at the bus stop. The Blue Peanut was nowhere to be found. By now it was probably sitting in a tow pound on Twelfth Avenue.

It dawned on me that my briefcase with the keys to my apartment were sitting on the passenger seat of the car. I left spare keys in the Temple and thought better of trying to retrieve the Blue Peanut. Asking the NYPD to release the car to me with four beers in my system wouldn't improve my situation. Tomorrow's problem was for tomorrow. I started walking towards Times Square.

As I rode the long escalator up to the lobby, workers streamed out of the building. There always seemed to be a meeting or a shift ending any time day or night. My office felt fresh when I stepped into it. My desktop was disinfected, and the carpet looked recently vacuumed. I stood on my tiptoes and reached my hand to the top of my bookshelves. I felt for my spare keys. As I strained upwards I realized my shelves looked empty.

I grasped my keyring with my index finger and stepped back. All of my white National Union binders were gone. The binders that Tripper gave me were nowhere to be seen along with a binder of materials I used to prepare the jury research script and the binder where I kept the scripts themselves. I felt panicked. Did Chuck tell someone I was in the Backwater? Maybe he had seen me going through the boxes. And the offer of beer was just to kill time while my office was cleaned out.

I inventoried the rest of my shelves. My books and other binders were still there. My notebooks with illegible scribbles and doodles still sat on my desk. I opened my closet. My emergency shirts and suit were hanging where I left them. I looked at my computer monitor and noticed my laptop was missing. Oh, shit. Then I remembered it was in my briefcase on the passenger seat of the Blue Peanut. I prayed it would stay there. Otherwise, I'd be having an extremely awkward conversation with firm security on Monday.

I poked my head out into the hallway and looked both ways, but there was no one visible. Am I being paranoid? I dug my cellphone out of my pocket and found Knuckles' contact info and tapped it. The phone rang for a long time, but he finally picked up. It was after midnight and I wondered if he was still out.

"Will, hold on! Let me step outside." It was a full shift. Maybe it was soda the whole time. "All right. Tell me something good. Watcha got?"

I took a deep breath. "I got nothing."

"Nothing?"

"Nothing."

"They beat you there?"

"Worse. I got nabbed by a partner and watched a Yankees game with him while they carried the boxes away."

"Holy shit. I'm sorry, Will. You made the effort, though. That's all you can do."

I felt my eyes getting glassy and didn't want to crack in front of Knuckles, even if it was only over the phone. "Thanks, Kevin." I sighed deeply.

"Listen, don't beat yourself up. Even if you got there first, there was no guarantee it was going to work. A lot of things could've gone wrong. And, importantly, you would've had to get Sarah Moore to bite. And that wasn't a sure thing. It could have all gone sideways. And you know that. In the realm of bad things that could've happened, this was the least-worst bad thing. And you get to still be a lawyer and live another day. So, we'll do what we have to do. We'll regroup and get our shit together next week and we'll go from there."

Knuckles' reminder made me feel a little better. But just missing walking away with red-flagged documents was a bitter pill. If I had them, maybe it wouldn't have worked. Or maybe it wouldn't have seemed like a good idea after all. But at least we would've had the option.

"You ok? Hang in there. We're going to keep trying. That's all we can do."

"Thanks, Kevin. I'm ok. I just wish I had the documents." Knuckles could hear the disappointment in my voice.

"Hey, Mickey's no worse off right now than he was when you were in Boston this afternoon. And he might not have been better off anyway. I know he's your brother and it's hard. But you gotta keep your chin up. We have work to do. Call me next week and we'll move the ball forward. I'll be waiting by the phone."

A smile creeped across my lips at the thought of Knuckles waiting by the phone for anyone. After our call ended, I sat at my desk and stared into the sanitized atmosphere of my office for a long time.

CHAPTER TWENTY-FIVE

Full of Surprises

After a nearly sleepless weekend, I dragged myself out of bed to be at the NYPD tow pound before it opened. On Saturday I learned it was closed for the weekend. When I finally sat on the Blue Peanut's cloth seats I was reunited with my briefcase, keys, and laptop. Soon after I was back at the Temple. As I sat down next to Erika at 1:58, I still didn't know why the binders were missing from my office.

"Rough weekend?"

"You don't know the half of it." Before we could get into it, Harry walked into the room and began talking.

"Everyone, thank you for being here. This meeting is going to be short, but I wanted to get everyone together to say thank you in person for all of your hard work." Members of the firm's catering department pushed two rolling trays loaded with champagne on ice into the conference room. "This is a little token of appreciation. After I emailed everyone on Friday, the situation with Austin King and Sarah Moore became very fluid."

"We were already working on papers and basically have the deal done, with whatever minor nits might remain. Of all the class actions and complex cases I have worked on, this was among the smoothest. And getting client buy-in at an early stage was huge. And that's thanks to Patrick and the jury testing team. And a testament to the client 'getting it.'" He punctuated the air with quotation marks. Patrick was sitting on camera and perked up at the sound of his name.

"This is a celebration, so I'm not going to go on and on. But it goes without saying, this is top secret information. National Union, again to its credit, took the allegations seriously and agreed to a large settlement. It didn't want it to drag out. Instead, it wanted to do what it thought was the right thing. And as part of that, the bank made a substantial proffer of documents and information to Austin King and the government. That proffer included some highly confidential information. We have been tasked with mitigating the risk of any of that information becoming public." I wondered how doing the right thing involved hiding dirty documents from the government.

"To that end, someone may be stopping by your office asking for your National Union materials. We're going to collect them and warehouse them. It's a top priority. So, if a member of office services stops in, turn them over. And if they already stopped by, my apologies." I felt relieved that the mystery was solved. "Ok. Really now. I'm going to shut up." Harry smiled at his team. "I'm going to shut up after I say one more thing. Does everyone have a glass of champagne?" He looked around the room and surveyed the participants' hands. He looked at Patrick on the television monitor. "How about you, Patrick?"

"We have mineral water." Barbara appeared on the screen next to him and they both held up glasses of clear liquid.

"Mineral water?" Harry laughed.

"Yeah, Harry. It's not even noon."

"Californians." Harry shook his head. "Have it your way, but after the judge signs off, you're coming out here and we're all going to party for real. No mineral water."

"We'll be there." Patrick grinned.

"Good. Now that I said a lot of things after I said I wouldn't say anything else, I'm going to shut up. But first, everyone raise a glass. Champagne, mineral water or whatever else you have. I've told everyone this is a special place. And those aren't just words. This is a special place. I knew it before I arrived. And that's why we came. This is a special place and you're all special attorneys. And without you, this deal wouldn't have happened. It's a great result. So, cheers everyone!"

Champagne flutes clinked around the room. I wondered how many firms Harry had toasted as being "special." One every three years or so based on his track record. Erika and I clanged glasses and I took a big sip and immediately felt its effects in my head and in my knees.

"I don't know about you, but I'm done for the day."

"Me, too," Erika replied.

I raised my eyebrows. "You? Done for the day? You should get your temperature checked."

She smiled. "I know. I stopped by earlier, but you weren't there. I need to tell you something."

"Sorry. Crazy morning. Shoot."

"This isn't a good place." I shook my head and half-smiled.

"Want to tell me over something other than champagne?"

"Sure."

I sheepishly wandered into St. Pat's just before 3:00 and ordered a beer. Erika strolled in with her briefcase and I waved her over.

"What can I get you?"

She disentangled herself from her bag and beige raincoat. "Buffalo Trace. Neat."

"Wow, a bourbon girl." I teasingly looked at my watch. "I wouldn't have figured it."

"Well, it was passed down to me by my grandmother. All the women in my family drink bourbon."

"That's as good a reason as any."

"She was my hero. She went to Portia School of Law in Boston before there were a lot of law schools admitting women. Because of her, Blanche Barfield, all the Barfield women drink bourbon. I may be a Tavares, but I'm also still a Barfield."

"You know I'm from Dorchester up there?"

"I know that, Will. Anybody that hears you speak knows that. Maybe not Dorchester, but Boston for sure." I smiled and shook my head and realized that even working side-by-side, I knew very little about Erika's personal life other than she was engaged and lived in the Upper West Side.

"I'm pretty sure I know what's coming, but do you want to let the bomb drop, or what?"

Erika took a sip of her drink. "Yeah. I'm out of here."

I nodded my head in an exaggerated way. "Yup. Congrats."

"I've worked on pharmaceutical cases, asbestos cases and some tobacco litigation. But I never worked for a client like that. Even Patrick Cooley was running away. And he defends some of the worst of the worst. And what if I did stick it out? I'd be living my life in the hallways of the firm. I can't tell you how many times I cancelled plans and trips already in just three years. Maybe I'm delusional, but there's gotta be a balance somewhere."

"So where are you going? Doesn't sound like big law if you're looking for a balance."

"No, not big law. I'm going to Aronoff Shepsky."

"That place is a powerhouse. Good for you."

"I feel lucky."

"Well, congrats to that." We clinked glasses and each took a sip.

"So, when are you getting out of here, Will?"

I exhaled deeply. "As soon as I can, but Aronoff Shepsky isn't exactly beating down my door. I can't walk out without another job lined up first. And, frankly, I'm not going to match my salary here anyplace else. And it's really helpful right now."

"Right now?"

"Want another drink?"

"Hmm, you answered a question with a question. Now I'm even more curious." She looked down at the shallow end of the bourbon pool. She circled the tumbler in her hand releasing the bourbon's honey aroma. "If you're gonna talk, I'll have a drink. But it better be good. I don't usually have three drinks before 4:00 on a Monday." She looked at me with a sideways glance as she sipped the last of the Buffalo Trace.

I sipped the last of my beer. "I think I'm going to have to get one of those first."

"Ooh, this must be good, but beer before liquor? That's a rookie move."

"It's a risk I'm going to have to take."

"I'm dying now. What could it be? You cracked up your dad's Ferrari and he's making you pay for it?"

I smiled and shook my head. "Not quite."

"You, um, have a crazy drug habit. And you're blowing four hundred dollars a day on coke." I shook my head again. "Am I getting close at least?"

"I'm not saying a word until my drink gets here."

"Ok. Wait. I got it. You have a baby mama in every borough!" Erika's eyes and mouth opened wide with excitement. "That's it! You're secretly a lothario with Will Duggan franchises all over New York . . ."

"I wish. Well, I don't really wish that, but it's a better story."

Erika looked anxiously down the bar for our drinks. "Here they come!"

I felt slightly buzzed and apprehensive when the bourbons arrived. We lifted room-temperature glasses off of the wooden bar.

"To Aronoff Shepsky!"

Erika replied, "to good stories!"

We clinked glasses and the bourbon awakened my senses as it crossed my tongue and slipped down my throat. I suddenly felt very alive.

"All right. So spill 'em!"

"The beans?"

"No! Your guts!"

"Ok. But you gotta promise me this is under a vow of trust and secrecy. I need you to keep it in the vault."

"You're making me more anxious. I promise. I won't tell. It's our job to keep secrets."

"And to spill them strategically," I cracked.

"You have my word, Will. I won't tell a soul. Tell me! Please! I'm begging you!"

"Ok, ok." I took another sip of bourbon and scanned the bar. I looked down at the bar top for a moment while I found the words. "My brother. My older brother Mickey. Well, his name is Michael. Um, he's in prison."

The excitement that had just crested on Erika's face crashed suddenly and her expression went blank. "Holy shit!"

"Yeah. He's been in prison for almost twenty years."

"Jesus! For what?"

"For felony murder. But it's not what you think."

"Oh my God. What happened?"

"He was in the wrong place at the wrong time, basically. He, um, picked up his friend at a donut shop and a few minutes later they were pulled over by police." Erika watched with wide eyes. "He goes to the stationhouse and starts answering questions. He hasn't done anything wrong and waives the right to an attorney. He figures he doesn't need one. He tells the cops he picked up his friend, who told him to get out of there fast, so he did. Turns out his friend had just robbed the donut shop and shot a sixteen-year-old cashier to death. Felony murder."

"Jesus Christ . . ." Erika looked stunned.

"The friend doesn't say a word to anyone and doesn't speak at trial. Mickey's public defender tells him to take a deal because he's cooked. So, he takes life with parole eligibility after fifteen years. The first year in prison his friend kills himself. No note. Never tells anyone what happened. And Mickey stayed in prison. He was denied parole at fifteen years. And was just denied again. He won't be up for another three years."

"Shit. Will, I'm so sorry."

"It is what it is, but thanks. He's why I went to law school. I thought I'd figure out how to get him released. But that didn't work out that way. Thankfully, though, I got a job and made contacts. And my salary allowed me to hire a great attorney in Boston."

"What about your family?"

"He's kind of my only family. Different dads. They're gone. And our mom died years ago. He was taking care of me when he was arrested."

"I don't know what to say. I, I feel embarrassed. If I ever complained about anything. I had no idea."

"No, no. Don't worry about it. No one knows. Just you now. Oh, and Knuckles."

"Knuckles?"

"Sorry. Kevin Sullivan. The criminal lawyer. Everyone calls him 'Knuckles.'"

"He must be a character."

"You don't know the half of it." I circled the bourbon in the glass. "It was probably kind of pointless. All of it. The parole board wants to see rehabilitation and remorse. He wouldn't admit to anything and he wouldn't say he's sorry for something he didn't do. And they only have the record in front of them. So he's been denied."

"There's no one?"

"Literally no one. Knuckles had investigators turn over every rock and there's nothing. I saw Mickey last week and he seems ready to say what he has to say to get out. The only problem is he's not up for parole for almost three more years."

"Oh, crap."

"Yeah. So, unless something big happens . . ."

"How big?"

"Real big. Big like Mickey's friend comes back from the grave or the governor pardons him."

"Shit."

"I know. Knuckles is going to see if he can do something on an emergency basis, but it doesn't seem like it's going to work."

"Why's it an emergency?" I sipped my bourbon. "Some guys found out he's in there for a teenager's murder . . . and, um, they aren't too happy with him."

"Holy shit . . ."

I looked towards the floor and my mouth pursed to the side as I thought about the National Union scheme.

"What? What is it?" Erika craned her neck to look at me.

"Nothing."

"That doesn't look like nothing. What's going on?"

"I guess it doesn't matter. Are we still under the vow of trust and secrecy?"

"Of course."

"Promise?"

"I promise."

"Because this is big."

"You're making me nervous. But tell me. Gimme some dirt!"

"Another round?"

"If this is big, sure."

"Ok. Yeah. But I'm going back to beer."

"Yet another rookie move. You're going to regret that."

"Probably, but at least I'll be able to walk out of here."

"Well, there's that, I suppose."

"Alright. Vow of trust and secrecy. Remember during the jury testing there was that 'dark and underrepresented' email? And then Aaron told me it was the tip of the iceberg?"

"Yeah."

"And he said he saw the n-word and a bunch of other stuff?"

"Um-hmm."

"Well, obviously, Smith Stevens and National Union never told Austin King or Sarah Moore. At least as far as we know."

"Right."

"Maybe not so much with Austin, but with Sarah, since she was doing an investigation for the DOJ, those documents should've been disclosed. And any false statement Smith Stevens or National Union made to the DOJ to hide their existence is a crime."

"Alright. What were you going to do? Report them?"

"Kind of. If the DOJ was interested, I wanted to try to work out a deal for Mickey."

"What about the attorney-client privilege? Wouldn't you get disbarred?"

"Usually that's right. But there's an exception to the attorney-client privilege. The crime-fraud exception. If National Union communicated with

Smith Stevens about hiding bad documents from the DOJ, the privilege doesn't apply."

"That sounds tricky. I'm no expert, but it seems kind of thin."

"It's definitely tricky. My problem was the DOJ might not have been interested."

"And maybe they saw the stuff anyway and it was useless," Erika offered.

"It doesn't matter anyway."

"Why not?"

"Smith Stevens destroyed all of National Union's documents. I was in Boston and raced back, but it was too late. I saw them leaving the building."

"Your word isn't enough?"

"Nah, Knuckles said I needed something to back it up. Or I'd get flattened."

"Shit. What about your binders?"

"They're gone, too. They cleaned out my office while I was in Boston. There wasn't anything in there that was useful anyway. I didn't even have a copy of the 'dark and underrepresented' email."

"That's not what I'm talking about." I had no idea and shook my head. "BestRateLoan."

I tried to find and capture a memory, which was increasingly obscured by beer and bourbon. I mouthed, "BestRateLoan."

"BestRateLoan. Tripper gave us the binders. Remember?"

"Tripper told me about the loan ratings. They changed and he said sometimes they change and that it was BestRateLoan's job to do its due diligence."

Erika's eyebrows raised towards her hairline. "Well, yeah. For sure. BestRateLoan should do its due diligence, but that's not the only interested party." She looked at me like a law professor waiting for an answer.

"The FDIC . . ."

"Yes!" Erika looked excited. "The FDIC. Because BestRateLoan is insured by the FDIC. If National Union misrepresents the value of the loans to BestRateLoan it's fraud. It's a violation of FIRREA."

"Ferea?"

"Yeah, FIRREA. The Financial Institutions Reform, Recovery and Enforcement Act of 1989."

My head was spinning, but Erika was only getting more excited. "Nerd alert!"

Erika smirked and shook her head. "You're going to thank me in a minute."

"Ok."

"Remember the residential mortgage-backed securities scandal? That was FIRREA. The federal government used it to go after banks that sold those securities and misrepresented the quality of the underlying mortgages to purchasers. It used FIRREA because some of the entities that invested in those securities were insured by the FDIC."

Erika nodded at me for an acknowledgment of understanding. I wasn't entirely following where she was going. "I'm listening . . ."

"Alright. Every misrepresentation made by the banks to investors insured by the FDIC could result in a fine of more than a million dollars. And when there are thousands of mortgages involved and misrepresentations were made about each one of those mortgages, the millions of dollars turn into billions of dollars in fines. And that's why some of the banks paid multiple billions of dollars in fines to the government after they were caught. It's huge."

"But National Union isn't selling securities."

Erika sighed. "No. National Union isn't selling securities. It's selling mortgages. And it's selling mortgages to BestRateLoan, which is insured by the FDIC. So, if National Union is misrepresenting the risk ratings of the mortgages it's selling to BestRateLoan, it has violated FIRREA. It's fraud and triggers FIRREA's penalty provisions. And National Union would be subject to a one-point-one-million-dollar penalty for every misrepresentation. Think about it. There are thousands of loans being sold. And every single misrepresentation could trigger a one point one million dollar fine. If they misrepresented the quality of a thousand loans, that's over a billion dollars in penalties."

"That's a lot of cheese."

"A lot of cheese! I researched it and this is just the kind of thing the DOJ would love to sink its teeth into. Fraud committed by a bank. The hardest part, and there have been some court decisions about it, is for the DOJ to prove that a bank intended to commit fraud at the time it entered into an agreement. But I think we can serve that up pretty easy here." Erika seemed more enthusiastic about turning in National Union for fraud than I had been to trade information for Mickey's freedom.

"You seem like you've done a lot of homework. I'm just wondering why."

"Well," Erika took a sip from her tumbler. "That class action settlement is bullshit. I can't believe what Aaron saw and that National Union is getting away with it. Something seemed fishy about the BestRateLoan deal when I first saw the binders. I told you. It just started to gnaw at me. I did my research and figured out the FIRREA thing. I was thinking about blowing the whistle myself on the DOJ's anonymous tip line. And then the Aronoff Shepsky gig came through. I didn't want to blow the whistle and light your client and maybe you on fire on the way out the door. Now I'm really glad I didn't. I think this is the bait you need. I don't know. Maybe this is the way it was meant to be."

"I'm glad you didn't, either. But I have one small problem. Maybe that's one huge problem."

"What's that?"

"The binders. I don't have the binders anymore. They got cleaned out with my jury testing stuff. I was lucky anything was left in my office."

"Shit. They came by and I turned over all my stuff, too. I wasn't planning on using it, so I handed it all over." We looked at each other grimacing. I stroked my chin as I tried to think of a solution. No matter how much I rubbed it, one didn't materialize.

"Charlene!" Erika nearly screamed. "Charlene the paralegal. She works on all of David's stuff. And she has that wall of binders. They have to be in there."

I was momentarily lost in the tranquil warmth of the alcohol streaming through my veins, but snapped to attention. "Shit! You're right! Charlene! But how are we going to get them? She's going to get curious if I ask for them. And she locks her door behind her. Even when she gets a coffee from the breakroom. She guards that room like it's full of state secrets."

"What about Tripper?"

"Also too weird. He'd be very curious if I asked him for copies again."

"Hmm. What if you just told the DOJ?"

"What if I'm wrong? Knuckles was adamant that I have something in hand to back up what I'm saying. I don't want to get flattened."

Erika chewed on her thumbnail as she looked at the ceiling lost in thought. "What if we stole Charlene's keys?" She gazed into space without looking at me.

"She's going to realize it the second she can't get back in her office. And they're going to change the locks for her."

"Will, you're such a pessimist. What if she doesn't know they're gone?"

"And how do you plan to make that happen?"

"Perhaps I'll invite her to a liquid lunch to thank her for smoothing out my path here at Smith Stevens." Erika was smiling widely. I could see she was enjoying the thought of taking a swing at National Union.

"I haven't known Charlene to turn down a free cocktail or two."

"Or three or four. And I owe her a few," Erika followed with a wry smile.

"So, what are we going to do?"

Erika looked devilish. "I'll take care of getting the keys. And you take care of getting the binders."

"How are you going to get those?"

"At some point she's going to have to use the bathroom. Right? And I'll just borrow them from her purse. And you get the binders and bring the keys back to me before she realizes they're gone."

"Sounds pretty straightforward." I lifted my half empty pint glass and grinned big. "To your retirement from Smith Stevens!"

"To nailing those fuckers!" Erika laughed as we clinked our glasses together.

CHAPTER TWENTY-SIX

Execution

My cellphone buzzed and I placed a half-full bottle of Xingu on the neat wooden bar in front of me. It was just after 2:30 on Thursday afternoon. Portuguese drifted around Via Brasil. I looked at a message from Erika. "Go Time!"

I left a twenty-dollar bill on the bar and skipped out the front door. I passed a group of tourists strolling and smoking cigarettes and took a quick right turn into St. Pat's. I immediately saw Erika sitting alone at the bar. There was an empty seat to her right. Charlene's black purse hung from the barstool. Erika waved at me furiously. Before I could reach her she flung a set of keys in my direction that spun like blades on a ring in the air.

I snatched the keys from their flight and hurried towards the door without saying a word. As soon as I stepped onto the concrete in front of the bar I broke into a full sprint. I ran as fast as my wingtips' leather soles would carry me. I dodged and weaved my way through tourists and strode off the curb and began running down 46th Street against traffic. I crossed Sixth Avenue and continued sprinting for Times Square. I took for granted how much sidewalk separated Sixth and Seventh Avenues.

My necktie flapped around my chest while my unbuttoned suit jacket formed wings behind me as I ran. I carried an empty black backpack in my left hand and pumped furiously with my right arm as I raced towards the Temple. I could hear Charlene's keys jangling in my pocket. My heartbeat accelerated before I started running. Now it felt as though my heart would explode in my chest. I was breathing heavily. Sweat rolled down my forehead and dampened the back of my dress shirt.

I finally spotted the glass façade of the Temple from across Times Square and bolted towards it. I hoped no one from the firm saw me running wildly. I stopped before crossing the street and quickly rearranged my tie and buttoned my jacket to hide my shirt, which was now soaked. I used my pink silk pocket square to wipe sweat from my forehead and stuffed it back into my pocket. I took a heavy breath with my belly extended. As collected as I could make myself, I strode across the street and stepped inside of the air-conditioned escalator bank.

The ride up was an eternity, followed by another eternity in an elevator. The doors opened to the 48th floor. I repeated "go time" to myself out loud. As I walked down the quiet hallway, not a single person looked up at me or in my direction. I took Charlene's keys out of my pocket and found the one that looked similar to the key to my office. I pushed her door in and the ceiling lights turned on as the door passed the motion detector. Shelves covered every inch of available wall space from floor to ceiling. An open binder sat on her desk.

I looked at the thousands of white binders resting on her shelves. Each one was labeled and there were multiple copies. All of them were arranged alphabetically by client name and then matter name. I touched my finger to the shelves in the middle of the wall and worked my way to the N's. "National

Union" was first and there were hundreds of binders for open matters. I located binders that read "BestRateLoan Deal Documents" and pulled the first copy I found. It was a newer copy of the one Tripper gave me. I shoved the thick binder into my backpack.

My phone vibrated in my jacket pocket. "Hurry! She says she has to go. Trying to stall."

"Fuck!," I yelled in a whisper. I typed back. "Hurrying!"

I began searching for the Wampanoag deal binder. I quickly scanned all of the National Union binders, but there was nothing that began with W. There was a knock on the door then silence. I froze in my tracks and stood motionless. Frosted glass framing the doorway separated me from whoever was outside. I didn't know if he or she could see my shadow. Another knock was followed by a man's voice. The doorknob twisted, but it locked when the door shut behind me and didn't open.

"Charlene are you in there?" My heart skipped a beat. I tried to remain motionless. Then it began to beat so hard I thought he would hear it through the door. "Angela, do you know if Charlene's in there?" The knob twisted again, but still didn't open. I couldn't hear the woman respond. "Maybe she's on the phone," the man said. His shoes scuffed the carpet as he walked away. I let out another deep breath.

I doublechecked for a W and there was nothing. I checked the binder on Charlene's desk, but it belonged to another client. I went back to the shelf where I found the "BestRateLoan" binder. I scanned it with my finger and reviewed the remaining copies of the "BestRateLoan Deal Documents" binder. I followed it to the end this time. The next binders were labeled, "BestRateLoan Due Diligence." I pulled a copy and stuffed it into the backpack. I traced my finger along all of the remaining National Union binders, but there was nothing else that said BestRateLoan or Wampanoag.

Another text buzzed in my pocket. "Hurry!!!" A shiver ran through my body.

"Tell her I'm coming for a drink. On the way!!!" I zipped the black backpack closed and slid it over my shoulder. I cracked the door open quietly and heard nothing. I cracked it open wider and peered down the hall in the direction of the elevator bank. The coast was clear. I stepped out and closed the door as quietly as I could and paced towards the elevators.

"Hey, was Charlene in there?" I froze and Xingu nearly released down my pant leg.

"Hmm?" I turned around. Tan khakis, a plain black polo shirt and a pair of black sneakers. No self-respecting Smith Stevens attorney would wear black sneakers into the Temple.

"Was Charlene in there?"

I channeled Chuck MacPherson. "Charlene?"

"Yeah. Charlene Parent. Didn't you just come out of her office?"

"Nope." I turned and marched down the hall towards the elevators without looking back. It was probably the third or fourth time something like that had happened to him that day in the Temple. I was sure he just added me to his lifetime hitlist. I hoped he couldn't figure out who I was from the firm's website.

I passed through the glass doorway without being noticed further and waited for the elevator to arrive. The now-heavy black backpack draped awkwardly from my left shoulder and crumpled my suit jacket. My body heat pressed wrinkles across the shoulder and sleeve. The elevator chimed as it arrived. I nearly gasped as the brushed steel doors parted and revealed David Bell standing next to a man I had never seen before. We immediately made eye contact and having no other choice, I stepped in.

"Will, where have you been? I wanted to introduce you to Mr. Saito. Jiyu, this is Will Duggan. He's one of our litigators." Mr. Saito looked in my direction.

"Nice to meet you, Will Duggan." He bowed his head slightly and I returned the bow.

"Nice to meet you, Mr. Saito."

"Will, see me tomorrow. I want to discuss Mr. Saito's matter." Mr. Saito looked at David and frowned slightly. "Or should I say his company's matter."

Mr. Saito smiled and nodded at David's correction. "Thank you."

"That is if you're going to be here tomorrow. You going camping or something?"

"Aah, hah. Ah, no. No camping. Just bringing some stuff home."

David deliberately looked at his watch and clucked his tongue. "Must be nice."

"I'll be back," I said in a panic. I could feel my cheeks blush and I wondered how sweaty my hair looked. All of it was suspicious and I wouldn't have been surprised if he thought I was having a breakdown.

"Take it easy. I think you're entitled to an afternoon off. Jiyu, Will here was a huge help on a big problem for a client recently. He worked night and day. And through his efforts and those of others it turned into a huge success. We're lucky we have him." I was less prepared for that response than just about anything else David could have said to me at that moment.

"Well, then we are lucky to have him, too." Mr. Saito smiled. Before I could respond, the doors chimed open.

"Get some rest and come in here fresh tomorrow. We have a lot to catch up on." David led Mr. Saito to the reception desk and I hurriedly walked towards the escalator.

My phone buzzed again. "Where are you????"

"Running!!!!!"

I pushed my way through revolving doors onto the street. Without knowing if I was in view of David and Mr. Saito, I began to sprint back to St. Pat's. The black backpack wouldn't stay put. I slipped the empty strap over my right shoulder and snapped the backpack's belt shut in front of my stomach with its plastic buckle.

The backpack rocked back and forth with my alternating strides. I reached the front door of the bar and panted with both hands on my knees. As I looked at the sidewalk and corralled my lunch in my stomach, I noticed I had worn through the toes of the leather soles of my wingtips. I could feel the pavement with what remained of my striped socks. I wiped my forehead clean with my pocket square, unsnapped the backpack, and draped it over my shoulder like a college student.

Erika's eyes were shooting arrows at the door as I walked in. She mouthed, "what the fuck?," as we made eye contact.

I mouthed, "sorry," back in an exaggerated fashion.

She put her fingers in front of her lips to shush me and then pointed at Charlene's black Michael Kors purse hanging from the back of her barstool by a long strap. Chatter and the sound of the jukebox masked my footsteps. I pulled Charlene's keys out of my pocket and as I stepped closer I stretched my right arm downwards and quietly dropped the keys through the open zipper.

"Charlene and Erika!"

"Thank God! The second shift is here! I gotta get back. Joe Moriarty is having a panic attack and has been harassing me since I got here. He can't find a document and I couldn't lead him to water. He's probably going to be at my door when I get there. Angela says he's been stalking my office." Charlene stood up. "Alright, sweetheart. Give me a hug. I'm gonna miss you. You're one of the good ones. Don't forget that." She gave Erika a sloppy hug that wrapped up Erika's small torso.

"But this guy." She pointed her thumb at me. "He's just the worst." Charlene then mock-punched my chest and laughed. "Just kidding! You're one of the good ones, too." She pointed her finger at me. "Don't get any ideas, mister. You're not going anywhere." Little did she know.

Charlene gave me a strong hug and pulled her purse by the strap from her barstool. She looked down at it after it was on her shoulder. "Hmm," vibrated out of her pursed lips. She drew the zipper shut. "Don't stay out too late, kids." I took over her barstool and hung the backpack where Charlene's purse had been.

"Buffalo Trace?," Erika teased. I looked at her for a long time. "So how'd it go?"

"Well, I feel like I might drop dead. I had no idea I was in such bad shape. Then I had Joe Whatshisface breathing down my neck looking for Charlene. And afterwards I rode the elevator down to the street with David Bell."

"Holy shit!"

"I know. It was heart attack city, but I think I hit paydirt." I scanned the bar and put the backpack on my lap. I unzipped it and revealed the two large white binders inside.

"Let's see what you got!"

I pulled out the first binder and read out loud. "BestRateLoan Deal Documents."

Erika put it on her lap and angled it open against the edge of the bar. She began leafing through the pages until she found the schedule of the mortgages being transferred from National Union to BestRateLoan.

"What's that?," she asked looking at the second binder.

"BestRateLoan Due Diligence."

"What is it?"

I opened it and looked inside. "It looks like a copy of the Wampanoag deal binder. It must be a copy of what National Union sent to BestRateLoan during due diligence."

"Find the schedule of mortgages that were transferred from Wampanoag to National Union."

I began flipping through the pages until I located the schedule. "Here."

Erika lined the schedules next to each other and began to run her index fingers down the corresponding pages. "On the first page there were risk ratings that didn't match up. That's weird."

"What?"

"All the risk ratings match up." She flipped the pages and did the same exercise with her fingers. After a couple of minutes of concentration, "same here." She flipped page after page with the same result. She scrunched her face and turned to me. "Will, either I'm going crazy, or someone switched the schedule in the Wampanoag binder given to BestRateLoan."

"I don't think you're crazy. I wouldn't put anything past National Union."

"There are too few high-risk loans for this to be the original Wampanoag schedule. And that would explain why BestRateLoan's lawyers haven't figured it out. That's some shady shit."

"What else would you expect?"

"And that was it? You couldn't find the original Wampanoag binder?"

"I searched for it, but it wasn't there. Everything was in alphabetical order. And there was nothing under W. I was lucky I found the due diligence binder before I came running."

"Do you think it's enough?"

"I don't know. Knuckles said I needed to have something to show the DOJ. I hope it is. It's all I got."

"Can you call him?"

I punched Knuckles' contact information. "My favorite big shot New York City attorney!" I could hear music and the chatter of a crowded bar. "Willy Boy, what's up?"

"Kevin, I think we got something. Something I think I can use to help Mickey."

Knuckles paused for a moment and I could only hear bar noise. "Wait, what? Sorry, Will. It's loud in here."

Erika watched with fascination as I yelled into the phone. "I have something I think can help Mickey."

"Really? That's great. I'm not in a good place to talk. Call me tomorrow and we'll hash it out. I'm in the office all day. Or at least until two-ish. Call me in the morning, but not too early."

"Ok, Kevin."

"Hey Will!"

"Yeah?"

"You're the best brother. Don't forget that!"

Before I could say thanks, the phone clicked off and I turned to Erika. "He said to call him tomorrow."

"He can't talk tonight?"

"He's not exactly working Smith Stevens hours. And nothing's going to happen tonight anyway."

"Must be nice."

After another round, Erika and I parted ways in separate cabs. When I returned home, I hid the binders in my kitchen cupboard. The evening turned to morning and I lay in bed awake too excited to fall asleep. I hoped what I dragged out of Charlene's office would be enough for the DOJ. I waited anxiously for my call with Knuckles.

CHAPTER TWENTY-SEVEN

So Close

Knuckles groaned on the other end of the line. "You're breaking my heart right now, you know that?"

"And why's that?"

"Why's that? Why do you think? You know how close I was to being rich beyond my wildest dreams? And you, too!" I sat silently on my cellphone. The only noise in my office was the sound of cold air being forced down from the vent in the ceiling. "Attorneys dream of this kind of thing walking into their office. So close . . ." Knuckles' voice trailed off.

"If you weren't National Union's attorney, you could've been a whistleblower and gotten a cut of the government's recovery. We would've filed a *qui tam* complaint and neither of us would've worked another day in our lives. If the government's case against National Union is worth billions, our award could've been hundreds of millions."

"I'm sorry to disappoint you," I jested.

"It's not real, you know that. What would I do if I were rich? Eat caviar all day and sleep by the pool. That's not living. And I wouldn't have any new stories to tell. It's not the natural order of things."

"I guess not."

"So you're sure about this?"

"A hundred and ten percent."

"If you're wrong about the fraud, you've breached the attorney-client privilege and there's no crime-fraud exception to save you. I could be representing you in a criminal case. Got it?"

"I got it. The BestRateLoan binder is the latest version. Someone changed the schedule of the mortgages in the Wampanoag binder given to BestRateLoan during due diligence. It doesn't have as many high-risk loans as the original, even on the first page. This thing is probably going to close any day."

"Then we have to do this immediately before someone else figures it out and reports it."

"When you say immediately—"

Knuckles cut me off. "Today. There's no time to waste. I have a contact in the DOJ in Boston, Imani Walker, and I'll call her as soon as we're off."

"Not Sarah Moore."

"No. First, I want to keep this in Massachusetts. It gives us the best chance to have pressure applied where we need it. And second, let's just say Sarah Moore has enough going on with the class action. I don't want this thing buried somehow to save face. You're sure you're sure about this? I've already told you you're the best brother. You don't need to do this to win the award."

"I'm sure, Kevin."

"Alright. But if you're wrong about the schedule in the Wampanoag binder and it gets back to National Union or Smith Stevens—"

I didn't let Knuckles finish. "I know. I know. I'm probably going to get disbarred and then prosecuted."

"And you're still sure? You could be sharing a cell with Mickey."

"I'm still sure. Whatever happens happens. But I have to try."

"Best brother ever. Hands down. I'll call you as soon as I have news."

Knuckles hung up the receiver without saying "goodbye." I sat in my office and felt the drumbeat of my heart. It was Friday morning and Smith Stevens was a morgue. David opted to have a long weekend and pushed our meeting about Mr. Saito's case until next week. A coffee in Times Square was a needed distraction. I meandered slowly down the hallway, as if eating up time with a slow walk would make the day pass more quickly. I tapped the down button in the elevator bank. The pocket in front of my heart began to buzz. I contorted my right arm and struggled to pull the phone out of a small opening inside of my suit jacket. The phone trembled in my shaking hand.

I clicked the answer button and blurted, "So what happened?" I was so anxious I couldn't help myself.

"No promises, but Amani is interested."

"That's great news!" My heart raced and I felt momentarily elated. "We have some traction, right? It's not going in the wrong direction."

"True. But I don't want to get our hopes up. And I don't want to jinx anything, so let's be cool."

"I'll try."

"I need those binders. How fast can you get them to me?"

"They're in the cupboard in my kitchen."

"In the cupboard in your kitchen? You're even more paranoid than me! So how soon?"

"I'll get out of here and drive them up this afternoon. Is that soon enough?"

"That's great, but you could just overnight them."

"Too paranoid for that. I don't want to let them out of my sight. What about the original Wampanoag binder? Did Amani ask?"

"The DOJ can get it. Either from regulators or Wampanoag's former lawyer. If the DOJ bites, National Union isn't going to find out until it's too late to play hide-the-ball."

"See you in about six hours or so."

"Alright, Will."

As soon as the phone clicked, I returned to my office to pack up my laptop and briefcase and snuck out of the firm. Around 4:30 I passed through security and pushed the button in the elevator bank of a building on Custom House Street in Boston. The elevator glided to the seventh floor and opened inside of a glass cube in the middle of an open-style office space. A reception desk sat facing the glass cube. As I pushed open the door, I was immediately greeted by a twenty-something man, who had started packing his things to leave for the weekend.

"Hi. Who are you here to see?"

"Kevin Sullivan."

The office space was dotted with workstations, and similar to Smith Stevens, the floor was ringed with offices, each one with a view of the surrounding area. The Rose Kennedy Greenway on one side and Faneuil Hall in the other direction.

"There he is!," Knuckles bellowed moments later. I stood up and shook his hand. He held my elbow as we shook. "Can I get you anything? How about a beer?" He pointed towards the glass wall of a conference room. There were buckets filled with ice and cold bottles of wine and beer.

"Sounds good."

"Friday afternoon we always have wine and beers. It's called the 'wine-down.' This is your first time here?" I had never visited Knuckles' office. I imagined him sitting at a large wooden desk in an aging space surrounded by stacks of dusty boxes of closed client files. Instead, the space was open, full of light and airy. And also full of people.

"I thought you were solo."

"I am. This is a shared space. All lawyers, but I'm the only criminal guy. There are trust and estates, personal injury, and other civil litigators. You name it. It's good for referrals."

The floor was emptying out, but those that remained greeted Knuckles as if he were the mayor. His office had a long view of the greenway and was filled with sunlight. His desk was black and sleek, and a large computer monitor sat to one side. Bookshelves framed a large leather couch against the opposite wall. Two comfortable looking leather chairs interrupted the space and faced his desk.

"Ok. Let's see what you got." I hauled the two white binders, one after another, out of my black backpack. "I never would've guessed they'd be white binders."

"This is the BestRateLoan deal binder." Knuckles eased into his desk chair and I slid the binder across the table with the text facing him. "This is the agreement and starting here are all the exhibits and the schedules. And if you flip back here, you'll find the schedule of the mortgages National Union is selling to BestRateLoan. This has all of the mortgage information, including the risk ratings. High, low, average." Knuckles leaned over and examined the schedule.

"And this is the Wampanoag deal binder. It says, 'Due Diligence,' and I believe it's a copy of the binder National Union gave to BestRateLoan during the due diligence process. And here is the schedule of the mortgages that were transferred to National Union when it acquired Wampanoag." I slid the binder in front of Knuckles, and he lined the schedules next to each other. "See. It has the risk ratings. They're here." Knuckles leafed the through pages of both documents and scanned the lines. He traced individual mortgages and risk ratings.

After reviewing page after page of the schedules intently, he finally came up for air. "These look the same to me."

"I think they are the same."

"And the original Wampanoag binder had a different schedule?"

"It did."

"Ok. Walk me through what happened. I need to be conversant for Amani."

"We were doing the jury testing and I was tasked with putting up a business defense. We were given a lot of binders by a corporate attorney who works on National Union's deals. He didn't know what to give us, so he gave us everything he had, including the Wampanoag binder and the BestRateLoan binder. While I was doing the script for the defense, the associate who was helping me started reviewing all of the binders and she noticed the ratings changed between the Wampanoag binder and the BestRateLoan binder.

"I asked the corporate guy and he said that the ratings change sometimes. But a lot of ratings had improved. High-risk loans became average-risk. And average-risk loans became low-risk loans. And there were very few high-risk loans left. It seemed strange that the loans improved over time."

"Like with plumbing, that's not likely." Knuckles smiled. "So, you saw this? Or did just she see it?"

"She showed me, and I saw it. You can see there are thousands of loans. But I saw at least a few hundred loans and probably more than a thousand that had been changed for the better."

"That's good. And what's her deal? This associate?"

"She's leaving the firm to go to another shop. She said she was going to blow the whistle, but didn't want to burn me on the way out the door."

"You sure she kept it to herself?"

"I am. If it weren't for Erika, I wouldn't have this stuff."

"That's good. And the original Wampanoag binders?"

"They're gone. The firm came around and took the National Union stuff from everyone that worked on the jury research."

"That's ok. Like I told you, the DOJ can track them down without alerting Smith Stevens or National Union. It's the DOJ after all. Got anything else we can use? Actual smoking guns? Compromising photographs?"

"Naw, that's it. Do you think it'll be enough?"

"If everything you're telling me holds up. And I mean if the risk ratings were tampered with, then that looks like fraud and the DOJ has a helluva case under FIRREA."

"So, I've been told."

"Who told you that?" Knuckles seemed uneasy for a moment.

"Erika. The associate. She knew it in and out."

"You sure she didn't talk to anyone about it?"

"I'm sure. She's smart as a whip. She figured it out on her own."

"Good. Let's keep it that way. There's another thing."

"What's that?"

"If I were you, I'd get ready to get the hell out of Smith Stevens. You prepared for that?"

"I can't say I'm prepared for it. But if this works, then I don't really care what happens."

"If this blows up, you're going to be in a very awkward space. There are some protections for whistleblowers, but you're going to end up with everyone at National Union and Smith Stevens coming after you once they figure out what you did. The DOJ will want to protect its case and will protect you to protect its case. But beyond that, you're on your own."

"This is my last bullet. It's why I went to law school. If this doesn't work, I tried everything else."

"I get it. I'm not going to say it again, but you know how I feel about you. Just be ready to step out. I don't think I'd keep anything important in my office if I were you."

"I don't and I won't. Should I give notice?"

"I wouldn't light myself on fire just yet. We don't know what's going to happen. But it wouldn't hurt to get your resume out there." Knuckles rocked back and forth slightly in his chair after the words left his mouth. "All right, I need to take these binders for a walk."

"A walk?"

"Yeah. I'm heading over to the US Attorney's office to see Amani."

"Can I tag along?"

"I'd love to bring you, but I think as a witness you should stay back and let me run interference. I'm not mentally prepared to defend an interview right now. And I think you're better off giving them space to let them figure out if they can run with it."

"Alright."

"Walk out together?" I stood up to go and Knuckles looked down at a half-empty beer bottle sitting next to my visitor chair and then up at me. "It's one thing to leave a wounded soldier when you have to run out. But this is simply alcohol abuse."

I picked up the bottle and swilled the rapidly warming remainder of the lager. "Satisfied?"

"I don't know if that's the word, but at least I'm not embarrassed for you. C'mon."

When we stepped outside, the streets were buzzing. "I'll let you know if Imani says anything interesting. Otherwise, the ball's in her court and we have to play the waiting game. So, you just sit tight. And I'll let you know as soon as I know anything."

"Sounds like a plan."

"I don't know if it's a plan, but it's all we can do. See you around."

"Thanks, Kevin."

We shook hands and I watched him vanish out of view as he ambled towards the federal courthouse on the edge of Boston Harbor with a white binder under each arm.

CHAPTER TWENTY-EIGHT

Last Stand

Weeks rolled by after Knuckles met with Imani Walker and nothing happened. While I was trying to get used to life after Erika, Aaron's team announced it was leaving Smith Stevens to open the New York office of an Atlanta firm. With my courthouse visits drying up and with Erika and Aaron among the "dearly departed," as we called those who left the firm, I felt much more alone than I had at any prior time in New York.

My work life became a blurred cycle of pushing paper in my office bookended by arriving and departing from the Temple. My human points of contact were limited to my discussions with David and my occasional check-ins with Amanda. My relationship with Tripper became more tenuous after Aaron left, as we found we didn't have much to talk about in Aaron's absence. As I continued to muddle through projects in my grey and sanitized work environment, my cellphone began to buzz and seemed to draw itself to my hand, which was covering a black mouse tethered to my keyboard.

I picked up the phone and answered almost out of breath. "Kevin!"

"Will!" He seemed as excited as I was. "I think I would tell Mickey to start packing his bags if I were you."

"Why's that?"

"Because we got an order from the parole board today?"

"What? What does it say?"

"It says 'Michael Glynn is hereby found eligible for conditional release as of June 14, 2019. Mr. Glynn shall remain within the territorial boundaries of the Commonwealth of Massachusetts for a three-year period from the date of this order. Mr. Glynn shall meet with his parole officer within three days of his release and periodically afterwards during the pendency of this parole period.'"

"Wha . . . What does that mean?"

"It means that Mickey is getting released on Friday."

"What? Why? That's just three days away. What else does it say?"

"Nothing. That's it."

"No decision?"

"No decision. It's just an order."

"Did you file something?"

"I didn't file anything."

"Holy shit!" My heart nearly floated out of my chest. I felt a massive wave of relief wash across my body. "I kind of expected the governor to sign something."

"I would've told you not to hold your breath on that one. My sense is Amani found enough on her own without having to pull you in as a witness. And if she did, she can avoid fighting over the attorney-client privilege and the crime-fraud exception. That could've been a mess. And now you won't have to be in the middle of it. I'd take this as a 'thank you.'"

"That's a hell of a thank you!" I took a moment to gather myself. "So what's next?"

"Well, he's going to have to stick around Massachusetts. He has to meet with a parole officer, and he needs to get a place to stay and a job. There are halfway houses that offer counseling and a place to live—"

"No way! I'll get him an apartment. He's been institutionalized too long already."

"Will, you're going to have to take it easy with him. He's been in there for a long time. And he hasn't had to take care of himself in a long time. You can't just throw him into the world and expect him to thrive."

"Then I'm giving my notice today. I'll get up to Boston tomorrow and start looking for a place. What do I have to do on Friday?"

"Basically, you just wait outside until he walks out a free man. I'll go with you. There'll be other guys leaving. It's kind of like watching a graduation."

I smiled at the thought of it. "Graduation," I repeated. "In the meantime, do you need anything from me?"

"Will, we're square. I'm going to miss you. You're a good kid. You gotta stop by and pay me a visit here and there."

"You got it. Your office on Friday?"

"Meet me at 11:00 and I'll drive us to Cedar Junction."

"Sounds like a plan."

After I hung up the phone, I took a deep breath. Four years of college, three years of law school and more than half a decade in law firms, but my goal of seeing Mickey released was about to be realized. It wasn't how I had planned it, but it didn't matter in the end. Mickey was going to be free. Fueled with adrenaline, I marched down to David's office and gave my notice. Associates leaving for greener pastures was such a common event at Smith Stevens David didn't seem to miss a beat.

On Wednesday morning, I climbed onto an Amtrak Acela to Boston to get a jump on apartment hunting. The train smoothly glided out of Manhattan into Connecticut and Rhode Island. Its gentle rocking was relaxing, but I couldn't completely let go, as my excitement over Mickey's release kept me on edge. As the train pulled out of Providence, my cellphone began to buzz. Aaron. I realized I hadn't told him or Erika I quit.

I clicked the receiver and coyly said, "Hey, stranger," and prepared to be chided for not spreading the news.

Aaron replied excitedly, "Dude, what the fuck is going on?"

I was taken aback. "Ahh . . ."

"Are you at the office?"

"No, no. Why? What's up?"

"I just got a call and was told the FBI was there with a warrant and they took a bunch of files. And they took Tripper away in handcuffs!"

"What?," I nearly yelled, but pulled the word back into my mouth remembering I was in a quiet car.

"You didn't hear?"

"I didn't hear anything. I, I just gave notice yesterday. I'm on the way to Boston."

"Wait, what? You quit?," Aaron yelled. "What the fuck is going on?," he added loudly.

My heart was beating through my chest. "I have no idea. I missed all the excitement. I left yesterday afternoon and haven't heard a thing."

"Holy shit! The most exciting day ever at the firm and we both missed it! Alright. You good?"

"I'm fine. I have no idea what's going on. Your call was the first I heard of it."

"Good good. I'm going to work the phones. This is crazy! Why Tripper? Stay cool. Peace out."

I knew why. Tripper controlled National Union's deal documents and was most likely responsible for switching the Wampanoag schedules given to BestRateLoan. But I didn't want to connect myself with the raid, the FBI, the DOJ or FIRREA. Before I could put my phone back on the tray in front of me it buzzed with a text message from Erika.

"Will, check the news!!!"

I opened my mobile browser and started to sift through the headlines. "FBI Raids Offices of National Union Bank & Trust and Smith Stevens."

"Holy shit," involuntarily rolled off of my tongue.

I feverishly read the article. "Federal agents raided the offices and offsite storage facilities of National Union and its lead counsel, the New York office of international law firm Smith Stevens. In a press statement, the United States Attorney's Office for the District of Massachusetts said that it was acting on an anonymous tip provided by a whistleblower. The FBI executed warrants related to counts of wire fraud, mail fraud and violations of the Federal Institutions Reform, Recovery and Enforcement Act of 1989. A law enforcement source that asked not to be identified stated the investigations concern several deals between National Union and other federally insured banking institutions related to packaged mortgage sales." "Anonymous tip," I thought to myself. I wondered if there was more to the story with Imani Walker than Knuckles had let on.

"Holy shit!," I typed back to Erika. "Aaron called me and told me Tripper was taken away in handcuffs."

"It's crazy! I heard it's not just BestRateLoan. There are other deals where National Union did the same thing."

"Anonymous tip!"

"I think Smith Stevens is in big trouble. You better get ready to jump ship!"

"I'm one step ahead of you!"

"Holy cow! That's great! Where are you going?"

"Boston. To live with Mickey!!"

"Wait, what!?!?"

"I know!! He's getting released on Friday!!"

"That's great, Will!!! Congrats!!!"

Before I could respond, my phone began to ring again. I clicked to answer and in a yelling whisper, "Kevin, holy shit! I can't believe it! It's all over the news! They raided Smith Stevens and National Union!" It took me a couple of moments to realize Knuckles was completely silent. "Kevin. Kevin . . . Can you hear me?" I heard a deep sigh on the other end of the line. "Kevin?"

"Will. Where are you?"

"I'm on the train. Is everything ok? Are they looking for me?"

"No, but we need to talk when you get off."

"What's going on? Just tell me."

"No, no. It's not a good time."

My heart began to pound and my mind began to race. "What is it? Is it Mickey? The investigation?"

"Just call me when you get off. What time are you getting in? It's important."

"Oh . . . ok. 2:30. I'll call you."

The excitement washed away as I wondered what Knuckles wanted to talk to me about. I continued scrolling through coverage of the FBI raids until the train groaned to a stop at South Station in downtown Boston.

As soon as I stepped outside, I called Knuckles on my cellphone. "Kevin?"

"Will, look to your left." I looked and saw Knuckles standing in front of his battered old Mercedes. He waved at me to walk in his direction.

"What's up?"

He opened the dinged door. "Get in and I'll tell you on the way."

He shut the door behind me and put my rolling suitcase in the trunk. Knuckles plopped onto an aging and cracked blue leather seat behind the black steering wheel and pulled away from the curb. The old engine puttered as we stopped at a red light.

"Where are we going?"

Knuckles looked down at the thin steering wheel, seeming to examine the ridges designed for fingers to grip. "Will, there was a fight."

"What? Is Mickey ok?" I felt panic spread from my eyes to my knees and my hands began to shake.

Knuckles shook his head. "It's not good, Will. They stabbed him." Knuckles looked pale and the skin of his face seemed to droop towards his chest.

"Fuck! Those fuckers stabbed him? Where is he?"

"I'm so sorry, Will. Norfolk Medical Center."

"Jesus Christ! What? With a shiv? What the fuck? Will he be ok?"

"We're going to get there and get you in."

"Is he going to . . ." Knuckles pursed his lips, and I held my face in my hands. Tears began to stream out of my eyes and my chest started to heave uncontrollably. I felt Knuckles' hand patting my back.

"It's going to be ok, Will. If anyone can make it, it's Mickey. He's tough as nails."

Knuckles sped towards Norfolk Medical Center and pulled the silver Mercedes in front of the emergency room entrance and let me out. "Go. I'll be right up. ICU."

I staggered into the emergency room and looked around panicked. An unattended man with a bleeding headwound compressed with dirty gauze sat alone at a bank of chairs. I hurried to the reception desk.

"My brother was admitted. He was stabbed. He's in the ICU."

"Name."

"Mickey. Uh, Michael Glynn."

"Eleventh floor. Elevator down the hall to the left."

I jogged down the hallway to the elevator bank avoiding pedestrians using walkers along the way and punched the up button. I reached the eleventh floor and ran to the front desk.

"My brother is in the ICU."

"Name."

"Michael Glynn."

"Eleven forty-one." The woman pointed down the hallway to the right. I walked rapidly avoiding patients on carts and beeping electronic equipment being wheeled from one room to another. I finally reached the room. I carefully pressed open the door and peered my head around its edge. The room was quiet. A heavy-set man in blue hospital scrubs was making a bed.

"Michael?"

"There's no one here," the man replied quietly shaking his head.

I felt a new wave of panic. I stumbled away from the door and saw a woman with dark hair in pink scrubs. "I'm looking for my brother. I was told he was in eleven forty-one, but he's not there. Do you know where he is?"

"Hold on. Come with me." I followed her back to the front desk, and she sat behind a computer and began to type. "What's his name?"

"Michael Glynn."

She looked at the screen for a long moment and sighed. "Ok." She looked around. "Where's Dr. Charles?"

"Eleven fifty-three," another woman replied. "Take a seat here. I'll be right back."

"Will!" Knuckles yelled loud enough for me to hear. He looked harried as he trotted down the hall towards me. "Where's Mickey?"

"I don't know. I went to his room, but he wasn't there."

Knuckles immediately went into action and began quietly talking to a man sitting behind a computer at the front desk. Moments later a tall man in light blue scrubs with a surgical mask dangling from his ear strode towards me.

"Michael Glynn?," he asked into the air looking around. Knuckles spun on his heel and I sprang from the chair. Beeps and alarms filled the air.

"That's me. That's my brother."

"And I'm his lawyer."

"Please follow me." We followed him back towards Room 1141. He knocked and opened the door to the now-empty room. He pushed the door open wide. "Come in." Knuckles and I followed him in. "Take a seat. Anywhere you like." The door slowly drifted closed and the room was completely quiet. The man took a deep breath. "I'm Devin Charles. I'm a trauma surgeon here and I operated on Michael Glynn. You're his brother?"

"I am? I'm Will and that's Kevin. He's Mickey's lawyer."

"Gentlemen, I'm afraid I have some bad news. Michael. Mickey . . ." He nodded and I nodded back. "Mickey passed away about an hour ago."

"Wha . . ." Tears began to stream down my face. "What do you mean?" Knuckles stepped towards me and put his arm around my shoulder.

"I am so sorry. Mickey was a fighter and he put up a hell of a fight. He lost a lot of blood. He arrived just after four this morning. He wasn't conscious. Are you ok?" I couldn't speak and nodded to the doctor. "I don't want to tell you too much."

I looked at Knuckles' blurry form through my teary eyes. His face was pale, and I could barely see his features. "Do you want to know, Will?" I was going to find out anyway eventually and nodded. "You can go ahead," Knuckles replied.

"He was stabbed eleven times, including three stab wounds to his neck. His jugular was severed. He lost a lot of blood before he received compression. It's remarkable that he arrived here alive. Like I said, your brother was a fighter. He hung in there. He was stable after surgery, but unconscious. Unfortunately, he began to crash this afternoon. We attempted to revive him and performed CPR, but we couldn't bring him back. I am so sorry. I've seen this kind of thing before. Too many times, sadly. And most people don't make it as far as your brother did. But I'm truly sorry. Do you have any questions?"

I still couldn't speak. I mouthed a sticky sounding, "thank you, Doctor." Knuckles patted my shoulder.

"Thank you," Knuckles responded.

"This room may be needed shortly, but at least for the next few minutes it's yours."

"Alright, we'll clear out of here," Knuckles replied. The doctor left the room quietly. "Just breathe, Will. That's all you can do right now. Take a deep breath. And then another and another. I'll get you a water. Ok?" I nodded my head, still stunned and unable to form words. I finally found the strength in my rubbery legs and stood up and Knuckles led me out of the hospital's emergency entrance to the old silver Mercedes across the street in a parking garage.

"I'm so sorry, Will. I'm so, so sorry." I sipped from a plastic water bottle Knuckles gave me inside the hospital.

"It's ok. Thanks for getting me, Kevin."

"Where you staying?"

"Downtown."

"Why don't you crash with me tonight? I know you don't have family."

"It's ok."

"Nah, I'm serious."

"Thanks, Kevin. I'm just going to try to sleep this off."

"You sure?"

"I'm sure. Thanks."

"Ok. I'm going to clear my deck tomorrow. I'll help with arrangements."

Knuckles dropped me off at my hotel and before I closed the door I said, "You're the best."

"Nah, you are. Don't forget that. And call me if you need anything."

CHAPTER TWENTY-NINE

Free Man

On Friday morning, instead of standing outside of the gates of Cedar Junction waiting for Mickey's release, we stood inside of the gates of Cedar Grove Cemetery in Dorchester waiting to lay Mickey to rest. With no family and no friends to speak of on the outside after eighteen years on the inside, Knuckles and I were the only witnesses to Mickey's burial. The June sun cast a warm glow on the old cemetery, which was in full bloom. Birds chirped a farewell as Knuckles and I watched Mickey's casket being carried out of a long black Cadillac hearse.

I finally felt in control of my emotions and was starting to come to terms with burying Mickey when I noticed a black BMW 5 Series with yellow New York plates pulling up behind Knuckles' old Mercedes. The water works started again when the doors opened and Aaron and Erika stepped out of the car and into the sunlight.

Knuckles tilted his head towards me. "Do you know these two?"

I nodded and replied, "yep," through my quivering upper lip.

As they approached, Aaron teased, "you better not be crying on account of us or we're getting back in and going home."

I chuckled through sniffles and Aaron wrapped me up in a bear hug. "I'm so sorry, buddy."

"Careful. I don't want to snot on your pinstripes."

"Don't worry, I'll send you the bill." We both chuckled a little and Erika hugged me next.

"I'm so sorry, Will." She stepped away and before I could introduce her to Knuckles, she asked, "is this Knuckles? Who I've heard so much about?"

Knuckles turned to me. "You call me 'Knuckles' to other people?" I could feel my face blushing.

"Uh—"

"Yeah," Erika interrupted. "But only in an endearing way. Will says you're the best criminal lawyer in Massachusetts."

"He did, did he?"

"Yes, he did. He says a lot of good things about you."

"Well, Will, looks like I'm going to have to take back some of the things I said about you." Knuckles elbowed me gently in the ribcage as he said it.

"Kevin, this is Erika."

"Will told me all about you. Says you're a real shark."

"Well, gee, thanks, I guess." She rocked onto her tiptoes and back down as she said it.

"And Kevin, this is Aaron. He kept me sane at Smith Stevens. I wouldn't have made it as far as I did without him."

"Any friend of Will . . ." Knuckles and Aaron shared a strong handshake.

"Sorry we're meeting under such sad circumstances," Aaron added.

Knuckles acknowledged the gravity of the moment with a silent nod. Pallbearers from the funeral home carried Mickey to his grave and placed his casket onto a metal framework over a long freshly dug rectangular hole in the ground. A thin Catholic priest named Father Jude from St. Gregory's stood patiently wearing long black robes in the hot summer sun. After a few more minutes of our group becoming acquainted he cleared his throat and we walked in his direction and stood graveside.

Father Jude prayed and read from Ecclesiastes. "'For everything there is a season, a time for every activity under heaven. A time to be born and a time to die. A time to plant and a time to harvest. A time to kill and a time to heal. In sure and certain hope of the resurrection to eternal life through our Lord Jesus Christ, we commend to Almighty God our brother Michael, and we commit his body to its final resting place.'" As the priest said the words, I felt detached from my body as if I were watching a movie and not real life.

His final words brought me back to earth and to reality. "And finally, as Michael was a nice Irish boy from the neighborhood, who I knew since he was a little boy, I want to leave you with one final prayer this morning. 'May the road rise up to meet you. May the wind always be at your back. May the sun shine warm upon your face. May the rains fall soft upon your fields. And until we meet again, may God hold you in the palm of His hand.'" With the Irish Blessing, I felt the waterworks starting to return. I noticed Erika sobbing and the waterworks returned full blast. Knuckles placed his arm on my shoulder, and I managed to regain my composure.

As the priest stepped away from the grave, Knuckles said, "thank you, Father Jude."

"Good to see you, Kevin. And Will, I am so sorry about your brother. He was a good kid and I always liked him. But he's in a better place now. I hope you find peace in that."

"Thank you, Father," I sighed.

After he stepped away, Knuckles looked around at the group. "Good friends. Both of you. Will's a lucky guy." Aaron and Erika appeared embarrassed by the compliment.

"It's nothing," Aaron said as he looked down at his shoes.

"Well, you both drove a long way for a fifteen-minute funeral. How about we get something to drink?"

"Sounds good," Aaron replied.

"I'm in," followed Erika.

"Thanks, Kevin," I added.

"Follow me. That's my car." Erika and Aaron got into the BMW and I hopped into Knuckles' Mercedes.

"Thanks for everything, Kevin."

"For what? You're a good kid. A great client. Best brother I ever met. My pleasure. Anything you need, let me know."

"Well, thanks for everything. Including everything you did for Mickey."

"Let's not forget what you did for Mickey. It wasn't the ending anyone wanted, but Mickey died a free man because of you. His papers were signed, and he was on the way out. That was all you."

"Thanks, Kevin."

We pulled up outside the ancient Dorchester landmark The Bowlegged Woman on Dorchester Avenue. I hadn't been inside in years.

"How's this?"

"This is great."

The BMW pulled up behind us and the four of us headed inside. We took a table across from a long bar in the dark and quiet tavern. An old sailor was regaling the bartender with a tall tale when we sat down.

"Guinness?," Knuckles asked. We all nodded.

"No bourbon for you?," I asked Erika.

"Bourbon?" Curiosity crested Knuckles' face. "I think they can pull that off."

"No. No thank you. I only drink those after 11:00."

Knuckles chuckled. "All right then. Sal, four Guinness, please," he hollered towards the bar. After a few minutes, an elderly bartender came from behind the long bar and brought Knuckles the four pints of Guinness on a round tray.

Knuckles held up his chilly glass with tan foam leaking over the side. "To Mickey, may he rest in peace," he toasted.

"To Mickey," we repeated.

We sipped our black draughts and each of us had a foam moustache on our upper lips afterwards.

"So you both worked with this guy? How was that?"

"Great," Erika responded. "He's smart and dedicated. I loved working with Will. I just hated our client."

"So, I heard," chuckled Knuckles.

"We didn't really work together," Aaron added. "Mainly we just got our shoes shined. And went out for beers."

"Must be nice," Knuckles responded.

"Thanks, dude," I added playfully smirking at Aaron.

"So do tell us, Master William, what lays next in your path? You left your job. As far as I know, you don't have a wife or a kid. Or even a dog. Isn't that right?"

"It's true. All of it's true," I responded.

"So what's next?"

"I really don't know." I sipped my Guinness.

"I told him to throw a resume my way," Aaron chimed in.

"And I'm sure he could get into Aronoff Shepsky, where I work," Erika added.

"Whoa, whoa, whoa. Let the man think," Knuckles replied. "Give him some time. He needs space." Knuckles turned to me. "So, what will it be? You can't just hang out and be a man of leisure. You have to have a job."

"True. Very true," I nodded.

"So, I was thinking, why don't you work with me while you figure it out?"

"With you?"

"Yeah. With me."

"I'm not even a criminal lawyer. I couldn't do that."

"Well, you got that *pro bono* guy off, didn't you?" Erika and Aaron craned their necks at me in surprise.

"Well, yeah. But that was really him. He did the work."

"Bullshit. He never would've gotten there if it weren't for you."

"Even if it's true, I don't know what I'm doing. I was shaking in my boots."

"Everyone's scared at first. It's normal. You'll pick it up fast. You're smart."

"What if I send someone to jail?"

"You won't. You won't be doing murder one out there. You'll learn the ropes. I bet you'd love it."

"But the stakes are so high. Aren't there other people out there? That are better suited than me?"

"Maybe more experienced, but you have big firm training. I know you can spell and speak in complete sentences." Erika and Aaron chuckled. "No, I'm serious. You'd be surprised at how many lawyers can't speak in complete sentences in court. Half of them don't know their clients' names. Am I right?"

"Well, yeah, sometimes," I replied.

"The thing is, Will, you have the intangibles. I know how hard you worked for Mickey. You have heart and, pardon my French, stones. You either have them or you don't. And I don't think you can learn them. And you got them. And those things will carry you a long way."

I smiled at the compliment and sipped my Guinness. "I don't know. I don't think I could work with you. You're too tough."

"Me? Too tough? I'm a teddy bear. I'm not tough."

"That's not what I heard."

"They're always talking, aren't they? What did you hear?"

"You really want me to tell? I don't want to embarrass you." Knuckles looked curious.

"I won't be. You can't embarrass me. Tell me."

"Well, I heard you had a murder trial and had just hired a new associate to work with you." Knuckles seemed to be deep in thought and his face contorted as I spoke. "I heard it was the associate's first murder trial. And the defendant—your client—was found guilty at the end of the trial. And when the jury foreman came out and read the guilty verdict, the young attorney began to cry. And when he did, I was told you leaned over to him and said, 'what the fuck are you crying for? He's the one going to jail.'"

We all looked at Knuckles, who looked amused. "That's the story?" Knuckles' head bobbed.

"That's just what I was told."

"And who told you that story?"

"I don't know. That's just the story they tell."

"Well, let me tell you something. They should get their facts straight before they start telling stories. That never happened."

"Never happened? That story is a legend," I cracked.

"Never happened. I never said that to anyone."

"So, it's not true?"

"Not at all. Not the way you tell it, at least."

"Then what's the true story?"

"You want to hear the truth about what happened?" Erika and Aaron were watching the conversation intently.

"Yeah," I replied, and they nodded along.

"The truth is . . ." Knuckles sipped his Guinness. "That was me, but my boss said it. Not me. It was my first job after being an ADA."

"Wait, what? You were the associate?"

"I was, indeed." Knuckles nodded and took another sip.

"And you broke down after a guilty verdict. I don't believe it!"

"I did. What did I tell you? You have to have heart. If you don't care, then what's the point of it all?" Aaron, Erika, and I all smiled. Knuckles took a big sip of his Guinness. "So what do you think about that?"

"I think I have it all wrong."

"And what are you going to do about it?"

"Can I get back to you?"

"You certainly may, but don't make me wait too long."

"I won't."

After we finished our beers, Knuckles asked, "Another round?"

"Sadly, we gotta get back to New York. Fiancés await," Aaron replied.

"Too bad. I have more stories to share."

"I want to hear why they call you 'Knuckles,'" Erika chimed in.

"Well, that's a long one. It'll take more time and more Guinness, so you'll both have to come back again."

"I'm in," she smiled.

"Can I hook a ride back to Manhattan?"

"Of course," Aaron replied.

"There's one hitch. My suitcase is at my hotel in downtown Boston."

"Naturally."

Aaron looked at Erika and she said, "no problem."

"Not going to stay here?," Knuckles asked.

"Ah, all my stuff is down there. I think it's better to go home and figure out my next move. I'll call you next week."

"Don't forget." He gave me a strong hug.

"I won't forget."

"All right you kids. Take care of this guy. He needs it."

Erika and Aaron each hugged Knuckles and we departed the old bar for the BMW. As the six-cylinder engine purred down Route 95 towards New

York, my future lay more open and less clear than ever before. Mickey gave me a singular purpose for becoming a lawyer. I began to question what the point of it had been. After all the years and the effort, Mickey was gone anyway. But I refused to believe it was all for nothing. As I searched for meaning, I began to wonder if Mickey had not only given me a reason for becoming a lawyer, but maybe had also introduced me to my calling.

THE END.

ACKNOWLEDGEMENTS

Huge thanks to Molly Lewis, Cate Hoff, Chris Ryan, Juan-Luis Acevedo, Lori Watson, Brendan Recupero and Yonaton Aronoff. As always, my utmost love and gratitude to my parents and my children for their love and support. I can't adequately express how grateful I am for my beautiful wife, Alyne—I love you to the moon and back! Always and forever! Por último, pero no menos importante, nuestro amor y gratitud a nuestra familia fuera de casa en México Lindo en New Rochelle, New York.

ABOUT THE AUTHOR

John Cader is a freelance writer and author of crime and legal stories. John was born in Boston and has lived much of his adult life in New York. He draws inspiration from his New England roots and his time in the Empire State. When not writing, John can frequently be found surrounded by characters with a taco in his hand.

Website: johnnywords.com
Instagram: @johnnywords
Facebook: @totallyjohnywords

Made in the USA
Columbia, SC
20 August 2021